Abbeys & Priories

Abbeys & Priories

GLYN COPPACK

TEMPUS

First published 2006

Tempus Publishing Limited
The Mill, Brimscombe Port,
Stroud, Gloucestershire, GL5 2QG
www.tempus-publishing.com

British Library Cataloguing in Publication Data.
A catalogue record for this book is available from the British Library.

ISBN 0 7524 3022 X

Typesetting and origination by Tempus Publishing Limited
Printed in Great Britain

CONTENTS

PREFACE

I was asked to write a general book called *Abbeys and Priories* by Peter Kemmis Betty in 1987 and the book I produced for the English Heritage/BT Batsford series (now long out of print) had a remarkable effect on the study of monastic sites. In 2002 Peter asked me if I would revise the book for the Tempus series. My reaction was that because the book was by then seriously out of date I would need to rewrite it substantially. In rereading it I saw that many of my ideas had developed over the past 18 years; some of the views expressed were perhaps, with the benefit of hindsight, unwise. My own research had developed substantially over that period, and a lot of research by others that I was aware of was finally moving towards publication. Though parts of the old book can still be detected, and for that I make no apology, this is essentially a new book that has benefited from the generosity of many people working in the field of monastic studies, both in Britain and further afield. The views expressed are still my own.

With nearly 1000 sites to chose from in Britain it is obvious that I have had to be highly selective in the monasteries I have used to illustrate my account. Some are well known, others have never been of more than local importance. Those I have used were chosen because they provide the best evidence known to me. This book is a personal view; the choice of sites reflects the extent of my own research and that of close colleagues. When the original book was published I was taken to task for including sites which were 'not significant' in the international context of monastic studies. That many of those sites have survived into this version is hardly surprising – their significance is now accepted because of the story they have to tell and they are the sites that have produced the information which is now driving research.

Monasteries were an integral part of life in England from the later seventh century to the early 1530s, and from the mid-twelfth century there were few parts of medieval England that did not have a local abbey or priory. Monks and nuns were a part of everyday life, though they set themselves apart from society to praise God in often elaborate and costly buildings. They were supported in their religious life by landed estates, the gifts of founders, patrons and ordinary people. They provided charity for the poor, hospitality for travellers, education for some, and a place of burial for many. They supported a way of life which is now foreign to us, swept away in the early stages of the Reformation, and though religious life is no longer an integral part of our society, the remains of medieval religious life are still with us, in many of our cathedrals and parish churches, in surviving buildings, ruins, earthwork sites and even place names. After parish churches, monastic remains comprise the greatest collection of surviving medieval architecture. What survives today is a small part of what we have lost since all abbeys and priories were suppressed in the sixteenth century, but it is a significant portion which can tell us a great deal if we look it closely.

Monastic research has had a long history with its origins in antiquarianism, and until well into the twentieth century was largely the preserve of historians and architectural historians. Archaeology came late to monastic sites, only really beginning in the 1960s, though there were some remarkable earlier interventions. The result was that before my generation of archaeologists were able to begin our study, research agendas had largely been set. The concept of what comprised a monastery was largely dictated by what survived and could be identified; the ruins of churches and cloister buildings. The different orders of monks and nuns were studied individually, though they might be compared one with another. There was also a concentration on twelfth-century and later monasteries because this is what survived, not only in buildings but also in documents relating to monastic life. The 1970s and '80s saw a move away from this approach, with a concentration on the monastic economy, perhaps initially at the expense of the spiritual side of monastic life. Large-scale excavation enabled the study of the wider monastic precinct, establishing for the first time how monasteries were able to function, what drove their building campaigns, and what the day-to-day connections were with the outside world. The late '80s and '90s saw this economic research balanced by a study of the early development and planning of individual orders – my own work on the Cistercians and Carthusians, Roberta Gilchrist's work on nuns, the military orders and the less obvious aspects of monasticism, and the Museum of London Archaeology Service's analysis in depth of the capital's monasteries. The last 10 years have seen a new generation develop this work, with important work by Barney Sloane on burials in monasteries, by Jackie Hall and Mark Samuel on the development of monastic architecture from detached fragments, and by Tim Pestell on the siting of monasteries and the reasons for their foundation. At last, serious research is being done on the planning of late medieval monasteries and the archaeology of suppression and conversion.

That I was ever able to write this book is a testament of the generosity of many friends and colleagues who have shared their research with me (and argued with me about my own work) over many years and the willingness of English Heritage to allow me to continue my research in a changing world. The original book was largely inspired by the influence of the late Roy Gilyard-Beer and Stuart Rigold who started me in my monastic interests. The late John Hurst and later Christopher Young encouraged my research and ensured it was adequately funded; Peter Fergusson gently steered me through the minefield of Cistercian research and continues to provide those thoughtful insights which guide my thinking. I am particularly indebted to Jackie Hall, Mark Samuel and Stuart Harrison for their advice on monastic architecture, to Evelyn Baker, Stephen Moorhouse, Stuart Wrathmell, Sue Wright and Sue Hirst, Judith

Roebuck, Andrew Davison, Roberta Gilchrist, Barney Sloane, Peter Huggins, Martin Foreman, Mick Jones, Rob Atkins, Jim Hoff, Rachael Hall and Paul Cope-Faulkner for their advice on individual sites and sharing their ideas with me. Thanks also to Laura Perehinec at Tempus Publishing for her thorough and considerate editing of the text. Any errors of fact are my responsibility, not theirs, and any variation in interpretation they will immediately recognise as my own. Simon Hayfield, Miranda Schofield, Jim Thorn and Dawn Flower provided many of the drawings used in this book.

Glyn Coppack
St David's Day, 2006

I

THE ARCHAEOLOGY OF MONASTERIES

There were more than 1000 monasteries in medieval England, ranging from the small and inconsequential to the great and powerful. Some were only occupied for short periods before moving sites or combining with other communities, others were occupied for four or more centuries, some dating from well before the Norman conquest of 1066. Those that did not fall by the wayside were ruthlessly suppressed between 1536 and 1540, leaving only a pitiful number of surviving buildings, rather more broken ruins, and dispersed contents. No complete medieval monastery survives in England, though after parish churches they comprise the largest group of surviving medieval stone buildings. The concept of monastic life, once an integral part of our social history, is now foreign to us, and Shakespeare's 'bare ruined choirs' are objects of fascination and mystery. Even the cathedrals and parish churches that survived the wreck of the dissolution have been altered physically to suit new liturgies. Elsewhere, stripped and quarried ruins are all that remain of institutions that were intended to last for ever as perpetual reminders of their founders' piety and communities' devotion. Some were destroyed so completely that the only indications of their existence are the earthworks that cover their buried foundations or spreads of rubble, tiles and pottery in the ploughed soil of arable fields. Others are lost below housing, with even their precise locations uncertain. Together, though, these thousand or so monasteries contain the evidence for the nature of monastic life in medieval England, and in their structural remains they show the aspirations, customs and economy of their long-dead inhabitants. The developing and careful study of their remains, using the skills of archaeology, the reading of their fabric and the interpretation of their surviving documents, can now give a clear insight into their building, use, economy and communities.

There was no such thing as a typical monastery because the monastic movement was one of continuing reform and extension. From the early ninth century all medieval monks and nuns lived by the precepts of St Benedict, who compiled a rule for the monks of his abbey of Monte Casino in the early years of the sixth century. The followers of this rule became known as Benedictines and remained the predominant order of religion until the late tenth century. By this time, the Benedictine rule was found to be too easy for many groups, and the next two-and-a-half centuries saw the growth of many reform movements within the order, particularly those of the Cluniacs, the Savigniacs and the Cistercians, all of whom lived enclosed lives. Each different rule observed its own particular customs, which were reflected in dress, liturgy, architecture, manuscripts, strictness of life and position in society. In every case, their buildings differed in details of planning and in the degree of decoration and fittings. In addition to the enclosed monks and nuns of these orders, a movement had grown up among bodies of clergy who served collegiate churches yet sought a similar form of monastic community. Bodies of canons banded together, living under a modified version of the Benedictine rule and precepts developed by St Augustine. From their rule, they became known as Augustinian canons, as austere as the fundamentalist Cistercians but living less enclosed lives and serving parish churches as well as their own monasteries. Other groups of canons and canonesses, the Premonstratensians and Gilbertines, developed their own rules, strongly influenced by the Cistercians. Again, their buildings varied according to their rule and liturgy.

All houses of canons, canonesses, monks, nuns and friars were established for a purpose: to house and sustain groups of religious who would pray for the souls of the founder and his descendants, and to provide them with a place of burial. They provided a home for those who chose to withdraw from the distractions of the world to serve God in a continuous round of prayer and devotion as part of an ordered community. A monastery therefore had to consist of a church, domestic buildings in which the community would live, a place for their burial, buildings to process their foodstuffs and agricultural estates to feed them and provide capital for building; a concept it is difficult to gain from the surviving buildings and ruins which tend to comprise only the nucleus of a once greater whole. In theory at least, monasteries should be self-sufficient, and for the most part they were, with farms and manors that exploited their estates.

Most monasteries were established in rural areas, often on marginal land, although a number were built in or just outside towns, often on the sites of pre-conquest monasteries. Some, like Battle Abbey in Sussex or Bridlington Priory in East Yorkshire, established towns and markets at their gates, which were an important source of cash revenue, though like most they were supported primarily by agriculture. They formed an important element of the national economy, and in producing scholars and trained administrators provided the first civil servants. Their presidents enjoyed the rank of major landowners, an honour that carried responsibility for the administration of justice, with the abbots of the greatest houses actually sitting in parliament. Their accumulated wealth and lands, coupled with their separation from an increasingly secular society, led to their downfall, in many ways marking the effective end of the Middle Ages in Britain. In little more than four years, Henry VIII and his chief minister, Thomas Cromwell, destroyed what had taken centuries to create. Their churches were dismantled, their cloisters turned into private houses or simply used as quarries, the contents dispersed or ruthlessly destroyed, and their lands sold off or added to the royal estates.

THE ORIGINS OF ANTIQUARIAN INTEREST

Interest in the cultural wealth of monasteries, their buildings, plate and libraries began before their destruction, when John Leland, the King's Antiquary, travelled the country in the 1520s. Leland found them to be treasure-houses without equal, and from his accounts it is possible to gauge the scale of loss that resulted from their suppression. His own claim in 1549 that he had 'conservid many good autors, the which other wise had beene like to have perischid' is palpably true. He was followed in little more than a decade in 1534/5 by the Royal Commissioners of the *Valor Ecclestasticus*. These commissioners were not charged with recording the cultural treasures of the monasteries; rather their task was to value them as real estate, for, since the king became Head of the Church in England, all Church property had become a state asset. The commissioners were to list the lands and rents of each house (*1*); to survey and describe the buildings, particularly those with valuable lead roofs; and to list any debts. They were followed by other commissioners whose job was to assess the quality of monastic life, men like Richard Leyton, Thomas Legh, and Edward ApRice, whose motives might easily be questioned from the scurrilous and partisan reports they made. These surveys, the first stage in the destruction of monastic life, are the starting point for any study of monasteries in England and being government records, many have survived. They tell us a great deal about the buildings and their contents at the end of their life, and they present a good secular view of monastic life when it was still an integral part of everyday affairs. One particular survey made for the *Valor*, that of the poor Cistercian nunnery of Kirklees in West Yorkshire, has been used throughout this book to describe through contemporary eyes the precise nature of monastic buildings.

The first interest in suppressed monasteries became apparent during the second half of the sixteenth century and continued up to and beyond the Civil War. Following the wholesale destruction of monastic libraries and service books, antiquaries like Sir Robert Cotton and Edward Fairfax collected what remained, saving many chronicles, histories, collections of charters, spiritual works and even service books (*colour plate 1*). Some of the finest books had been reserved at the suppression for the royal libraries, but works of the quality of the Lindisfarne Gospels found their way into Cotton's collection, which ultimately became the nucleus of the British Museum library in 1753. More prosaically, the new owners of monastic estates retained the collections of charters that proved the title to the estates they had bought, and protected these as jealously as their more recent deeds. Others were retained by agents of the government for identical reasons. The legal status of many former monastic landholdings in the north could be ascertained from the collection of original monastic charters stored by the Council for the North in a tower on the precinct wall of York Abbey, the abbot's house of which became their headquarters. A sad consequence of the royalist defeat at the battle of Marston Moor and the subsequent siege of York in 1644 was the destruction of the tower and many of the collected charters.

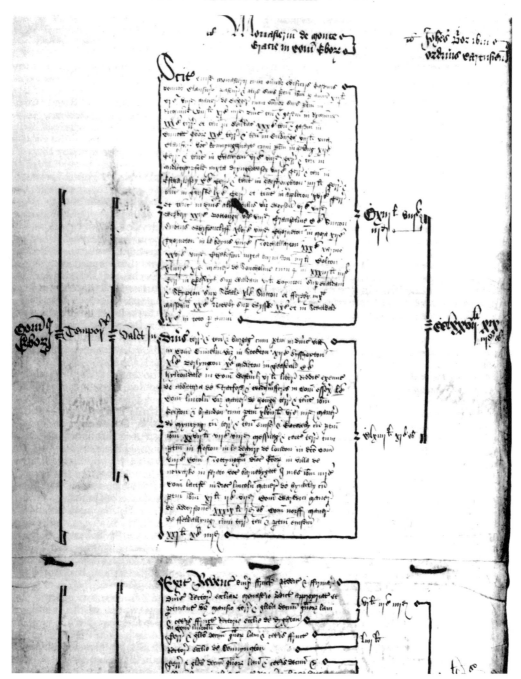

1 Part of the first membrane of the *Valor Ecclesiasticus* roll for Mount Grace Priory showing the value of the house's estates in 1534/5. *National Archives*

Antiquarian interest in the muniments of defunct abbeys continued throughout the seventeenth century, exemplified by Sir William Dugdale, Garter King of Arms, who produced with Roger Dodsworth the *Monasticon Anglicanum* in three volumes between 1655 and 1673. The *Monasticon,* the first synthesis of English monastic history, was compiled from transcriptions of documents recovered from the spoliation of the suppression that extended back to the eleventh century or before. Its timing was critical, coming in the recovery from the Civil War. Though the subject smacked of popery in a country which had just experienced the horrors of a civil war, the emphasis was on patronage, estates and individuals. For a nation in search of a non-partisan identity, the ruins and documents of the long-dead abbeys and priories provided a satisfactory outlet.

In the 1660s, John Aubrey, thinking back, no doubt, to the golden days before the Great Rebellion, described the remains of Waverley Abbey in Surrey thus:

The Abby is situated, though low, in a very good Air, and is as Romantick a Place as most I have seen. Here is a fine Rivulet runs under the House and fences one Side; but all the rest is wall'd. By the Lane are stately Rocks of Sand. Within the Walls of the Abbey are sixty acres: The Walls are very strong and chiefly of Ragge-Stones ten foot [3m] high. Here also remain Walls of a fair *Church* the Walls of the *Cloyster* and some Part of the Cloysters themselves, within and without are yet remaining: Within the Quadrangle of the Cloysters was a Pond, but now is a Marsh. Here was also a handsom Chapel (now a stable) larger than that at *Trinity* College in *Oxford.* The Windows are of the same Fashion as the Chapel Windows at Priory S' *Mari'es* in *Wiltshire.* There are no Escutcheons or Monuments remaining only in the Parlour and chamber over it (built not long since) are some Roundels of Painted Glass, *viz.* S' *Michael* fighting with the Devil, S' *Dunstan* holding the *Devil* by the Nose with his Pincers; his Retorts, Crucibles, and Chemical Instruments about him with several others; but so exactly drawn as if they were done from a good modern Print. They are of about eight Inches [20cm] Diameter. The *Hall* was very spacious and noble with a Row of Pillers in the middle and vaulted over Head. The very long Building with long narrow Windows, in all Probability, was the *Dormitory.* There are many more ruins.

Though Aubrey was an exceptional antiquary, the points he examined at Waverley identify the interest that was current in monastic sites: what remained, what it compared with, the possible identification of buildings and the survival of heraldry and window glass.

Not only did the *Monasticon* encourage an academic interest in monastic ruins, but also they began to be recorded artistically as objects of wonder and curiosity for the first time. The first such venture was Daniel King's *Cathedral and Conventual Churches of England and Wales*, published in 1656, and using drawings by Thomas Johnson (*2*), a valuable indication of how much or how little had survived the first century after the suppression. From this beginning, a valuable series of drawings, paintings and prints continued well into the nineteenth century, recording with great clarity more recent losses of fabric.

MONASTIC SITES IN THE EIGHTEENTH CENTURY

A more general interest in monastic sites grew in the second quarter of the eighteenth century, with the growing interest in medieval architecture that gave rise to the Gothick style of building typified by Horace Walpole's Strawberry Hill and by Viscount Camden's villa at Bayham Abbey in East Sussex (*3*). Bayham offered the chance to build a fashionable house on the site of a real monastery, but the house was built in 1754 at the expense of the ruins, the thirteenth-century roof being removed from the eastern part of the church that had survived as a barn (*4*) for reuse in the new house, walls demolished and new 'ruins' created to improve the melancholy aspect of the site.

Though there was a growing awareness of the value of monastic ruins, their survival was still very much a matter of luck. Indeed, the middle of the eighteenth century was a bad time for surviving fabric. Dr Stukeley observed of Bardney Abbey in Lincolnshire in 1753: 'Mr Rob. Banks gave me the following inscriptions on tombstones now under the turf at Bardney Abby. The abby is intirely demolished and was so when I saw it many years ago. Tis now a pasture, but the rubbish of the sacred structure has covered up the pavement of the church which they are now digging for the sake of the stones'. Though interest in ruins was to increase

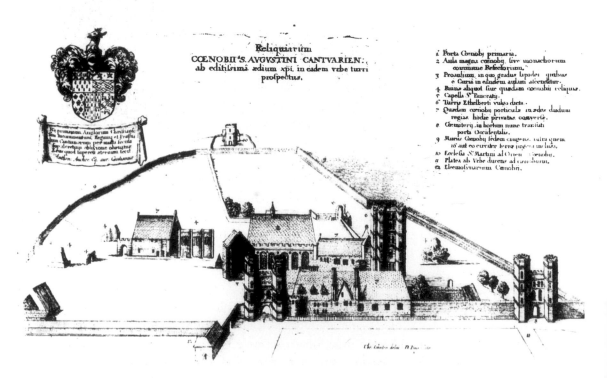

2 The site of St Augustine's Abbey at Canterbury as it was in about 1650. Many of the buildings shown still survive, though the tower that marks the west end of the nave collapsed in 1822. *From Daniel King's* Cathedrals and Conventual Churches of England and Wales

3 The gothick villa built by Viscount Camden to the west of the ruins of Bayham Abbey in the 1750s

4 Camden's removal of the thirteenth-century roof of the eastern part of the church at Bayham made the building into a romantic ruin much more in keeping with the tastes of the eighteenth century as this watercolour by James Lambert demonstrates

throughout the later eighteenth century, little was done to preserve them as relics of the past. William Aislabie, when he added the extensive ruins of Fountains Abbey in North Yorkshire to his father's gardens at Studley Royal, felt no concern in removing those parts that got in the way of his garden scheme and increasing the dereliction of the site to improve his vista. Lord Scarborough's gardens at Sandbeck Park were reorganised by Lancelot 'Capability' Brown in 1774, the contract specifying that his design should accord with 'Poet's Feeling and Painter's Eye', the intention being to create an appropriately picturesque setting for the ruins of Roche Abbey in South Yorkshire. To achieve this, Brown demolished the greater part of the cloister buildings, an action that was even then seen as unnecessary vandalism. Until the site was excavated in the 1870s, the only visible ruins of Roche were the walls of the transepts and eastern arm of the church and small outcrops of masonry, for Brown chose to bury the greater part of the site below parterres that were removed only after the First World War.

A SCHOLARLY APPROACH

The turn of the nineteenth century saw some improvement in the preservation of monastic ruins, however, as the value of the evidence they contained became more widely appreciated. At Bayham, for instance, when Humphrey Repton was advising on the extension of Lord Camden's villa, William Wilkins was being consulted on the best means to preserve the ruins of the nave of the church. His advice – to rebuild missing buttresses in such a way as the new work could not be mistaken for old, using appropriate mortar – has a strangely modern ring to it. It marked the turning tide in the fortunes of monastic ruins

Just as Lord Camden's work at Bayham was modified for a more subtle taste by Wilkins and Repton, the unscholarly 'gothick of the 1740s and 50s had given way to a true academic interest in medieval architecture by the last years of the century, reaching its peak in John Britton's studies of the great cathedral priory of Norwich (1817) and Bath Abbey (1825). The first half of the nineteenth century saw intense work done, principally on the surviving monastic churches, which were undergoing extensive 'restorations' to return them to an approximation of their original form. J. and C. Buckler produced a remarkable record of St Alban's Abbey in its parlous but untouched state in 1847. At the same time Robert Willis was subjecting Christchurch cathedral priory at Canterbury to a highly analytical survey, identifying breaks in building with surviving documentation to read the history of the monastery in its stones. Restoration and repair bought scaffolding, allowing scholars to have proper access to medieval fabric for the first time. This interest soon spread from surviving buildings to the more important ruins, and monastic sites played a crucial role in the understanding of medieval architecture.

ARCHAEOLOGY AND MONASTIC SITES

The scholarly interest in monasteries that was so well established by the first quarter of the nineteenth century did not stop at studying their architecture and the surviving documentation. The next stage was to recover lost sites or details of surviving ruins by the developing techniques of archaeology. In 1790, John Martin of Ripon had been inspired by John Burton's *Monasticon Eboracense* to search the chapter house at Fountains Abbey for the tombs of the abbots whose burial there had been recorded in the abbey's 'President Book'. Persuading the non-resident owner's gardener to clear the room out for him, he did indeed reveal many of the grave slabs he sought, as well as a 'very curious ... pavement', and the bases of the columns that supported the vault. The vault itself, which had fallen, was simply barrowed out into the cloister where it remained until 1851, obscuring the bottom 2.2m of the chapter house facade. No plan was made or any note published, but Martin's exercise had demonstrated that excavation could be used to prove the evidence of medieval documents.

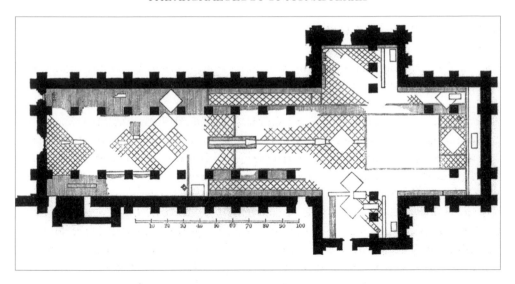

5 Plan of the church at Jervaulx Abbey, recorded by J. Ward in 1845, showing the extent of the tiled floors. Shading indicates plain red tiles, the diamonds indicate the position of highly decorated roundels of mosaic tile. *From Henry Shaw 1858*

To search for burials was one thing; to recover the plans of lost or buried buildings was another. The excavation of the church of Jervaulx Abbey in North Yorkshire, thoroughly demolished in 1537–8 and buried below fallen debris, by John Claridge, agent to the Earl of Ailesbury, between 1805 and 1807 followed his growing interest in the site, the gradual clearance of fallen debris and the repair of the ruins. Not only was the church cleared out to reveal its plan, fittings and elaborate floor tiles (5 and *colour plate 2*), it was also planned in detail, an important development in the growing concept of monastic archaeology. Fallen architectural detail, though not recorded, was stacked along the lines of walls, which were reduced to a few courses above floor level, close to their original findspots where they can still be seen today. From these, the form of the lost superstructure can still be recovered. The chapter house was also excavated to reveal the grave markers of six abbots and to enable the re-erection of the fallen columns that had originally supported the vault. Like Bayham and Roche, the intention was to develop the ruins at Jervaulx to form a feature in a landscaped park. The difference was that an appreciation of the abbey buildings and the layout of the precinct were allowed to influence the landscape in a way that had previously not been considered. Jervaulx today is as important for its early nineteenth-century setting as it is for its late twelfth-century buildings.

In the 1820s, the wealthy Benedictine Abbey at York was excavated before a new museum was built on its site by the Yorkshire Philosophical Society, revealing substantial remains of the cloister ranges standing up to 2.4m or more in height (6). Whilst the new museum building, of impeccable neo-classical design, was to occupy the site of the east range, such was the interest caused by the discovery that the excavators went on to examine the whole area of the claustral nucleus,

6 A view of the excavations of St Mary's Abbey in York in 1828 by F. Nash which shows the excavation of the chapter house and refectory in advance of the construction of the Yorkshire Museum. *York Minster Library*

producing in 1829 one of the earliest detailed plans of a monastic ruin. Though most of the site was subsequently reburied, the quality of record produced at the time of its excavation, coupled with the mass of fallen architectural detail recovered, enables the buildings to be reinterpreted today. Though the excavators were unable to resolve the building phases apparent in the walls they uncovered, it is clear that they realised they were dealing with many rebuildings and remodellings, a number of which were recorded in contemporary documents. This site gave the first indication of how complicated the archaeology of monastic sites could be and demonstrated the potential of buried sites, as both sources of architectural detail and confirmation of documented history. Martin Stapylton's excavation at Byland in North Yorkshire in about 1820 began as a search for the tomb of the founder Roger de Mowbray and became a hunt for capitals, corbels and other architectural elements, which were then removed to Myton Hall where they remain as garden ornaments. Similarly, Captain Chalonner's excavation in the church at Gisborough Priory in Cleveland in the 1840s led to the recovery of vast amounts of architectural detail, much of it found in place but sadly removed. It still lies on site in the displays that Chalonner created.

THE REASONS FOR NINETEENTH-CENTURY INTEREST

Monasteries held a fascination for early Victorian society which sought to break free from eighteenth-century classicism and re-establish its medieval roots, a move led by both the Evangelical and the Anglo-Catholic wings of the Church of

England. Abbeys rather than castles offered a tangible link with the medieval past that a highly motivated society could identify with: with piety, with patronage and with the newly-popularised Gothic architecture. Not all of society was interested – in 1816 Lord Yarborough bought the site of Thornton Abbey in north Lincolnshire from his neighbour to prevent its continued quarrying for road stone. His son excavated the ruins up to 1835 and recovered much of the ground plan. In 1835 the sometime quarry was opened to the paying public with a paid Keeper of the Ruins. So popular did the site become that it even acquired its own railway station. Indeed, the increased mobility afforded to the general public by the railways in the second half of the nineteenth century did much to popularise monastic sites, whilst also bringing scholars to them in great numbers.

The growth of new towns in the middle years of the nineteenth century led in turn to a need for instant and respectable history. At Birkenhead, Cheshire, for instance, the ruins of the priory, long converted to a farm, suddenly assumed a new importance that resulted in their study and publication. They gave a past to a new industrial town and gave a new lease of life to buildings that were then at risk. The same was true of the Cistercian abbey of Kirkstall in West Yorkshire on the banks of the River Aire to the west of Leeds. When painted by Turner, Cotman, Girtin and Richardson, Kirkstall stood in open countryside. As early as 1783 there were calls for the prevention of quarrying for building stone and the preservation of the ruins, work which was finally undertaken in 1799. In the early years of the nineteenth century the abbey ruins were opened to the public. In 1889, the site was finally acquired by the City of Leeds, and after archaeological study it was repaired and incorporated in a public park.

A new phase in the archaeological study of monastic sites began in the 1840s, starting with the work of Richard Walbran, who began his monumental excavation of Fountains Abbey in 1840, a project coupled with his extensive study of documents that was not completed until 1854. Walbran was first and foremost an historian, but his interest in Fountains was strictly archaeological. He was one of the first people actually to use the objects he found in his excavations to interpret the buildings he was studying and to reflesh the bare bones of a ruined site. Although he was frequently mistaken in his interpretation of particular buildings, mistaking for instance the ruins of the infirmary for those of the abbot's house and the warming house for the kitchen, his published descriptions were full, with a wealth of detail that would be commendable in a modern study, and easily capable of reinterpretation. Many of his finds can still be identified. By the standard of his day, his method of excavation was unexceptionable, but the sharpness of his observations was remarkable. Whilst excavating in the choir area of the church:

> the wheel of a cart that was passing over this part suddenly sank a foot or more deep
> in the earth and, on being raised, it was found that the slip had been occasioned
> by the fracture of a large earthenware vase that was buried immediately below the

surface. As it had evidently been placed there at a remote period, the soil around was particularly examined, when it was discovered that, on the east side of the screen, and divided by the processional pathway, were two spaces of the form of a Roman letter L walled on the sides and flagged on the bottom. In that on the south side nothing was observed; but in the other, a large quantity of charcoal ashes; and to the astonishment of all who have seen them, nine vases or jugs of rude earthenware, each sufficiently capacious to have contained nearly two fluid gallons, fixed on their sides within the walls of the space, and also partially filled with charcoal. These ashes may have been cast here from the adjacent furnace, where the lead stripped from the house had evidently been melted into a marketable shape at the time of the dissolution; but why the vases should have been introduced is, so far as I can understand, on precedent, a case unique and unaccountable.

He had found the resonance pits below the late medieval choir stalls, instantly recognisable from his description, and filled as he correctly supposed with the debris of spoliation. Walbran's recording of small and seemingly insignificant detail was a sign of the growing archaeological interest in monastic sites which was to increase throughout the second half of the nineteenth century. He was an enthusiast, an amateur in the true sense of the word, taking his lead like John Martin before him from extant documents and not necessarily understanding what he found. His concern was to recover the plan of the buildings that did not survive above ground level and to examine the finer detail of those that did remain, and this he most certainly achieved.

Whilst Walbran was working amid the standing ruins at Fountains, a more remarkable excavation was being carried out at Lewes Priory in East Sussex, the senior Cluniac house in England. The coming of the railways to the Sussex coast in 1845–6 required the driving of a cutting 12.2m wide and up to 3.6m deep through the slightly raised site of the thoroughly demolished house. The heavy work of the navvies was supplemented by a group of local archaeologists led by A.M. Lower and J.L. Parsons, who recovered the plan and some architectural detail of the eastern end of the church and the greater part of the chapter house. The excavators found clear evidence of the mines used by Thomas Cromwell's engineers to throw down the church. They also examined a large number of burials, recovering from the chapter house lead caskets containing the bones of the founders, William de Warenne and Gundreda his wife, and the well-preserved body of a prior, with his habit, undergarments, shoes and red hair surviving. Further investigation of the site, revealed in the railway cutting, included the monastic cemetery with more than 100 stone-lined graves being identified in addition to a great charnel pit aligned on the main axis of the church and only 2.4m from its easternmost chapel, which the excavators chose to associate with the Battle of Lewes in 1264. It could just as easily have been connected with the late twelfth-century rebuilding of the church, which had been extended into the monastic cemetery. This rebuilding was also the

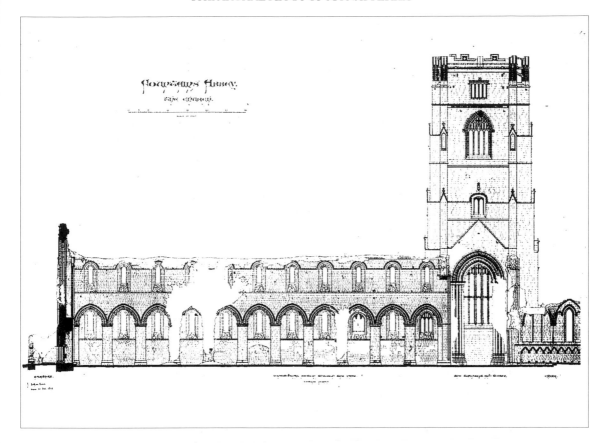

7 Stone-by-stone elevations of Fountains Abbey by J.A. Reeve, an assistant to the architect William Burges, remain the most accurate record of much of this important site

probable context of the removal of the founders' remains from the choir to the chapter house, and it was this rather than the recovery of lost buildings that most interested the excavators.

Monastic archaeology was to assume a more ordered form in the last quarter of the nineteenth century, the principles that were developed then having a lasting effect well into the twentieth century. Interest became more precisely architectural, with excavation used to answer specific questions. The architectural component was the detailed study of surviving fabric and the appreciation that it contained good evidence of the original form of buildings and their modification through time. The most remarkable manifestation of this can be seen in the stone-by-stone record of Fountains Abbey undertaken by J.A. Reeve at the suggestion of the architect William Burges in the 1870s (7). It remains the most complete analysis of any abbey ruin and comprises an effective record of the buildings that were cleared of debris by Walbran a quarter of a century earlier. The most important aspect of this work was its publication as a permanent record of the largest monastic ruin in Britain.

THE INFLUENCE OF SIR WILLIAM ST JOHN HOPE

The study of monasteries in the last three decades of the nineteenth century and the first decade of the twentieth century was dominated by one man, William St John Hope. He took his lead not from documents, but from the buildings themselves, seeking to establish ground plans from both standing masonry and buried foundations. He had a remarkable career, producing definitive analyses of every major class of monastery, surveying and excavating four Benedictine, two Cluniac, six Cistercian, four Augustinian, six Premonstratensian, one Templar and two Carthusian houses as well as one Augustinian nunnery and two houses of friars, towards the end of his career collaborating with two architects, John Bilson and Harold Brakspear. His method of working was basic. Describing the excavation of Alnwick Abbey in Northumberland specifically cleared for the Newcastle meeting of the Royal Archaeological Institute in 1884 on a site where only the gatehouse remained standing, he observed 'a more hopeless site for excavations could hardly be met with but trial trenches soon laid bare foundations of walls and by following these up in a scientific manner, the entire ground plan of the abbey was gradually disclosed'. This technique, if destructive of archaeological stratification, was used effectively at the Cistercian house of Waverley, one of the few Hope excavations for which a photographic record survives (8). The plan of Alnwick that Hope produced (9) was not phased to show periods of construction but it did show precisely what was found. Areas not excavated were labelled as such. What is remarkable about the excavation of Alnwick is the inclusion of the buildings of the inner court or service ranges. Previously, it was only the church, chapter house, and perhaps other cloister ranges, all buildings of some architectural sophistication, that had been studied. Hope was at a loss to interpret them for lack of parallels, describing them as 'a singular collection of chambers, ovens, fireplaces, etc., of which it is difficult to fix the precise age'. He was not even sure they were medieval.

8 Hope's excavation of Waverley Priory was very much an exercise in following walls, as this trench along the west wall of the east range shows. Wall following might be expanded in interesting areas, doing untold damage to the archaeological deposits he cut through without record

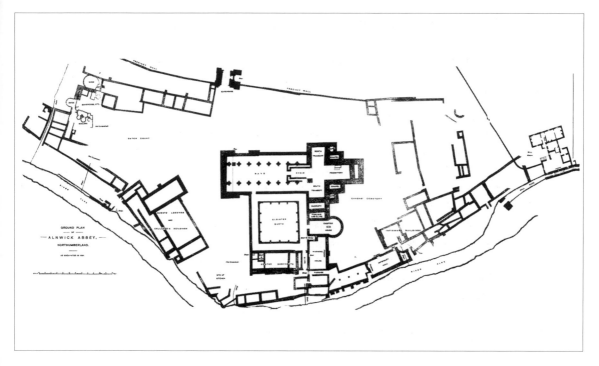

9 Hope's published plan of Alnwick Abbey made in the 1880s records every wall uncovered, providing a remarkably complete plan of the site, though it does not attempt to show the date of any of the buildings

In dealing with standing ruins, selective clearance was carried out to establish the outline of buildings and small trenches, seldom more than 0.3-0.6m in width, were dug to examine key intersections. Where these have been re-excavated at Fountains Abbey and Mount Grace Priory in North Yorkshire, it is clear that they were placed with considerable skill and remarkable economy. They also indicate that the plans he produced required a great deal of intuitive guesswork and may not necessarily be as simple or as accurate as he assumed. A change can be recognised in his later work, with the production of coloured phase plans and more detailed descriptions of architectural detail, reflecting the influence and collaboration of Harold Brakspear at Beaulieu (Hampshire), Jervaulx and Fountains (where Brakspear drew the highly detailed and analytical plans), and John Bilson at Kirkstall.

The value of Hope's work lay in the identification of individual buildings and the establishment of a series of 'standard' plans, and his bringing of academic respectability to monastic archaeology led to others following in his footsteps. His detailed studies of Fountains and Mount Grace remain classics even though both sites have been the scene of major recent excavations. Because he was led by standing buildings, his efforts (and those of his imitators) were concentrated on the church, cloister buildings and gatehouse, leading to a failure to understand that the monastic precinct contained many other buildings of architectural sophistication which could often be identified from documents.

THE WIDENING CONCEPT OF MONASTIC ARCHAEOLOGY

Harold Brakspear, whose archaeological career began with Hope in the 1890s, had a much wider concept of monastic archaeology than his mentor. He broke new ground in three respects: the study of the precinct as a whole; the recovery of buried buildings by area excavation as well as trenching; and the understanding that early buildings could be traced on the site of their successors. His first major excavation, taken over from Hope in 1899, was on an important Cistercian site, the abbey of Waverley (*colour plate 3*), where his published report still stands the test of time. He worked from both surviving documents and the remaining ruins to identify the original church and cloister layout and its substantial rebuilding. His excavation, which was completed by 1900, did not simply look at the church, cloister and infirmary. He went on in 1901 to excavate substantially the lay brothers' infirmary and the inner court, an operation he completed the following year, together with a complicated brew house. In 1903, he excavated a further group of buildings to the north-west of the abbey church, badly disturbed by modern watercourses and difficult to identify, but probably the almonry. He then gave up, failing to find the inner gatehouse and gate chapel, known from John Aubrey's description of the 1660s, though not before he had carefully examined the 24ha of the enclosed precinct, identifying evidence of water management.

His interest in the whole of the precinct recurred in his excavation and survey of Stanley Abbey, Wiltshire, in 1905-6, though he was not able to examine outlying buildings. He did, however, locate them on the ground and planned their apparent robber trenches along with the major earthworks of the precinct. Within the claustral nucleus he was able not only to identify the surviving walls and footings of the church and cloister buildings but also to trace walls which had been totally removed by excavating their robber trenches, indicating that he was aware of the latest developments in excavation techniques. His plans included little in the way of supposition, a distinct improvement on the work of Hope, but his technique of excavation was more destructive of archaeological deposits, though he rarely excavated below the uppermost floors except in

10 Although the church at Bardney Abbey had been thoroughly demolished at the suppression, its floors and lower walls recovered before the First World War remained in excellent condition. The grave markers in the floor were broken and depressed by falling masonry

small trenches. Although he revealed the existence of an earlier church at Stanley Abbey on the same model as his primary church at Waverley, it was not followed up, and remains for future study.

The last great excavation of a monastic site before the First World War, was undertaken by the Rev. C.E. Laing at Bardney Abbey, a major Benedictine house on the Witham fen edge in Lincolnshire. The method of excavation – trenching followed up by clearance to floor level – was very much that of Hope and Brakspear. Indeed, Hope's advice was taken at the outset of the excavation, and it was Brakspear who did most of the recording and eventually published the site. At Bardney excavation was taken to its logical conclusion: the wholesale exposure of structures, and in particular the church (*10*). Work was stopped by the war and by Laing's early death, and some 70 per cent of the walled precinct still remains to be excavated. Only the central buildings and the gatehouses had been examined, and they were left exposed to public view within a wall built from fallen stone. Laing had unintentionally demonstrated the future for monastic ruins in the twentieth century. Unfortunately, the low walls were never conserved and began to fall apart, being reburied in the 1930s to protect them from the weather. Today they remain buried, and the site is only capable of reinterpretration from Brakspear's magisterial report and an incredible series of photographs taken during the excavation and sold as postcards to finance the operation.

MONASTIC ARCHAEOLOGY AND THE STATE

The Ancient Monuments Act of 1911 permitted the government to take into state guardianship any ruins or buildings of archaeological and architectural importance, and allowed for their repair and display to the public. The effect that this was to have on monastic studies was dramatic. Many of the most important abbey and priory remains were taken into the guardianship of the Office of Works and its successors, with the express intention of repairing and conserving their fabric for the first time. Because the emphasis was on conservation and display, however, it tended to be only the church and claustral ranges that were taken, divorcing the central group of buildings from the normally less well-preserved areas of the inner and outer courts and even placing these areas at risk. Many of the earliest guardianships were in the north of England, where the survival of fabric was greatest, and included several sites that had not been available to Hope or his contemporaries. Among many other sites, Rievaulx in North Yorkshire, a completely untouched site, was taken in 1918, Roche in 1921, Byland (North Yorkshire), again barely disturbed, in 1922, Furness (Cumbria) and Titchfield (Hampshire) in 1923, Egglestone (North Yorkshire) in 1925, Monk Bretton (South Yorkshire) in 1932, St Augustine's, Canterbury, in 1939, Shap (Cumbria) in 1948, Creake (Norfolk) and Lilleshall (Shropshire) in 1950, Thornton (north Lincolnshire)

11 Rievaulx Abbey was one of the few major monasteries that had not been dug into in the nineteenth century. Many of its buildings, including the nave of the church, were totally buried. *English Heritage*

in 1954, and Fountains in 1966. Central to the early policy of state care was the first Chief Inspector of Ancient Monuments, Sir Charles Peers. His own monastic interests can be seen in an active policy of acquisition and in the series of site guides he produced, and his policies were to have a lasting effect on monastic studies well into the 1960s.

Peers was not simply content to conserve the upstanding ruins, which he did with an exemplary respect for what he found, adding new masonry only where it was needed to support historic fabric, he also undertook the excavation of the sites to recover their full plans, recovering the remains of demolished walls and internal fittings. By modern standards, his excavations were brutal but effective, involving the clearance of all fallen debris, including the evidence for the latest occupation and demolition, but usually stopping at the latest floor levels. His approach developed those of Hope and Brakspear, but the resources he had at his command meant that, like Laing at Bardney, he could strip large areas and, with state funding, could conserve what he found for posterity. It is Peers who was responsible for the didactic display of vegetation-free masonry and closely-mown lawns that are still associated with monastic ruins.

Rievaulx Abbey, one of the first sites to be tackled by Peers in 1919 (*11*), remains today very much as Peers left it (*12*), stripped of its latest occupation and demolition levels by a small army of workmen, many of whom were

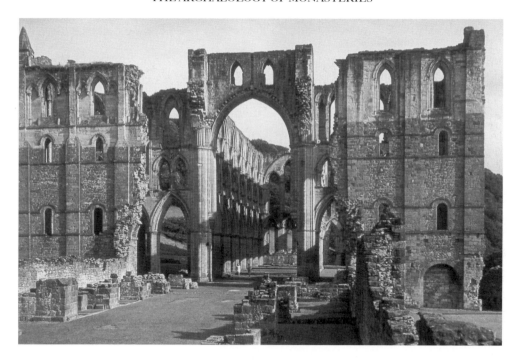

12 After 1921 the church at Rievaulx looked very different. It is seen here shortly after the completion of its conservation. Up to 3m of fallen debris had been removed to reveal one of the earliest surviving Cistercian churches in Europe

unemployed veterans of the First World War. There was little archaeological supervision of any kind, the day-to-day decisions being taken by the site foreman, who was a stone mason. In spite of this, rudimentary records were made of the most significant finds, and most, if not all, of the fallen architectural detail, coins, small finds, and even pottery can still be identified to a findspot. No attempt was made to excavate below the latest surviving floors, with the result that most of the structural archaeology that will identify phases of construction or even earlier phases of building is still intact (*13*). The loss of post-monastic deposits, which would include perhaps the evidence for the reuse of buildings after the suppression, was not considered important at the time and, though it had interested Brakspear, was thought to be a necessary price to pay for the large-scale recovery of important claustral plans. The simplistic idea that only monastic remains were significant on monastic sites was to continue into the 1960s, with the loss of many important post-medieval buildings, such as the seventeenth-century farmhouse built into the gatehouse at Monk Bretton Priory, and the post-suppression Cavendish house built into the west range of Rufford Abbey in Nottinghamshire (*14*), as inspectors trained by Peers pursued his purist approach. Few records survive to show how Peers and his workforce went about their task of clearing monastic sites, and photographs of work in progress are rare in the extreme.

13 The Office of Works clearance of Rievaulx was extensively recorded. The excavation of the mid-twelfth-century chapter house in 1921 demonstrates the method of working, with clearance to the latest surviving floor. Note the track of the Decauville light railway (post-First World War government surplus) and the adjacent heap of recovered masonry which would be used to cap the newly exposed walls

14 In 1950, the now ruined west range of Rufford Abbey remained a roofed building, a sixteenth- to nineteenth-century house that incorporated the twelfth- and thirteenth-century remains of the lay brothers' range. It was ruthlessly stripped away to reveal, none too successfully, the medieval fabric. Only the seventeenth-century kitchen survived long enough to be repaired and returned to use in the 1990s

Research excavation below the latest floors was rare, largely because of the need to conserve sites for public display, though it did happen occasionally. At Whitby Abbey (North Yorkshire) up to 2.7m of fallen masonry had to be removed to recover the plan of the church (see Chapter 6). The fallen debris was not simply rubble discarded by stone robbers but great sections of superstructure such as the western tower arch and three bays of the clerestory of the nave, which had fallen intact as the ruin decayed. Whitby was a site with an intriguing early history and Peers actually excavated below its latest floors. First, the remains of an earlier Norman church were excavated, and in 1924, following the discovery of Saxon buildings below the outer parlour on the south side of the church, the large-scale excavation of buried structures belonging to the Saxon monastery was undertaken, first to the west of the nave and then on the north side of the church (see 50). As with general clearance, there was a lack of constant archaeological supervision resulting in a poor quality of record, leaving the pre-conquest monastery both damaged and imperfectly understood. The work done by the Office of Works and excavations at non-guardianship sites, such as St Augustine's at Canterbury, Glastonbury (Somerset), Whalley (Lancashire) and Sempringham (Lincolnshire), set a new standard for monastic archaeology, however, and brought it firmly to the public's attention. Sites once conserved were opened to the public and proved immediately popular. Peers and his successors wrote a series of academically sound and remarkably informative guides to individual sites, all of which featured an accurate and phased ground plan, and which summarised the sites' history and architectural development. They also published more detailed considerations of their work in the academic press and both these media were to have a lasting effect, bringing scholarship to the general public and with it an appreciation of the monuments. While the study of monastic sites in the nineteenth century had been a matter for interested individuals, the twentieth century saw its exploitation for the masses. From those masses came the next generation of monastic scholars, who were to bring analytical excavation, detailed documentary research and a new appreciation of the potential of our monastic resources.

From the early nineteenth century, research on monastic sites had been driven by an obsession with the recovery of ground plans to the exclusion of the many other aspects of religious life that the sites could evidence. Perhaps the turning point was marked in the early 1950s, first by the aerial study of monastic sites which reawakened interest in non-claustral buildings and sites not in state care, and then by a growing interest in medieval archaeology which had previously been seen simply as a tool of the historian. Sites without standing masonry, so far largely ignored, were coming under threat from more intensive agriculture (15) and from housing or office development. Starting with the excavation of the London Charterhouse and part of the church of Bermondsey Abbey by W.F. Grimes, the active study of monastic sites passed from those who were primarily motivated by architectural history to those who were primarily archaeologists interested in recording all aspects of the site they excavated. The result has been that in the last 50 years far more has been learned about the origins, growth and demise of abbeys and priories in Britain, and a much fuller picture can be reconstructed of sites examined previously. Much work was government sponsored, initially on sites threatened with destruction: the Trinitarian house of Thelsford (Warwickshire), the Gilbertine houses of Haverholme and North Ormsby (both Lincolnshire), the Cluniac priory at Faversham (Kent), the nunneries of Elstow (Bedfordshire) and Sopwell (Hertfordshire), and the Templar preceptory of South Witham (Lincolnshire). Privately sponsored work ran in parallel with rescue archaeology, with major work undertaken by Leeds Museum at Kirkstall Abbey and by H.H. Swinnerton at Lenton Priory (Nottinghamshire). The results of these excavations inevitably led to a change in the way sites in the care of the state were treated. No longer were sites simply cleared of debris. Now they were properly excavated, leading to a fuller understanding of their potential. The pioneering work of Roy Gilyard-Beer at Gisborough Priory and Muchelney Abbey (Somerset) and Andrew Saunders at St Augustine's Abbey, Canterbury, was followed in the late

15 The great Gilbertine monastery of Sempringham, partially excavated in 1938-9, was cultivated from 1940 as part of the war effort and remains in cultivation. Below the square earthwork which is part of a post-suppression house are the foundations of the double church and north and south cloisters, visible as exceptionally clear cropmarks. *Cambridge Air Photography Committee*

1960s by large-scale excavations at Mount Grace Priory (North Yorkshire) and Rosemary Cramp's analyses of the Saxon and later monastery at Jarrow (Tyne and Wear), and more recently those at Bayham, Battle (East Sussex), Fountains, Gloucester Blackfriars, and Southwick (Hampshire).

NEW DIRECTIONS IN MONASTIC ARCHAEOLOGY

From the 1970s there has been an increasing interest in monastic archaeology and a further change in the direction of research, with a growing emphasis on the economic aspects of religious life. Major excavations have taken place at Norton Priory (Cheshire), Bradwall Abbey (Buckinghamshire) and Sandwell Priory (West Midlands), and continues at Bordesley Abbey (Worcestershire), providing, as did Birkenhead Priory and Kirkstall Abbey in the nineteenth century, a focus for new towns. Redevelopment on urban sites has led to the large-scale excavation of friary sites, most notably in Guildford, Leicester, Newcastle and Beverley (East Yorkshire), and other houses such as that of the Gilbertines at York. The difference is that the recent excavations have examined the sites involved totally, looking particularly at the way sites grew and were managed, using not only the buildings but also their cultural contents and the burials they contained. At Bordesley, for instance, not only are the cloister buildings involved, but the whole of the precinct has also been studied, with selective excavation of buildings in it – to date, the gate chapel and an industrial mill. At Norton, the tile kiln that provided much of the flooring for the church has been examined, and much of the precinct is preserved within a public park. In the field of rescue archaeology, three sites have made an important contribution to the study of the economic basis of monastic life: Grove Priory (Bedfordshire) (*16*), where the whole site has been examined in detail; Waltham Abbey in Essex (see *84*), where large areas of the outer court and home grange have been excavated; and Thornholme Priory (north Lincolnshire), where excavation has defined the development of the service areas of a well-preserved earthwork site (*17*) over four centuries. Additionally, work in the outer court at Fountains Abbey began the study of the economy of the richest Cistercian monastery in England with the analysis of two buildings central to its management – the mill (*76*) and the wool-house (*77*) – coupled with a re-examination of the church and cloister buildings that has substantially altered their accepted interpretation, and at the related Sawley Abbey (Lancashire) excavation below the south side of the cloister has revealed the largest known concentration of temporary timber buildings ever recovered. All of this work was driven by a developing research agenda that sought to expand our basic knowledge of monastic sites.

In the 1980s and 1990s some of the most important work on monasteries has undoubtedly been done in London, with large-scale excavations and multiple small-scale interventions on the sites of the Benedictine nunnery of St Mary of Clerkenwell, Cluniac Bermonsdey Abbey, the Carthusian charterhouse, the great Hospitlar priory of St John of Jerusalem, the Cistercian abbeys of St Mary Graces and Stratford Langthorne, and the Augustinian priories of Holy Trinity in Aldate and Merton in Surrey. These sites have demonstrated the value of combining modern excavation and recording with a systematic review of earlier antiquarian research, and extensive documentary analysis. Not only has it been possible to reconstruct complex sites from many excavations carried out under rescue conditions, but the emphasis has been placed on achieving an understanding of the whole precinct and its post-suppression development. Elsewhere, other sites have been examined for strictly research purposes. At Mount Grace Priory, the best-preserved Carthusian monastery in Britain, the excavation of the 1960s and '70s that examined individual monks' cells has been followed up by the excavation of the kitchens and communal buildings between 1988 and 1992, coupled with a full analysis of the standing fabric of the ruins which contain almost as much archaeological information as the ground around them, and the large collection of loose architectural detail from the site. Mount Grace is the most intensively studied Carthusian monastery in Europe. Aspects of archaeological research that were commissioned in the 1980s are now coming to publication, finally making them accessible. Peter Fergusson and Stuart Harrison's long-term research at Rievaulx places it on a par with Mount Grace for the Cistercian order, and Jennie Stopford's study of floor tiles from northern monasteries has brought together dispersed collections which alter significantly our perceptions of individual buildings.

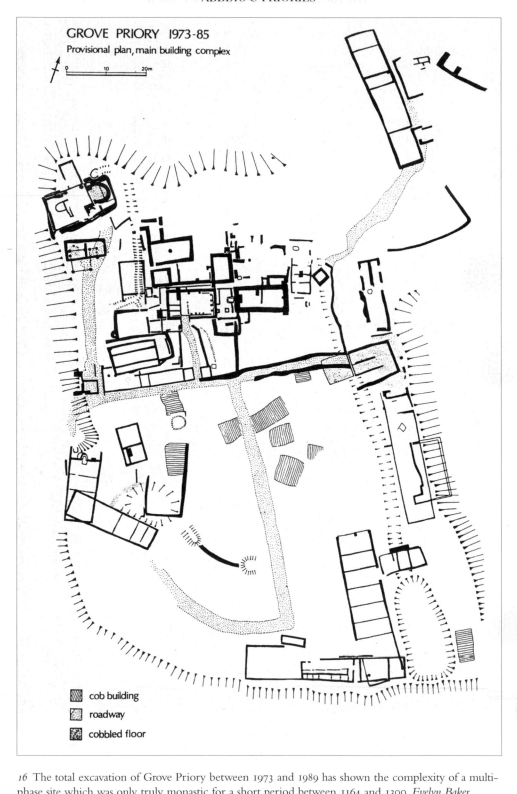

GROVE PRIORY 1973-85
Provisional plan, main building complex

0   10   20m

cob building
roadway
cobbled floor

16 The total excavation of Grove Priory between 1973 and 1989 has shown the complexity of a multi-phase site which was only truly monastic for a short period between 1164 and 1300. *Evelyn Baker*

17 Thornholme Priory, an earthwork site with no standing ruins, is a good example of a total precinct, with the cloister occupying the highest part of this island site (to the right of the ruined farm buildings). The remainder of the precinct is made up of enclosed courts containing many buildings. Large parts of the service areas of this Augustinian house were excavated between 1974 and 1980. *Cambridge Air Photography Committee*

Most recently, there has been a movement towards understanding the patronage and location of monastic settlement. In particular, the use of aerial photography and field–walking is being used to locate precisely the whole extent of monastic sites in cultivation and to date their origins by the pottery they are producing. Tim Pestell's work in Norfolk has produced remarkable results, and this is being repeated elsewhere. It has the benefit of being non–intrusive, leaving destructive research to the time when we actually understand which sites we need to look at as part of a wide–ranging research strategy. In a little over two centuries, the imperative has gradually moved from the study of individual sites to an understanding of the whole phenomenon of monastic settlement. The scale of past research has been substantial, with some excavation being carried out on nearly 200 sites since 1945, almost one fifth of those available. Much of this work has been small-scale, and some of it not very informative; some has been extensive and of international importance. Only now are we starting to understand what we should be looking at, and why.

Since John Martin persuaded the gardener to clear out the chapter house at Fountains Abbey in 1790, monastic archaeology has come of age and permitted an accurate impression of monastic life to be recreated. There are still many gaps in our knowledge, and every new excavation will add to our understanding. Monasteries are no longer simply churches and cloister buildings, no longer enclosed precincts with many other buildings, they are at last seen for what they were: major religious and economic corporations whose actions affected all of medieval England. They were, of course, much more than this, and in our attempts to understand their function we have tended to lose sight of their purpose, and very reason for being. They should be seen not simply as objects of curiosity, but understood as they were by their builders and users, as self-sustaining oratories to God and workshops of prayer.

2

THE MONASTIC CHURCH

The church was the largest and most important building of the monastery. Used for a continuous round of services, its scale, quality and fittings reflected the importance of the community and the aspirations of its patrons. A number of medieval monastic churches survive, among the greatest being the cathedral churches of Carlisle, Canterbury, Chester, Durham, Ely, Gloucester, Peterborough, Rochester, Winchester, and Worcester. Others survive at least in part as parish churches, like Binham (Norfolk), Bolton (North Yorkshire), Boxgrove (West Sussex), Bridlington (East Yorkshire), Christchurch (Hampshire), Crowland (Lincolnshire), Leominster (Herefordshire), Malmesbury (Wiltshire), Malvern (Worcestershire), and Selby (North Yorkshire). Others survive in varying states of preservation, ranging from the substantial roofless ruins of Fountains, Mount Grace, Netley (Hampshire), and Rievaulx, through more heavily ruined buildings like Bury St Edmunds (Suffolk) and Kirkham (North Yorkshire), to mere fragments like Kirkstead and Barlings (both Lincolnshire) or the Dominican friary at Boston (Lincolnshire). Others, like Temple Bruer (Lincolnshire) and Bordesley are known primarily from excavation. No church remains in its medieval state or retains its original furnishings or decoration, and most have been substantially rebuilt, extended, and altered in their four centuries or more of extended use. It is only by comparing surviving buildings, the evidence of excavation, and the evidence of contemporary documents that we can understand how monastic churches were originally planned and how they developed to suit changing liturgies and growing (or indeed shrinking) aspirations.

Reduced to its basic provisions, the convent church was a house for the altar, the monastic choir where mass and the seven daily offices or services were sung, additional altars for the religious who were priests and required to say a personal mass, and for the burial of the founder and his family. In some cases, a part of the church might be reserved for the laity. While changing liturgy, increasing wealth and growing communities might lead to changes in the planning of the monastic church, the need to provide these facilities remained constant.

THE CHURCHES OF SAXON MONASTERIES

The earliest monastic churches in England were built of timber, and few have been identified in excavation. The archetype was the church of Glastonbury, known in the twelfth century when it was still standing as the *vetusta ecclesia* (ancient church). Its date is unknown, though it must have predated the construction of a masonry church in the early eighth century, and it had been remodelled several times before it was destroyed by fire in 1184. It was associated with at least four other wooden buildings and a cemetery with two stone-built mausolea, all within an enclosing ditch.

What the Glastonbury church must have looked like can be judged from two Middle-Anglian buildings with associated cemeteries at Brandon in Suffolk, almost certainly the site of a seventh- and eighth-century monastery. Both buildings were rectangular, the larger some 14m x 7m, with walls of timber posts set either in post-pits or trenches, with doors at the centre of the side walls. A similar building at Flixborough in North Lincolnshire with associated burials may also be monastic. The buildings are indistinguishable from standard Middle-Saxon halls, and in plan and construction little different from the domestic buildings associated with them. The planning of these early monasteries derives not from continental monasteries, but is deeply rooted in the Irish monastic tradition, though the buildings are Anglo Saxon and not Irish in their method of construction.

The continental pattern was introduced to England in or after 597, with the mission of Augustine of Tarsus to the court of the Kentish King Æthelberht. Augustine was prior of St Andrew's monastery in Rome, and he brought with him monks from that monastery. Given a site in the Roman cemetery to the east of Canterbury, Augustine established a monastery, the church of which was excavated between 1900 and 1931, and partially re-examined in 1955. Dedicated to Sts Peter and Paul and most probably completed in 613, it is the earliest-known church in England (*18*). Reduced to low walling, and partly destroyed by the late eleventh-century church that stands on its site, it was built of reused Roman tile set in pink mortar and had mortar floors. It was a simple rectangular building, with a porch at its west end, no aisles but *porticus* or chapels ranged along its side walls, and an apsidal chancel which was destroyed in the mid-eleventh century. It was designed from the first to be a mausoleum church, the early archbishops of Canterbury being buried in the north *porticus* and King Æthelberht of Kent and his Frankish wife Bertha in the southern *porticus*. The church was built in the late Roman manner, and almost certainly masons had to be brought from northern France to build it. In 620 a second church dedicated to St Mary was built in line to the east, and a third church, dedicated to St Pancras to the east of that. St Mary's church, which lay on the site of the crypt of the Norman church, became the burial place of further royalty and the monastery's abbots; St Pancras' church survived to become the cemetery church of the later abbey.

The building of a series of small churches in line was very much a feature of Middle-Saxon monasteries, and similar arrangements have been recorded at Glastonbury, Winchester, Monkwearmouth, and Jarrow. The importance of the Canterbury churches is that they were observed to develop, and that process was elucidated by excavation and historical research. From the surviving excavated remains, and by analogy with the late seventh-century monastery church of Reculver in Kent which largely survived into the early nineteenth century, it is possible to reconstruct their original appearance (*19*). Gradually, between the eighth and eleventh centuries, the churches grew together to form a composite church, much more like the great monastic churches of continental

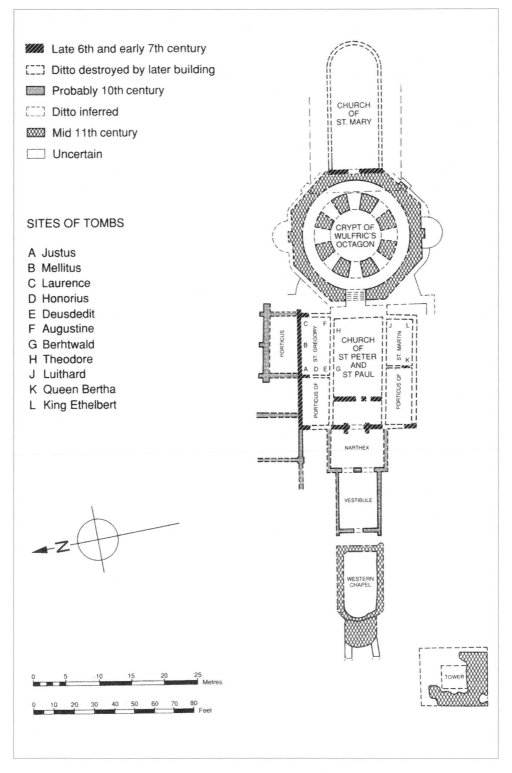

Late 6th and early 7th century
Ditto destroyed by later building
Probably 10th century
Ditto inferred
Mid 11th century
Uncertain

SITES OF TOMBS

A Justus
B Mellitus
C Laurence
D Honorius
E Deusdedit
F Augustine
G Berhtwald
H Theodore
J Luithard
K Queen Bertha
L King Ethelbert

CHURCH OF ST. MARY

CRYPT OF WULFRIC'S OCTAGON

PORTICUS

PORTICUS OF ST. GREGORY

CHURCH OF ST PETER AND ST PAUL

PORTICUS OF ST. MARTIN

NARTHEX

VESTIBULE

WESTERN CHAPEL

TOWER

Metres
Feet

18 The Saxon churches that lie below the great Norman abbey church at St Augustine's, Canterbury

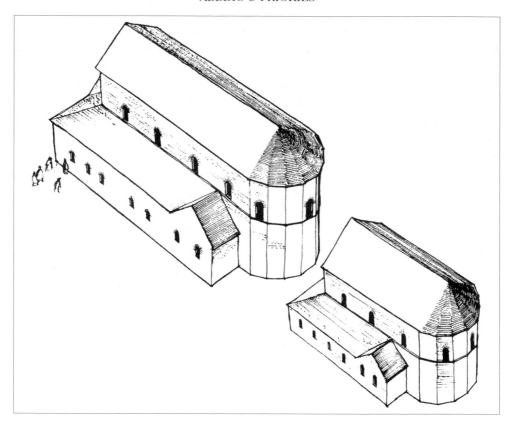

19 The earliest Saxon churches at Canterbury were more substantial than their plans might suggest, with the church of Sts Peter, Paul and Augustine to the left, and the church of St Mary to the right. *Terry Ball and Richard Gem*

Europe. An additional *porticus* was added on the north side of the church of Sts Peter and Paul between 731 and 792, and a major extension was carried out in the tenth century, completed by 978 when St Dunstan re-dedicated the church to Sts Peter, Paul and Augustine. The context for this rebuilding or reordering (*20*) was the monastic reform led by Sts Æthelwold, Oswald and Dunstan that brought Benedictine monasticism as it was practised in northern France to England and that occasioned the *Regularis Concordia* (Agreement about the Rule), a code of practice drawn up by the Council of Winchester in 973. Specifically, the *Regularis Concordia* defined three liturgical areas within the church, each with its own altar: at the west end (*oratorium* (oratory)); in the nave (*ecclesia* (church)); and at the east end (*chorus* (choir)) of the church. At Canterbury, this was marked by the western extension of the nave into the old narthex or porch, the building of a new narthex to the west, and a vestibule beyond that. A new screen was erected in the nave, and it is likely that the eastern *porticus* were converted into two-storey transepts and that the nave was raised in height to match them. The upper storeys of the transepts acted as galleries above the nave altar that was backed by a wall that separated the *ecclesia* in the nave from the *chorus* in the eastern apse.

The final stage of development at Canterbury can be dated to the abbacy of Wulfric II in the early eleventh century. In 1047 he helped fund the completion of a great bell tower then under construction, and he may also have been responsible for the westward expansion of the church, the construction of which is dated by early eleventh-century pottery in its foundation trenches. His greatest work however, was to join the church of Sts Peter, Paul and Augustine to the church of St Mary by the construction of a great octagon raised over a crypt, a project for which he gained papal approval in 1049. This involved the demolition of the eastern apse of the western church and the western porch of the eastern church and displaced the shrine of St Mildrith (who had been brought from Minster in Thanet) and many burials. It was also a major change in the planning of the monastic church and its developing liturgy. The work was never completed and was abandoned at Wulfric's death in 1061. William The Conqueror's invasion of England five years later ensured that work would not restart, and that a different model of monastic church (see below) would take its place. Two models exist for this momentous structure, the rotunda of St Benigne at Dijon and the smaller rotunda of the Benedictine nunnery of Ottmarsheim in Alsace which was dedicated by Pope Leo IX in the same year that Wulfric sought the pope's blessing for his project. Goscelin of Canterbury, writing in the twelfth century, acknowledged that it was a landmark building, but said that the inexperience of the workmen made it unsuitable for monastic use. It was the first instance in England of the separation of a monastic choir and altar from the main body of the church.

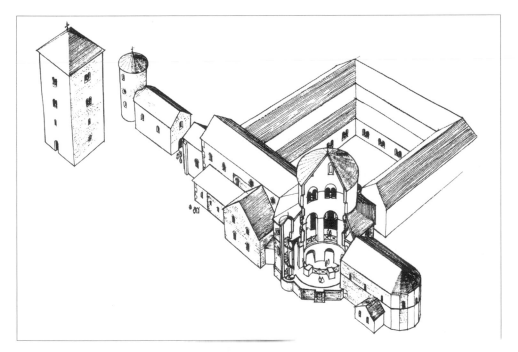

20 The growth of the Canterbury churches and the development of a cloister, first under St Dunstan and later under Abbot Wulfric was dramatic and closely related to developments on the continent. *Terry Ball and Richard Gem*

Similar development can be seen in the church of Glastonbury where a monastic community had existed from perhaps as early as the sixth century. Its early timber church survived (see above) and to the east of it King Ine of Wessex built a rectangular stone church at the turn of the eighth century (*21*), with flanking *porticus* and an eastern chancel of square plan set over a mausoleum. It was linked to the wooden church by a walled court or *atrium*. This building, known primarily from excavation, was modified substantially by St Dunstan, abbot from 944 to 956. His biographer, William of Malmesbury, records 'he added a tower to this church, considerably lengthened it and, so that it might form a square in length and breadth, he added aisles or *porticus* as they call them'. Ine's mausoleum was destroyed to build the tower, with its walls refaced and widened to carry the superstructure. To the north and south of the tower slightly irregular *porticus* were added in the form of transepts, much in the manner of the later work at Canterbury, and from a later documentary source it is clear that these were two-storeyed with galleries looking down onto the nave altar. To the east Dunstan built a new chancel with flanking *porticus* to north and south. Its eastern limit has yet to be confirmed by excavation.

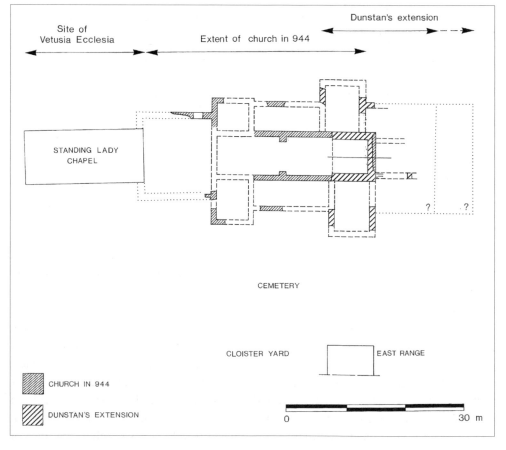

21 Excavation below the medieval church at Glastonbury has revealed fragmentary remains of the Saxon monastic church built by King Ine from about 700 and later extended by St Dunstan. *After Eric Fernie*

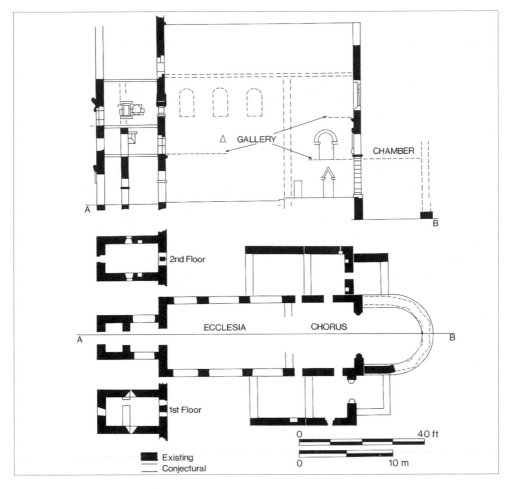

22 Deerhurst, the best-preserved Saxon monastic church in England, survives substantially as built, allowing its Late-Saxon form to be recovered. *After Taylor and Taylor*

In both these cases, excavation has recovered a ground plan, albeit fragmentary, but it can tell us very little about the elevation of the buildings. Documentary sources imply that Saxon monastic churches had more than one storey, and this is confirmed by the few buildings of the period that survive. The finest of these is Deerhurst in Gloucestershire, built by 804 and ceasing to be monastic before the Norman conquest. The archaeological study of its surviving fabric coupled with the excavation of demolished elements has revealed it to be a complicated structure (22). The first phase of stone building, which overlay an existing Christian cemetery, comprised a rectangular building with a porch at its west end and no separate chancel, its walls surviving in places to their full height of only 3.6m. At some point before the mid-tenth century an apsidal chancel was added. Although it was built from a level 1.5m below the floor of the nave it did not contain a crypt or mausoleum. The church was extensively rebuilt in the tenth century, perhaps as a result of the reform of the monastery by St Oswald in about 970. The nave was raised to its present height of 12.2m and a square *chorus* defined to the east of the *ecclesia* in the nave by the insertion of a cross wall. The apsidal chancel was rebuilt in polygonal form, its outer face decorated with strip-work at the angles. Two-storey *porticus* were built to the north and south of the choir, with wide round-headed openings at first-floor level, perhaps leading to timber galleries. Excavation demonstrated that further *porticus* were added, first to the west and then to the east, overlapping the construction of the new chancel. They, too, appear to have had an upper floor. An upper chamber in the chancel is evidenced by a wide opening in the east wall of the choir with a pair of corbels below it to support a gallery. Similarly, the western porch was rebuilt to form a tower, probably in two stages. At first-floor level, an oratory was created, its door offset to the north to avoid the altar and leading to a gallery at the west end of the nave. The room above had a door in its west wall, leading to an external gallery, and a pair of triangular windows looking into the nave. Here, in three dimensions, is a small church of the late tenth-century monastic reform which evidences the insular development of the monastic church at the height of Saxon monasticism.

THE CHURCHES OF NORMAN BENEDICTINE MONASTERIES

The traumatic conquest of England in 1066 sounded the death knell for the Anglo-Saxon monastic church with the introduction of new abbots, and with them new architectural models from Normandy that reflected the greater influence of the tenth-century reforms in continental Europe. The change had, in fact, begun before the Norman conquest with Edward the Confessor's rebuilding of Westminster Abbey, which was sufficiently complete for him to be buried there in January 1066. Limited excavation below the floor of its thirteenth-century successor has revealed sufficient low walling and foundation work to show that King Edward's work was closely modelled on the abbey church of Jumiège, and it is perhaps not surprising that he was supported in his endeavours by Bishop Robert of London, who, as abbot of Jumiège, had begun rebuilding the church there before 1044. At Westminster, the new church had a long, aisled nave with paired western towers, a crossing with fully developed transepts and a short eastern arm that terminated in an apse. What was innovative before the conquest was to become the norm when new Norman abbots were intruded into existing Saxon monasteries, and when new monasteries were established by the Norman aristocracy on their English estates. The destruction of the Saxon monasteries at Canterbury (both the cathedral priory and St Augustine's) and Glastonbury was only a matter of time.

The basic church plan introduced from Normandy was to survive up to the suppression of the monasteries in the sixteenth century, though it was modified to suit developing liturgies from time to time, and it can still be identified in its simplest form from many sixteenth-century surveys. At the Cistercian nunnery of Kirklees (*23*), where the church has been excavated, a survey made in 1534/5 describes the church thus:

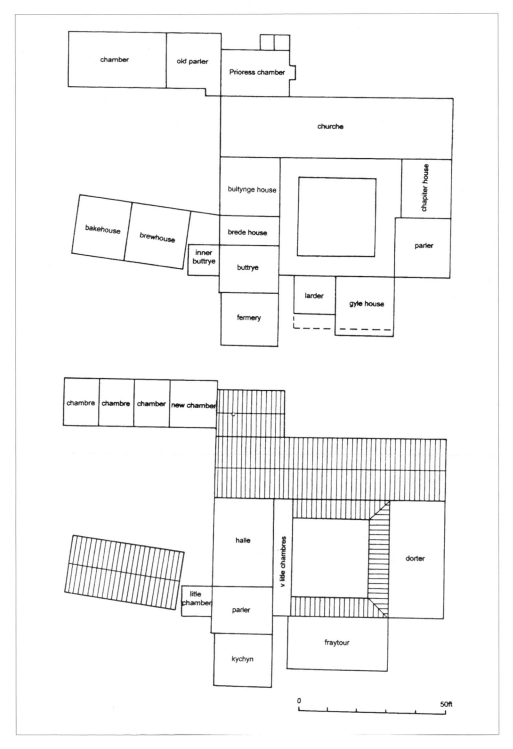

23 Reconstructed from a survey made in 1534/5 which gives approximate dimensions of all its buildings, Kirklees Priory serves to demonstrate a fairly typical monastic layout, with the cloister on the south side of a simple rectangular church

The churche conteyneth in length iiij^{xx} ffoote and in bredith xxi foote, w^t a high roofe coueryd w^t slates, hauinge [blank] glasse wyndowes conteynynge l foote of glasse, w^t the high alter, ij alters in the quere, and ij benethe, and xxij stalles in the quere for the nones.

Although the nuns' church at Kirklees was a simple rectangle, its internal arrangements were closely comparable with the cruciform churches favoured by most monastic orders.

The rebuilding of St Augustine's Abbey at Canterbury is remarkably well documented and attested by excavation, and shows that it was normal even for great churches to be built in stages (24). Abbot Scolland, formerly a monk of Mont-St-Michel started the building of a great cruciform pilgrimage church in, or after, 1070 on the site of the Saxon monastic church of St Mary to house the relics from the earlier Saxon monastery, building an aisled apsidal presbytery above a crypt. At his death only the presbytery, transepts, crossing and eastern two bays of the nave had been completed. This was sufficient to house the choir monks and their altars, a natural place to pause in the construction of a church. The monk Goscelin's contemporary chronicle, however, explains that there was a problem. The convent was divided over the demolition of St Augustine's original church of Sts Peter and Paul and disturbing the burials it contained. Almost certainly the dispute was between Saxon members of the community who resented the loss of their old church, and Norman monks who had no attachment to it. Scolland had no such qualms, for he had laid out the foundations of his intended nave around the old building. It was left to his successor Wido in 1087 to complete the rebuilding, and the bones of the archbishops and kings of Kent buried in the old church were translated to the new one three years later. He changed the intended plan, adding further foundations for two western towers that were not actually built until after his death in 1099. The architectural detail of the north-west tower, which survived until 1822, shows it to be the work of his successor, Hugh de Fleury. The architectural fragments of this church that survived its wholesale demolition in the sixteenth century show it to have been a building of the highest and most developed quality. The abbey church of St Augustine was not unique but one of a series of monumental Norman churches designed to change the architecture of the English church. A closely comparable church was built at Bury St Edmunds to house the shrine of the martyr King Edmund between about 1090 and 1142. Its model was very clearly the church of St Augustine's at Canterbury, and both followed the apse and ambulatory design established for the cathedral church of Rouen begun in the 1030s.

The majority of churches built within two generations of the conquest, however, were not large or elaborate. They were never intended to be places of pilgrimage. Quite often, they were intended as penance or thanks for the conquest of England provided by the new Norman aristocracy. Some re-colonised earlier Saxon sites or replaced minster churches staffed by secular clergy. Others were completely new foundations. First among these was King William's earliest foundation. The scale of his atonement was modest. In about 1170 the Conqueror decided to establish a small Benedictine abbey on the hill of Senlac, the site of King Harold's last stand at the Battle of Hastings, drawing four monks from the great abbey of Marmoutier (that explains its dedication to St Martin)

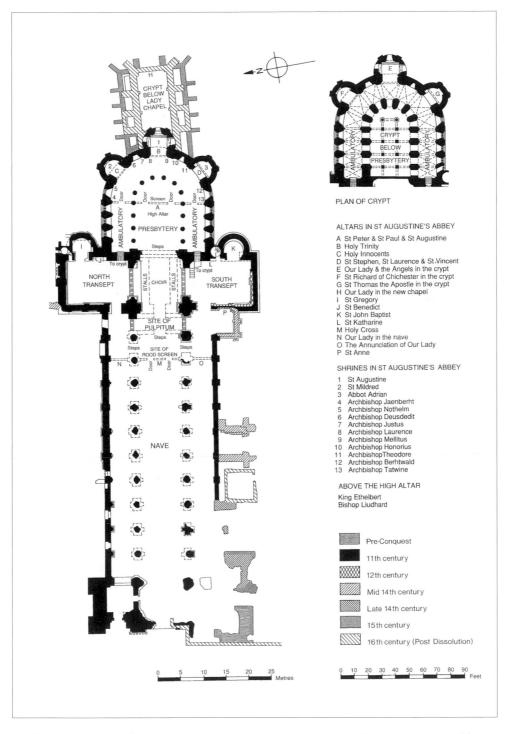

PLAN OF CRYPT

ALTARS IN ST AUGUSTINE'S ABBEY

A St Peter & St Paul & St Augustine
B Holy Trinity
C Holy Innocents
D St Stephen, St Laurence & St.Vincent
E Our Lady & the Angels in the crypt
F St Richard of Chichester in the crypt
G St Thomas the Apostle in the crypt
H Our Lady in the new chapel
I St Gregory
J St Benedict
K St John Baptist
L St Katharine
M Holy Cross
N Our Lady in the nave
O The Annunciation of Our Lady
P St Anne

SHRINES IN ST AUGUSTINE'S ABBEY

1   St Augustine
2   St Mildred
3   Abbot Adrian
4   Archbishop Jaenberht
5   Archbishop Nothelm
6   Archbishop Deusdedit
7   Archbishop Justus
8   Archbishop Laurence
9   Archbishop Mellitus
10 Archbishop Honorius
11 Archbishop Theodore
12 Archbishop Berhtwald
13 Archbishop Tatwine

ABOVE THE HIGH ALTAR

King Ethelbert
Bishop Liudhard

Pre-Conquest
11th century
12th century
Mid 14th century
Late 14th century
15th century
16th century (Post Dissolution)

24 The plan of the Norman and later church at St Augustine's Abbey at Canterbury, recovered by excavation since the late nineteenth century, clearly shows the form of the new 'pilgrimage' churches introduced from the continent. The multiplicity of altars and shrines, identified from medieval sources, amplifies the importance of the building

near Tours in the Loire valley to form the core of a new community. The intention was to place the high altar on the site where Harold fell, and the abbey was simply to be called Battle, a sure sign of the Normans' confidence and arrogance. The monks did not like the site. The narrow ridge had no water, the valley below was an undrained swamp, and they set up their temporary buildings a little to the west on a more favourable site. William forced them back to the original site, and paid for the construction of their church exactly where he wanted it (25). The eastern arm and crossing was completed by 1076 and could be consecrated. The remainder was not completed until 1094, seven years after the founder's death. Even with a wealthy patron, churches took some time to build and the death of the founder might considerably slow the process of building. The church that was raised was typical of smaller Benedictine churches in Normandy, a scaled-down version of the greater Benedictine churches. Its slow building was typical of the late eleventh and early twelfth centuries – only those parts needed to serve the immediate needs of the monks were a priority, and England was full of churches waiting to be completed, usually at the expense of the community rather than the founder. Cloister buildings also tended to follow and, for the first generation of monks on a new site, temporary timber buildings and no cloister were the norm.

A second plan form, established at the Conqueror's own abbey of St Etienne in Caen, which was begun in 1066, did not use the great apse and ambulatory seen at St Augustine's or Battle. Instead, the central vessel of the apsed presbytery was flanked by shorter aisles with apsidal terminations which might be square-ended externally, the plan chosen for Lanfranc's new church at Canterbury cathedral priory in 1070, St Alban's Abbey in 1077, Whitby Abbey after 1078, St Mary's Abbey at York in about 1088, and Durham cathedral priory in 1093. The east end of these churches presented an impressive facade of stepped apses, particularly if the inner chapels of the transepts were extended, in what is known as the echelon plan. It was used extensively for the churches of smaller monasteries of both the Benedictines and Cluniacs, and is best seen in the Cluniac churches of Castle Acre and Thetford (both in Norfolk) where the plans of the demolished eastern arms have been recovered by excavation (26).

How the church functioned can be seen at Canterbury (see 24). The high altar stood in the centre of the presbytery or eastern arm, raised above the rest of the church at St Augustine's by the vaulted crypt below, but normally by one or more steps, the *gradus presbyterii*. The choir stalls occupied the crossing and were enclosed to the west, between the crossing piers, by a timber screen with a central door and above loft called the pulpitum. At St Augustine's this was a full bay of the nave deep, though this was exceptional. Within or in front of the pulpitum, flanking the door, were a pair of altars, usually enclosed by wooden screens, and to the west of this was an open space called the retrochoir (literally *behind the choir*) where older monks could sit in more comfort during services, and to the west of that was a second screen that crossed the aisles as well as the nave. This was the rood screen, so called because on its loft was a large crucifix flanked by figures of St Mary and St John, the *rood* in Anglo-Saxon English. It marked the western extremity of the monks' church and had the nave altar against its western face, with doors to either side that provided the only external access to and from the convent's church. Entry from

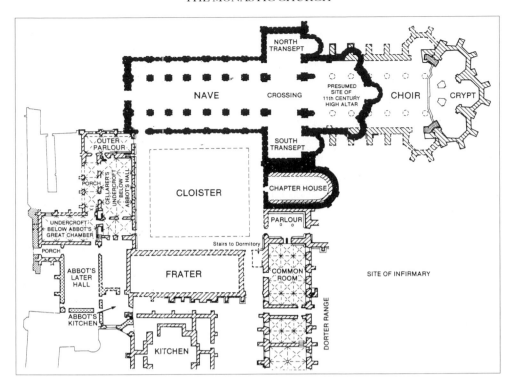

25 The first church at Battle Abbey, with its high altar within an ambulatory presbytery like that of St Augustine's, is typical of the scale and planning of many early Norman monastic churches, and its extension in the late thirteenth century is also fairly typical

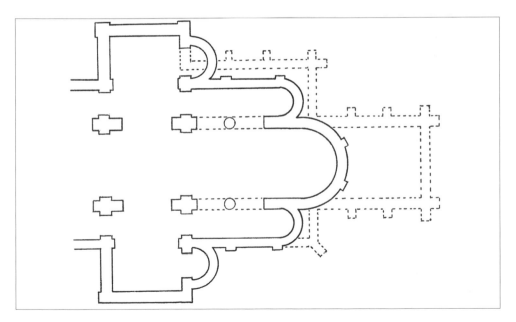

26 The church at Castle Acre Priory, extended in the fourteenth century, had an eastern apse and apsidal aisles, the alternate Norman monastic church plan

the cloister was normally into the aisle of the retrochoir. The nave might be parochial, as at Shrewsbury, Crowland or Wymondham (Norfolk), or simply for processional use, as at Castle Acre or Battle, explaining why it took so long to be completed.

Additional chapels were provided for those monks who were priests and thus required to say personal masses, always in the transepts and perhaps at the east end of the church, in the aisles or in projecting chapels if the presbytery had an ambuatory. The aisles were essentially corridors around the monks' choir and enclosure of the presbytery, and they tended to be vaulted, unlike the nave, presbytery and transepts which had wooden roofs.

In elevation, early Benedictine and Cluniac churches were tall buildings of three storeys as the surviving naves of St Albans (Hertfordshire), Norwich, Malmesbury (Wiltshire), and Ely (Cambridgeshire) demonstrate. Designed to be impressive, they were as much an expression of their founders' power as their occupants' piety. The purpose of their foundation was normally to provide a mausoleum for the founder and his family who would be buried in the presbytery and benefit spiritually from every office sung in the church.

The 'standard' Benedictine plan introduced by the Normans served in the main for independent monasteries. Many of the early monasteries, however, were gifts of land to monastic houses on the new aristocracy's home estates in Normandy on which they were expected to build a cell or outpost. Gilbert of Ghent, the Conqueror's nephew and a major landowner at the time of the Domesday Book, gave the site of the Anglo-Saxon monastery of Bardney to his family convent of Charroux in about 1087, and the church of that cell was to be an existing parish church that marked one of the centres of the earlier monastery. His grandson Walter gave chapels at Partney and Skendleby (27) (both Lincolnshire) to Bardney which were intended to become cells themselves, memorial chapels that marked the presumed (but mistaken) sites of other monasteries that had been recorded by Bede. Both have been excavated. Though both were modified in the mid-twelfth century, they remained rectangular single-cell buildings not unlike the nunnery church of Kirklees throughout their lives. Many of the Norman foundations were modest in the extreme, their revenues going to support existing family monasteries in Normandy and Flanders.

The change came with the second and third generations who now enjoyed fully developed English estates and had assimilated with the Anglo-Saxon and Anglo-Scandinavian landowners that the first generation had displaced. They had much more choice, too, for the Church was in the turmoil of reform in the late eleventh and twelfth centuries and new orders were developing. The Carthusians, Cistercians and Grandmontines were attempting to recreate an earlier form of monasticism, the former returning to the early monasticism of Sts Pachomius, Anthony and John Cassian, the last two the early sixth-century *Rule of St Benedict*. They formulated statutes to ensure that their churches were to be plain and humble. Other orders were completely new, arising out of the First Crusade in 1090, the knightly Orders of the Temple and the Hospital and of St Lazarus, developing new architectural forms derived from the centrally planned church of the Holy Sepulchre in Jerusalem. First to appear in England, however, were the Augustinian canons, not strictly monks but priests living a communal monastic life, appearing around 1100 with the active support of Henry I. They too set out as a reform movement though they lacked the centralisation of the other orders.

27 The rectangular church of the Bardney Abbey cell at Skendleby. Although this building was reconstructed twice it remained a simple rectangular building throughout its life

AUGUSTINIAN CHURCHES

We are fortunate that a number of early Augustinian churches survive or have been excavated, and their planning can be recovered to be compared with that of the early Benedictines. First among these is Kirkham Priory, established on the site of a pre-existing village in about 1120. It was founded by Walter Espec, lord of Helmsley and one of Henry I's justiciars in the north, the first of three monasteries he was to found on his extensive estates. Ten years later he was to invite the Cistercians to northern England and Kirkham was caught up in his conversion to the Cistercian reform. In about 1139, an agreement was drawn up whereby the Augustinian canons who wished to leave were given a new site and the promise of identical buildings to the ones they already had with their bells and glass windows; those who wished to remain would become Cistercian monks. The agreement was abandoned by 1143 when the prior himself left to become a monk of Rievaulx. It is the agreement that was drawn up, and the surviving remains of the contemporary church, which make this site so important. The agreement tells us that the church was built of squared stone and was covered with shingles. It had windows with coloured glass, and a tower is hinted at by the presence of more than one bell. The south wall of the nave and west wall of the south transept are still standing to a height of 1.4m, and were identified when the site was first conserved in the 1920s by Sir Charles Peers. From the surviving base of the eastern processional door from the cloister, this church could be dated to about 1130-40.

Peers went on to excavate the church at Kirkham, recovering the plan of not only the early church but also a later twelfth-century rebuilding and a monumental thirteenth-century reconstruction which had been abandoned unfinished. Though he never published his excavation sufficient information has survived to reconstruct what he discovered. The first church (there must have been a temporary church elsewhere) was a cruciform building of great austerity (*28*), without aisles, and of transepts without eastern chapels. The short presbytery had a square east end, and the crossing was marked by simple square opposed pilasters that could have carried a low crossing tower. The external walls were only 1.2m thick, suggesting a building of moderate height. This building was almost totally rebuilt on its original ground plan around 1160-70. The walls that butted the cloister on the south side were retained but thickened internally to 1.8m, and the north wall of the nave and north transept rebuilt from foundation level to the same width. The widening of the walls indicates that they were considerably heightened, perhaps to provide a second tier of windows. Chapels were added to the east wall of the transepts, and the eastern arm was rebuilt and extended from an original internal length of 13.5m to a little over 18m, its angles supported by clasping buttresses, and its lower walls internally decorated with blind arcading. The crossing retained its tower for the stepped plinths of elaborate crossing arches remain on three sides. The church was given a north door towards the west end of the nave, and the reason for this was the construction of a second axial tower at the west end of the nave.

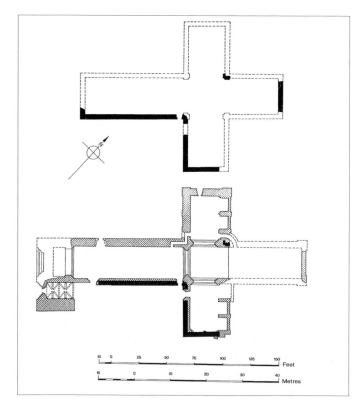

28 The early twelfth-century church at Kirkham (top) and its substantial rebuilding of the 1160s (bottom)

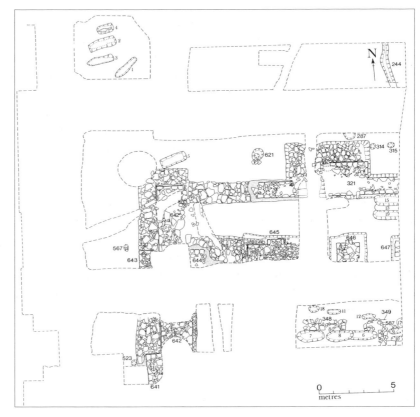

29 Excavation below the west end of the later nave at Guisborough Priory revealed the foundations of its twelfth-century predecessor

The unaisled cruciform church with squared east end was typical of many Augustinian churches in the twelfth century, and survives at Bolton (*colour plate 4*), and has been excavated at Norton and Thornholme. It was not the only plan form that the Augustinians adopted, as the surviving churches at Chistchurch in Hampshire and Waltham Abbey and the ruined church of St Botolph's Priory in Colchester demonstrate. These churches were aisled from the first half of the twelfth century. Excavation at Guisborough has revealed the western part of the nave of a mid-twelfth-century church with a western axial tower and aisles (*29*), probably closely contemporary with the first church at Kirkham and the reason for its reconstruction. The founder, Robert I de Brus, like Walter Espec, was one of Henry I's new men in the north, and he was building a church to be a burial place for his new dynasty. There are indications that Walter of Ghent's priory church at Bridlington (built for his own burial) was similarly aisled, and while the community may have preferred an aisleless church, wealthy patrons wanted something more fitting to their own aspirations. While the plan of the twelfth-century east end and transepts at Guisborough is unknown, excavation has recovered the plan of the east end at St Botolph's. Though undated, recovered architectural detail would suggest it was begun in the mid-twelfth century. The presbytery was short and square-ended, with square-ended aisles only a single bay long and little more than extended transept chapels. Essentially, this was the Benedictine plan derived from St Etienne at Caen simplified and not particularly Augustinian in its inspiration. What was exceptional here,

30 The west front of the nave at St Botolph's Priory, Colchester, showing the highly decorative arcading that was originally rendered and highly coloured. *After John Sell Cotman*

though, is that excavation revealed a crypt below the south transept and crossing, and possibly extending into the north transept and presbytery. The use of reused Roman brick and septaria (a conglomerate stone found on the Essex coast) for the superstructure of the church belies the original elaboration of the church. Its west front (*30*), completed about 1170, has elaborate intersecting arcading and a rose window above a central west door and flanking aisle doors, detailed in limestone. Within the nave were tall round-headed arches of two orders, a tall triforium and a clerestory with a wall passage, which has been lost. The whole of the building was originally rendered and all that remains is a framework for what was probably a highly decorative scheme that would have been picked out in coloured paint. The Augustinians love of detail, seen in the internal wall arcades of Kirkham and Bolton, can also be seen in the mass of loose architectural detail recovered by excavation from the heavily ruined church of Thornholme Priory (*31*).

The second agency of reform was the Cistercian order which first appeared in England in 1128, and was firmly established by 1140. The Cistercians were developing their philosophy of building throughout the 1120s to '40s. One site, Fountains Abbey, has revealed through excavation the process by which this happened, supported remarkably by a chronicle written in the early thirteenth century from the memories of an early member of the community. Excavation of the south transept of the great church that is still standing and which was thought to date to the late 1130s revealed it was the third church to be built on this site which was first settled only in 1132. The abbey's chronicle told that the monks settled the site in late December 1132, living first in caves and under a great elm tree before they built themselves an oratory and huts of turf and wattles, sending an envoy to Abbot Bernard of Clairvaux the following spring to seek admission to the Cistercian order. Bernard replied by sending them an experienced monk, Geoffrey d'Ainai to instruct them in Cistercian manners, including the correct form of building, in the summer of 1133. At the time of the harvest, the chronicle tells that carpenters and workmen were present on site, and excavation recovered the remains of two substantial buildings (*32*), a church, and a domestic building, evidenced by deep post-pits that had contained squared timbers. The church, which was aligned east–west, had its east and west walls cut away by later foundations, but was 4.9m wide and at least 7.6m long, with opposed doors in its north and south walls towards the west end, marked by double posts. The posts were all 0.40m^2 and carefully aligned, indicating a fully carpentered building that was professionally built. This church was designed for the founding community which comprised an abbot and 12 monks and was only intended to be temporary. Temporary churches were probably the norm on new monastic sites, but their finding is rare in the extreme. A fragmentary building below the nave at Guisborough which had burials associated with it might have been the temporary church there, but it was normal to build the temporary buildings away from the site of the permanent buildings to cause the least possible disruption to religious life. For some reason the Fountains monks became very attached to their first church and it remained within a few feet of their choir. In 1135, a building fund was established, and the following year saw the construction of a new permanent church.

The new stone church (33), of which the south transept and parts of the choir and presbytery have been excavated, is one of four early Cistercian churches known in the United Kingdom. Early churches were excavated by Sir Harold Brakspear at Waverley and Tintern, and one is known from geophysical survey within the cloister at Rievaulx.

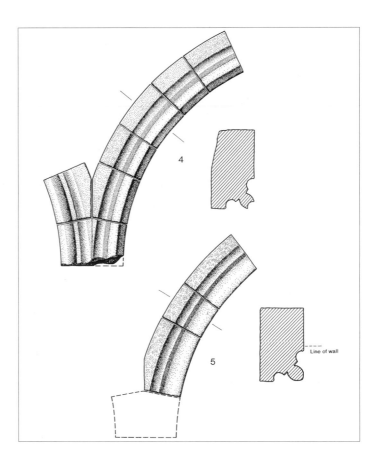

31 Arcading that had adorned the walls of the presbytery at Kirkham Priory. *Simon Hayfield*

32 Excavation in the south transept at Fountains Abbey in 1980 revealed the foundation of a smaller and earlier church that had been damaged by fire. Below that were the post-pits of the earliest buildings of the monastery, an east–west church that can be seen in the foreground, and a parallel domestic range to its south

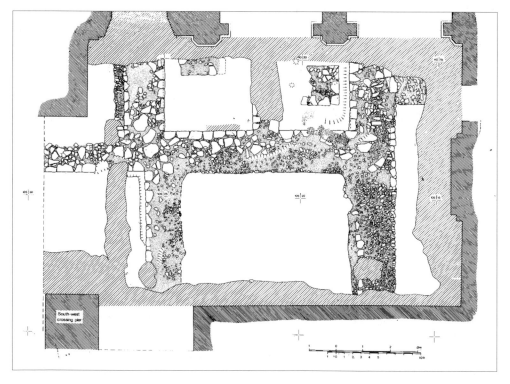

33 The south transept and parts of the choir and presbytery of the first stone church at Fountains Abbey as revealed by excavation in 1980

They all conform to a standard plan, and are cruciform and unaisled. The influence of the Augustinian canons cannot be ignored, particularly as later Cistercian churches were very different. Built partly around, and partly cutting through the remains of the timber oratory were the foundations of the south transept of a small church with two eastern chapels arranged *en echelon*, divided from the choir in the crossing by a solid wall. The transept had an earth floor, but the chapels were floored with mortar and retained traces of their wooden altars. The floor of the choir was also of mortar, and it was still covered with rushes that had been spread there when the church was in use. The south transept must have been entered by a small door at the east end of the choir and it, though not the choir, had been damaged by a serious fire. The chronicle informs us that the monastery was destroyed by fire in 1146, and that only the church had survived, though partly damaged, like a 'brand plucked from the burning'. It also tells us that the church was repaired, and new mortar floors in the transept chapels sealed the burned wooden altars, fallen plaster from the walls and melted lead from the gutters. New stone altars were provided. Though no superstructure remained in place, the rubble left by the demolition of this church included broken ashlar blocks. Though this was a small church, it was well built of high-quality materials. The plaster on its walls was tempered with crushed tile in the Roman manner and was painted white, probably externally as well as internally.

An aisled nave was added to this church in the 1140s, bringing it into conformity with Cistercian churches on the continent, and particularly with the church of Vauclair on the River Somme which had just been built by Henry Murdac, who became abbot of Fountains in 1144. For the first 20 years the Fountains community was not large. The many recruits the order attracted were spread around eight daughter houses. The last daughter house was established in 1150, and thereafter the community was allowed to grow, with some 80 choir monks by 1160. The first stone church, even with its extended nave, was simply too small and the decision was taken to build a larger church on the same basic plan (*34*). In the process of being constructed by 1154 it was built in sections and the nave was not completed before the late 1160s, even though it housed the choir of the army of lay brothers. The new church was substantial, a great barn-like building, and all but the short, square-ended presbytery survives. It had a simplified elevation of arcade and clerestory. There was no triforium or central stage, simply because it was not structurally necessary, and the building was painted off-white inside and out, with a plain masonry pattern lined out in white. The nave and transepts had wooden ceilings in the form of barrel vaults, but the aisles, transept chapels, and probably the presbytery, were vaulted.

The expansion of a church on the same basic plan was not a peculiarity of the Cistercians. The Augustinian church at Norton was similarly extended when its community became too large for the church that they had already built (see *42*). The provision of a timber temporary church is also unlikely to be a solely Cistercian habit. On many sites there is a gap of 20 years or more before a permanent church was begun. Excavation below these churches is rare in the extreme and temporary buildings simply have not been looked for.

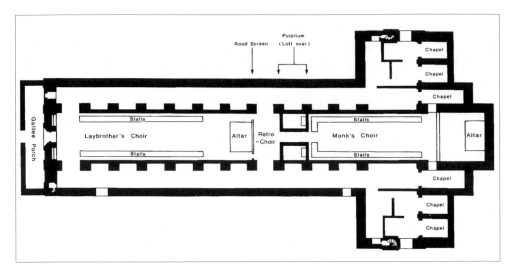

34 Plan of the second stone church built at Fountains Abbey in the 1150s and '60s. The nave and transepts of this building are still standing

THE CHURCHES OF THE MILITARY ORDERS

Of the new orders of the Temple, Hospital and St Lazarus we know even less about their early buildings. Three early Templar churches and one Hospitlar church have been excavated and their early plans at least partially recovered, and the second church of the London Temple survives in a modified form. These churches all had round naves with a short presbytery above a crypt that terminated in an apse. The origin of the plan, which does not appear before the first crusade in 1090, was the circular *anastasis* of the church of the Holy Sepulchre in Jerusalem, the holiest place in Christendom, though the architectural form was strictly contemporary. The Templar church of Temple Bruer in Lincolnshire (35) was first excavated in 1833 and its circular nave had been recorded by the Buck brothers in the 1730s. All that survives today is a squat, square tower of the 1190s, one of a pair that flanked an extended presbytery of the 1180s. The site was re-excavated by Hope in 1907, refining its plan. Originally built in the 1160s, the circular nave and its arcade survived only as foundations, but Hope uncovered a crypt below the apsidal presbytery with stairs down to it from the aisle of the nave. In plan it was virtually identical to the Hospitlar church of St John of Jerusalem in London, the crypt of which survives and the nave of which was partially excavated in 1900. The extension of the presbytery by a full bay and the provision of a squared east end took place a generation after the original building, and the provision of chapel space in the flanking towers (the southern of which is a rebuilding or remodelling of the 1190s) suggests developing liturgy. At the same period, the church of St John was given an aisled presbytery of three bays. In both cases the crypt was retained, in London it was extended. The Temple Bruer church was free-standing and this seems to be a feature of Templar churches. The London Temple, re-sited in about 1160 and consecrated in 1185, actually sat at the centre of the cloister.

The round church was not the only form used by the Templars and seems to have been restricted to their major houses or preceptories; it is otherwise only known at Dover, Bristol, Aslackby (Lincolnshire) and Garway (Herefordshire). The alternate form, best seen at South Witham in Lincolnshire (*36*), was a plain rectangular building 12.8m x 5m internally with a square east end. Architectural detail suggests it was built in the 1220s or 30s, suggesting it replaced a temporary timber chapel that was not excavated. South Witham was a dependency of Temple Bruer, in the same way that Temple Bruer was a dependency of the London Temple, and the difference in plan is probably an indication of status. Status was apparent too at South Witham. The church was two-storied at its west end, providing superior accommodation at first-floor level for the Knights and their sergeants above the *famuli* and servants who served the community. There are two surviving Templar churches of this form, the churches of Rothley and Temple Balsall, though both have lost their first floors in the nave, and a similar rectangular chapel has been excavated at Temple Newsam near Leeds.

CARTHUSIAN CHURCHES

Unlike other monks, the Carthusians used their churches only for mass and the first and last services of the day, saying their other offices privately in their cells. Their communities were usually much smaller than those of the Benedictines and their derivatives or Augustinian canons, and their churches were consequently much smaller. They were also detached from the cloister. Of the nine successful Carthusian monasteries in England, churches have been excavated at Hinton (Somerset), Beauvale (Nottinghamshire), London and Coventry (West Midlands), and substantial ruins survive of the church at Mount Grace in North Yorkshire (*colour plate 5*). In all cases, the original churches, built between the early

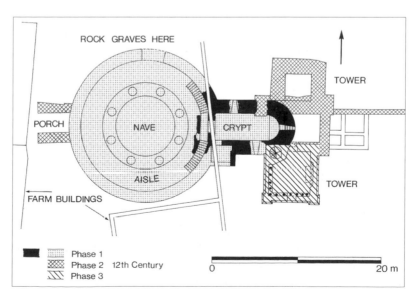

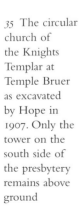

35 The circular church of the Knights Templar at Temple Bruer as excavated by Hope in 1907. Only the tower on the south side of the presbytery remains above ground

59

36 A reconstruction of the
Templar chapel at South
Witham, viewed from the west.
Jake Goodband

thirteenth and early fifteenth centuries were simple rectangles of four or five bays. The
eastern half was used by the monks, the western half by the lay brothers who might also
have a chapel in their own detached monastery. By far the clearest example is the church of
Mount Grace begun after 1398. There (*37*), the four-bay church, only 28m long and 7.3m
wide, was divided by a passage that ran across it just to the east of its mid-point. The passage
was defined by wooden screens, essentially the pulpitum and rood screen with a loft above
them. The monks' choir was immediately to the east of the passage, with the presbytery
and its altar to the east of that. As there were probably less than 12 monks when the church
was built, its scale could be economical. The building, though small, was architecturally
distinguished, with elaborate traceried windows. It was, however, barely larger than the
rectangular church of the poor nuns of Kirklees, and would have fitted comfortably into
the presbytery and crossing of Cistercian Fountains.

THE DEVELOPMENT OF MONASTIC CHURCHES

Monastic churches tended to be rebuilt as a house's economy developed, community
grew, the cult of saints was exploited and liturgy developed, and very few remained
as they were originally built by the early sixteenth century. Thus the scholar is
faced with having to untangle masonry, often fragmentary, of several periods in one
building. Alterations might be simple, modernising an old church by inserting new, larger
windows, reordering the interior, or demolishing redundant parts. Frequently, more drastic
action was taken, with extensive or wholesale rebuilding, particularly of the eastern arm.

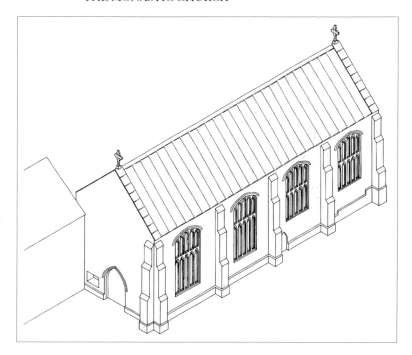

37 The first church at Mount Grace was a simple rectangular building of four bays, divided by a cross passage into the monks' choir to the east and the lay brothers' church to the west

At Kirkham Priory, it was not necessarily the community that was responsible for the rebuilding of the eastern parts of the church, though it must have seemed rather plain and unambitious in comparison with great churches like Guisborough and Bridlington. It was probably their patrons, the de Roos family of Helmsley. The de Rooses were also patrons of Rievaulx Abbey, only 2 miles from their castle of Helmsley in Yorkshire, but the Cistercians were reluctant to allow burials in their church. Kirkham was chosen to be the family mausoleum, and the first burial, that of William I de Roos, was made in the centre of the choir, the traditional burial place of a 'founder', in 1258. It was not the centre of the old, unaisled choir, but a massive aisled presbytery of eight bays (*38*) added to the old church. It terminated at a new pair of crossing piers that indicated that it was planned to rebuild the remainder of the church on a similar scale. Only a small part of the new presbytery survives, but that is sufficient to reconstruct its general form, a three-storied elevation probably vaulted throughout, and closely comparable with the great presbyteries built at Benedictine Whitby and Cistercian Rievaulx in the 1220s. Whitby's rebuilding (*colour plate 6*) was occasioned by the fortuitous but almost certainly fraudulent 'discovery' of the remains of its Saxon saints; the eastern arm of Rievaulx (*colour plate 7*) was built to house the shrine of its beatified third abbot, Aelred. In both of these cases, the partial rebuilding of the church for purely spiritual purposes virtually bankrupted the communities and work ceased at the crossing. At Kirkham, the reason for abandoning the rebuilding was more prosaic. The last de Roos burial there was in the 1340s, and subsequent burials were at Rievaulx, where the community had finally relented and allowed burial in the presence of their sainted abbot. Money for building quite literally dried up and Kirkham retained its old nave and transepts until the 1530s.

38 The form of the early thirteenth-century presbytery at Kirkham can be reconstructed from its plan and surviving elevation, loose architectural detail and eighteenth-century drawings. *S. Harrison*

The rebuilding of eastern arms, though it provided additional burial space, had as much to do with developing liturgy. The Cistercians at Fountains began the rebuilding of their presbytery (*39*) in the early thirteenth century because 'the congregation of monks was greater than usual, so that there were not enough altars to celebrate on, and the choir was too mean and insignificant and not large enough for so great a multitude'. The fact that their neighbours at Rievaulx were undertaking a similar rebuilding was perhaps as much a reason for the work, for they sought to surpass it in their new construction. Their choir remained in the 'mean and insignificant' crossing, but to its east they built an aisled presbytery of five bays that terminated in a great eastern transept containing nine altars ranged along its east wall. The presbytery was divided from the aisles by a screen of stone arcading which contained the sedilia for the celebrant priests to the south of the altar and separated the ritual area of the altar from the aisles that surrounded it. Though only fragments survive at Fountains, parts of a similar presbytery screen have been recovered and reassembled at Byland (*40*). It is not a Cistercian feature, but one used by all major monasteries and where stone was not used, timber screens would have been placed between the piers to enclose the sacred space. Smaller monasteries simply did without the aisles and additional eastern chapels.

Rebuilding because of a major fire was a fairly common event, though sometimes it seems to have been an excuse to update an old church that was perhaps repairable. The Saxon and Romanesque church at Glastonbury was burned in 1184 while the abbey was in the hands of Henry II during a prolonged abbatial vacancy. The king had been enjoying the abbey's revenues, but returned them to fund an immediate building campaign. First to be replaced was the 'ancient church' (the *vetusta ecclesia*) or wooden church of the early monastery, which would provide the monks with a choir while the major church of the monastery was rebuilt to the east. It was sufficiently complete to be consecrated two years later, and it survives largely complete (*41*). To its east a large cruciform church 122m long and 24.5m wide was laid out and building begun. Where the monastery's revenues were insufficient, the king himself paid for building work. Unfortunately he died in 1189, and neither Richard I nor John were likely to support the work, which ceased with Henry's death. The community, however, had access to the relics kept in their old church and the burials in their cemetery, two of which were exhumed in 1191 and identified as the legendary King Arthur and Queen Guinevere, which they then exploited in the same way as the monks of Whitby at about the same time. Work on the new church was slow, and it was not until the abbacy of William of St Vigor (1219-23) that funds were set aside for building. The thirteenth century was a troubled period for the abbey, with a long-running legal dispute between Glastonbury and the Bishop of Bath and Wells which diverted funds from building. Abbot Michael of Amesbury completed the eastern arm and transepts before his death in 1253, and was buried in the completed north transept. It was not, however, until

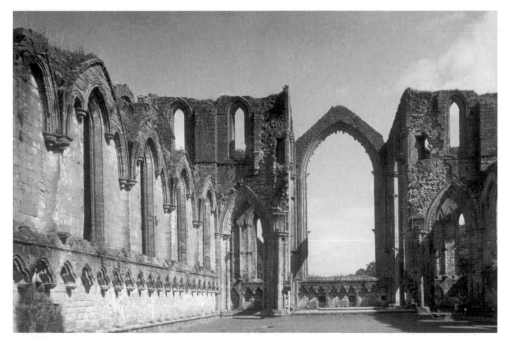

39 The early thirteenth-century presbytery at Fountains Abbey was a truly gothick structure, light and vaulted throughout, that terminated in a great eastern transept, the Chapel of Nine Altars

40 The presbytery screen at Byland, reconstructed from fallen masonry, enclosed the central area of the presbytery and the high altar

41 The chapel of St Mary at Glastonbury, built on the site of the ancient wooden church, served as the monks choir for half a century before their new church was complete enough to occupy

1278 that the high altar was consecrated, and the bones of Arthur and Guinevere translated to a new tomb of black marble before the altar in the presence of Edward I and his queen, Eleanor. By 1291 the western bays of the nave and the galilee porch between the nave and St Mary's chapel had been built, and Abbot Geoffrey Fromond (1303-22) completed the crossing tower and vaulted the eastern bays of the nave. His successor Adam of Sudbury completed the vaulting and decorating of the nave in the 1320s. While it was possible to complete St Mary's chapel in two years when money was available, it is an indication of the unsettled state of one of the richest monasteries in England that it took 135 years to complete the rebuilding of its church and 92 years before the high altar was rededicated.

Sometimes, rebuilding or extension was the result of success rather than disaster. The Carthusians of Mount Grace extended their church three times in less than 140 years (42) though the community itself barely grew above the numbers that the church was originally planned for. Following a strict rule, the Carthusians' prayers were thought to be particularly effective, and wills show that many people left money for obituary masses and some their bodies for burial in the tiny church. The first was Thomas Beaufort, Henry IV's uncle, who was given permission to be buried in the priory church in 1417. Between then and his death in 1427 the church was lengthened by a bay to the east and the screens between the monks' and lay brothers' parts of the church replaced by stone walls that carried a bell tower. Beaufort had provided the funding to support six members of the community and was responsible for building most of the great cloister and the monks' individual houses, and it seems that the community acquiesced to his remodelling of their church as a suitable place for his burial, even though it must have seriously inconvenienced them. The process by which the church was altered is visible in its surviving masonry and has in part been confirmed by excavation. Its fabric also provides evidence for the wooden elements that do not survive. At the east end of the nave and in front of the tower are the sockets for the rood beam and loft and the two enclosed chapels that lay beneath it. On the east face of the tower, surviving plaster indicated the line of the ceiling, following the curve of the braces in the wooden roof. In the north wall of the choir, grooves cut roughly into the wall face mark the supports for the canopies over the stalls above their excavated bases that Beaufort had provided for the monks in their enlarged church. Excavation recovered many fragments of tracery and the pictorial glass from the window they contained, as well as tiles from the church floor and Beaufort's tomb at the focus of the choir.

After Beaufort's burial, the pressure to receive the bodies of other laymen was such that to provide burial space the church had to be extended. The same thing happened in the Carthusian priory in London, where we know from documents that individuals sponsored the building of chapels for their own use. While it is not known who sponsored the chapels at Mount Grace, grave slabs in the floor indicate that they were used for burial in the same way as the chapels at London. The first to be built, on the south side of the nave in the third quarter of the fifteenth century, involved the removal of a window. Shortly afterwards, a matching chapel was added on a very cramped site on the north side of the church, entered through a tall, wide archway. Both were separated from the nave by screens and had altars with elaborate reredoses. Their appearance can be reconstructed from a description of one of the London chapels:

42 The church at Mount Grace was first extended and given a tower in the 1420s (top). Subsequently burial chapels were added to the south and north sides of the nave in the 1460s and '70s, and a further chapel was added to the south side of the presbytery in the 1520s (bottom)

In the Southe syde of the Churche a chappell of saint John thavaungelyste wyth an alter and a table of the Resurrecyon of alabaster with ij Imagys of saint John Evaungellyst and the other of saint Augustyne at eyther ende of the said alter. Item the sayd chappel is scealyd wyth oke waynscotte and other borde Rounde abougte thre quarters hygh.

Finally, a third chapel was added to the south side of the presbytery in the 1520s, its two altars separated by the base of a table tomb.

THE ARCHAEOLOGY OF CHURCHES

While the structure of monastic churches was for long the preserve of architectural historians, a proper understanding can only come from an archaeological study, combining the evidence of structure with that which survives in the ground. Not only does this often provide evidence of earlier phases which are not visible in the standing structure, it might also provide evidence of what has been lost from the ruins that survive. The excavation of the surviving church at Fountains Abbey recovered the partial plans of two earlier churches; the excavation and clearance of the church at Mount Grace Priory recovered a great deal of architectural detail discarded by stone robbers that permitted the reconstruction of its lost windows.

One of the most dramatic excavations of a monastic church was that carried out between 1911 and 1913 at Benedictine Bardney Abbey in Lincolnshire by the Rev. C.E. Laing, revealing not only the lower walls of a lost church (see *10*), but the whole of its floors, with the evidence for screens, altars, steps and burials, recovering the totality of its late medieval planning. Excavation stopped at the latest floors which were all carefully planned, leaving intact the archaeology of earlier phases. Ten years later a similar exercise was carried out by Sir Charles Peers in the shattered ruins of the great Cistercian church of Byland Abbey in North Yorkshire. The church at Byland, arguably one of the finest English churches built in the twelfth century, was a sadly shattered ruin before excavation began in 1922. Previous trenching by Martin Stapylton in about 1820 had recovered large quantities of architectural detail that lay close to where it had fallen. It was taken to decorate his garden at Myton Hall where it still lies. Peers stripped the whole of the church in 3m squares and recovered tons of carved stones that could be related to accurate findspots. Remarkably he did little with this material; some was stored, but duplicate pieces were reburied. It was only in the late 1980s that Stuart Harrison studied this material, re-excavating some of the stones that had been reburied. Relating particular stones to their original findspots by using contemporary photographs and surviving site records, and by using the critical evidence that remained in the surviving fabric, it proved possible to reconstruct the main elevations of the church (*colour plate 8*), not seen since the sixteenth century, with remarkable accuracy. It was also possible to identify particular elements to exact locations, showing how the masons had tackled particular parts of the church. Individual capitals from the arcades were identified to their findspots and their full forms regenerated from the plan of the surviving piers, demonstrating the sequence of building around a smaller but unknown church that may never have been completed before the standing church was begun. Many of the capitals retain their original decoration in red paint on a white background. What was remarkable was that the apparently later, plainer forms were painted to resemble their earlier carved fellows, something which may indicate a reduction in cost rather than architectural development. This kind of detail is lost in a weathered ruin or a stripped church interior reordered to a nineteenth-century interpretation of medieval design.

The accuracy of the Byland reconstructions resulted from the use of original but displaced structural elements and cannot be faulted. It demonstrates the importance of studying all the available evidence, a technique which can be used wherever there are important collections of loose architectural detail to supplement the often heavily reduced evidence of standing buildings.

Excavation has a critical role to play in the understanding of much more than the physical structure of the church. Monastic churches were not simply open shells, the impression given if one walks in through the west doors of Peterborough, Ely or Norwich, all great Benedictine churches that survived the Reformation as cathedrals. They were divided into function areas by screens and furniture which could be moved to suit changing needs and the growth or contraction of the community. Remarkably it was not until the late 1960s that archaeologists started to look seriously at the interiors of monastic churches, though the potential had been demonstrated by the stripping of the churches of Byland and Rievaulx in the 1920s by the Office of Works. A series of excavations designed to reveal the remains of buried monastic sites for public display has provided much of the evidence we previously lacked, and this has been extended by the excavation of many urban sites threatened by redevelopment, most comprehensively on the sites of urban friaries. Two sites in particular have seen extensive or total excavation, Augustinian Norton Priory and Cistercian Bordesley Abbey. Additionally, partial excavation at Guisborough Priory and Fountains Abbey and Thornholme Priory have demonstrated the potential for further research.

At Norton, Patrick Greene's excavation of the whole church, reduced to foundation level throughout, provided for the first time the total understanding of how an Augustinian canon's church developed and was used (43). The original church was a small cruciform structure, built in the mid-twelfth century to house a community of no more than 13. It had short transepts, each with a single chapel, a short presbytery, and a nave of six-and-a-half bays. Its floors were of clay and the choir must have been placed below the crossing because there was a door from the cloister in the eastern bay of the south nave wall, and an entrance into the north transept in the opposing bay of the north wall. To the west was the footing of the rood screen, and this would place the untraced pulpitum screen between the western responds of the crossing. East of the choir stalls were doors into the transepts which would otherwise have been blocked off by the stalls. To the east of these doors was the presbytery step and the raised floor of the presbytery on which the high altar was placed. As the community grew the church was extended, first to the west in the late twelfth century and within decades to the east. The inadequate transept chapels were replaced in the early thirteenth century. The north chapel was to be extended again, possibly as a Lady Chapel, in the mid-thirteenth century and was filled with burials, many in sandstone coffins. The Cluniacs of Thetford Priory in Norfolk had replaced the north aisle of their presbytery at about the same time with a Lady Chapel, and P.K. Baillie Reynolds recorded no fewer than 15 stone-lined graves packed into its western end when it was excavated in the 1950s. This chapel had contained a late Saxon image of the Virgin around which a cult had grown up, explaining the intensity of burial. At Norton, the presbytery was extended again to the east at the end of the thirteenth century, suggesting that either the liturgy had developed to need more space, or possibly that the new Lady Chapel had provided a new source of income that would fund an enhanced church. Unfortunately the floors of the presbytery did not survive.

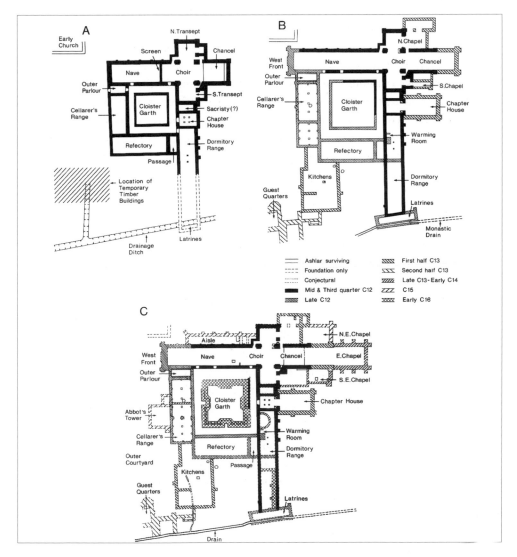

43 The excavated plan of the church and cloister at Norton Priory showing (A) the layout of the first stone buildings, (B) the thirteenth-century enlargement of the church and cloister for a growing community, and (C) the late medieval planning of the house that implies greater comfort for a reduced population

In the early years of the fourteenth century the canons of Norton laid a remarkable floor of mosaic tile (actually a ceramic version of *opus sectile* or coloured stones laid in geometric patterns) throughout the church to the east of the rood screen, around the two altars below the rood, and extending into the north-eastern Lady Chapel where it post-dated the earliest graves. Remarkably it extended below the choir stalls where the tiles survived unworn, suggesting that the tiling of the floor was part of a much larger refitting that included new stalls, which had not been fitted before the floor was laid. Wear patterns on the floor actually indicated where the canons had walked in procession.

THE ARCHAEOLOGY OF LITURGY

The architectural development of churches had as much to do with changes in the way they were used as it did with the aspirations of patrons and abbots. The excavation of the choir, presbytery and south transept of Bordesley Abbey, as well as setting the standard for the archaeological study of monastic churches, has demonstrated the potential for recovering the evidence for liturgical planning and change. Exceptionally, Bordesley (*44*) has seven distinct floor horizons between the mid-twelfth and late fifteenth centuries because its site was low lying and liable to flood. In most cases, four centuries of development are compressed into perhaps 100mm, with poor survival of the earliest features because of the constant cutting and recutting of graves, the replacement of screens and the relaying of tile floors.

Bordesley, in keeping with its Cistercian simplicity when first built, had earth floors strewn with reeds in the nave, transepts and crossing, while the presbytery, raised a step above the crossing area, had a stone-paved floor to mark its significance. The choir stalls occupied the eastern two bays of the nave, each bank evidenced by six slots cut into the floor for the timber joists of their wooden floor. Further slots to the west evidence the return stalls for the abbot and prior, but there was no evidence of a pulpitum screen closing off the choir from the nave with the lay brothers' choir to the west. The monks entered and left their choir from its upper entrances in the crossing or the lower entrance between the return stalls. A wooden stair in the south transept provided access from the dormitory for the night offices.

By the early thirteenth century, the original arrangements were no longer adequate; increasing numbers of monks, changing liturgy and structural problems with the church all led to modifications. The timber night stair had been destroyed by a fire which must have caused other damage that is not recorded in the archaeology or the surviving fabric and was replaced in stone. At the same time, the easternmost bays of the nave arcades were blocked with solid walls and the entrance from the south nave aisle into the transept was underbuilt, incorporating a narrower archway. Building work of this nature suggests a problem with the crossing, perhaps associated with the raising of a lantern stage on a low crossing tower – a fashionable development designed to flood the crossing with light much favoured by the Cistercians in the late twelfth century when light was seen as

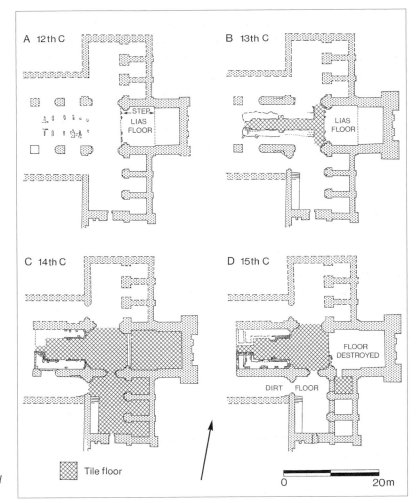

A 12th C

STEP
LIAS
FLOOR

B 13th C

LIAS
FLOOR

C 14th C

D 15th C

FLOOR
DESTROYED

DIRT FLOOR

Tile floor

0   20m

44 The
excavation of
the church
at Bordesley
Abbey has
shown how its
use and layout
varied from
the twelfth to
the sixteenth
century. *After
Rahtz, Hirst, and
Wright*

the personification of the Holy Spirit. Growing numbers required the extension of the choir into the crossing and new stalls of two tiers were provided, extending to within 1.8m of the presbytery step. Access to the upper tier of stalls was by narrow stairs at the mid-point of each bank, clearly evidenced in excavation. A stall end from this choir was actually recovered from a later context, showing that the stalls were undecorated and strictly functional. To the east of the stalls, a lead water-pipe was laid from north to south, running away across the south transept and into the east range beyond. It is likely that a branch was taken off it at the back of the southern bank of stalls to feed a laver. There was a recess in the blocking wall of the first bay of the nave arcade that marks its likely site. At Rievaulx Abbey a laver built into the back of the south bank of choir stalls has recently been recognised, and a water-pipe in the south crossing aisle at Jervaulx Abbey is probably connected to a similar laver. In the west wall of the thirteenth-century south transept at Wenlock Priory the laver still survives (*45*). These features all suggest that spiritual washing had become an important aspect of entering the choir.

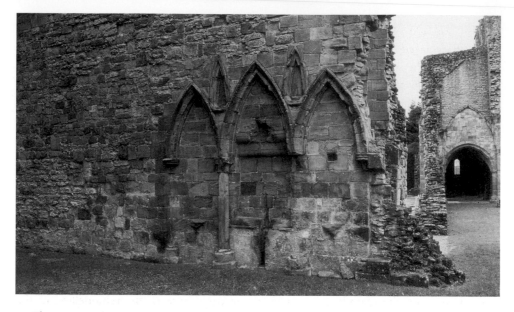

45 The surviving laver in the west wall of the south transept at Much Wenlock Priory

Sealing the water-pipe was the bedding for a tile floor that extended the length of the choir and extended into its upper and lower entrances and into the stairs that accessed the upper banks of stalls. The south transept and crossing aisle were also tiled in the thirteenth century and the wear pattern on the floor indicated that the normal processional route to the choir was along the south aisle and through the lower entrance. By about 1260-80, the north-west crossing pier was causing concern and needed to be underbuilt with new foundations, requiring the removal of the north bank of stalls. When they were replaced, the obviously worn choir floor was relaid with smaller tiles.

The start of the fourteenth century saw further reordering. New choir stalls were provided, now restricted to the two eastern bays of the nave and set on stone plinth walls. At the same time, the southern crossing arch was underbuilt, leaving a narrow arch little larger than a door for the upper choir entrance. Clearly the crossing tower was still causing concern. Narrow screen walls were provided in the second bay of the nave for the stalls to back on to, and for the first time the western end of the choir was enclosed by a timber pulpitum screen set on a stone cill wall. The stalls were only of a single tier and suggest a much reduced community, a fact demonstrated by the recording of only 34 monks at Bordesley in 1332. It is uncertain whether this reorganisation was completed when a catastrophic collapse of the north-western crossing pier, already underbuilt, occurred, rendering the central area of the church temporarily unusable. The evidence from excavation suggests that the collapse was expected, and that the stalls were removed from the choir before the pier fell. The lack of widespread damage, for the collapse of the pier would have brought down the corner of the tower above, implies that the superstructure had already been taken down, and that the pier was intentionally felled. The failure of crossing towers was not that unusual but it is rare to find such clear archaeological evidence for it.

The west side of the crossing was quickly rebuilt, with a new north-west pier that curiously retained some of the footings of its failed predecessor, and a matching respond was added to the south-west pier, indicating a new western crossing arch. The moulded bases of the new pier and added respond date this work to about 1330. Builders' rubble was then used to bring up the floor levels of the choir and presbytery, the choir stalls were refitted and new tiled floors laid. The greater part of the south transept floor was retained from the earlier phase, and a timber screen was inserted into the south upper choir entrance, effectively closing it. While few tiles remained in place in the choir and presbytery, the mortar bed in which they were laid retained evidence of their planning. While most tiles were laid diagonally to the axis of the church, bands of tiles were laid from the fronts of the choir stalls to the presbytery step which were parallel to the axis of the church. Similar bands survive at Byland and Fountains where their purpose is clear. They were processional markers that guided the community around their church, particularly for the night offices where lighting was limited. Monks with their cowls up and heads bowed simply had to follow the lines in the floor.

In about 1400 the church saw a major reconstruction with the remodelling of the nave, which was provided with a series of chapels in its aisles. At some point, the south transept had been flooded, damaging its tiled floor, and its floor level was raised by about 30cm. The new floor level brought the south transept up to the level of the new nave but it buried the bases of the crossing piers. The floor of the choir and crossing was similarly raised, and new choir stalls fitted. To their west were two screen walls that supported the pulpitum loft and gave it greater prominence. The third bay of the nave comprised the retrochoir, and beyond that the cill wall of the rood screen that extended across the aisles, with chapels against it in both the aisles and nave. A new tiled floor was not immediately laid and the south transept and choir simply had dirt floors that suggest a poor state of affairs in the house. It may be that the house was in debt because of the cost of remodelling the nave and that fine finishes were simply beyond its means at that point. The south transept in any case was ceasing to have a liturgical use. The eastern chapels were walled off, and the inner one was given a door into the presbytery that converted it into a sacristy, a fairly common late medieval feature. The central chapel of the south transept at Fountains Abbey (the inner one having become part of the presbytery aisle in the thirteenth century) was treated in exactly the same way at the same date. By the 1470s the choir and crossing were given a new tile floor, though the south transept was to continue with earth floors up to the suppression.

Bordesley is perhaps exceptional, but it is not unique. Many churches retain evidence for the movement, expansion and contraction of the choir, and the fitting of screens into existing masonry to reorder space. When the building is well preserved it is quite possible to read these changes in its masonry. What archaeology offers is a chance to understand the context of those modifications. At Thornholme Priory, the canons stalls were marked by L-shaped gaps in the stone paving of the choir floor (46). The stone base of the stalls had been removed, but lying in lines where they had fallen between the floor boards were rows of small objects: lace ends, buckles and pins from the canons' habits, clasps and mounts from the covers of service books, loose rosary beads, and the

46 The rood screen, retrochoir, foundations of the pulpitum and paved choir with the evidence for stalls at Thornholme Priory. Only the northern half of the church has been excavated

needles and thimbles lost by those who took their darning into church. The substructure of stalls is also very informative. Most were either set in the floor on wooden plates or stood on stone foundations like those still visible at Rievaulx Abbey and Mount Grace Priory. A feature of the late fifteenth and early sixteenth centuries, when plain chant was giving way to polyphony, was the creation of resonance chambers below the stalls, stone- or brick-lined pits up to 1m deep, with or without pottery jars set in the walls to amplify the singing. Certainly these were fitted below the early sixteenth-century choir stalls at Fountains Abbey; more surprisingly they have been recorded beneath the stalls of the Carmelite friars of Coventry and the Franciscan friars of Kings Lynn. Many monastic choir stalls survive. Those from Easby Abbey in North Yorkshire found their way to Richmond's parish church, as did those at Whalley Abbey in Lancashire to the local church. Others remain in place, like the late fourteenth-century stalls at Chester Abbey and those of 1308 at Winchester cathedral priory. Screens, too, were sold off at the suppression, and the early sixteenth-century pulpitum screen and loft from Bridlington Priory survives in Flamborough church. Few, like the pulpitum screen of Hexham Priory remain in place. We tend to overlook the other furniture. At Rievaulx Abbey in 1538 there was a clock 'of steple fashon' in the south transept, not unlike the surviving clock at Durham in the same position, a bookcase and a chest for copes in the south aisle of the presbytery, and another bookcase in the south aisle of the nave. At Thornholme Priory, hinges and locks suggest at least two chests in the north transept at the suppression.

The nave, being less interesting liturgically, tends to be overlooked in terms of its development, and many early naves survive little altered. In some houses they were parochial, as at Wymondham and Binham Priories in Norfolk or Bridlington, or partly parochial as at Crowland or where the north aisle remains the parish church, creating a tension between the community and the parish. Most, though were designed for purely monastic use, and that use changed through time. West of the rood screen that closed the western side of the monks' church was the nave altar. In Cistercian houses the nave was the site of the lay brothers' church until the fourteenth century; elsewhere it was an area for processional use and lay burial. Aisles, where they existed, were essentially designed as corridors around areas of liturgical use, but from the fourteenth century there was a tendency to convert them to chapel space. The best surviving example of this is at Rievaulx Abbey where the evidence for their fittings is exceptional, and for which there are sixteenth-century inventories of their fittings. Some might be used as chantries – at the east end of the south aisle at Rievaulx the grave slab in the floor indicates it was the chantry chapel of Abbot Henry Burton. In the same place at Bardney in Lincolnshire was a vestry associated with the nave altar, and to the west of that the monastic library, all screened in timber.

The processional use of the nave is demonstrated very clearly in houses of several orders. At Fountains Abbey a series of square limestone slabs with an incised circle on them were set in the nave floor, 23 along each side of the nave just over a metre inside the arcades, and two more to the east set further in, and a third, further east still, set centrally, all marking the positions that the convent took up when the Sunday procession entered the church by the west door. That this was not simply a Cistercian feature is shown by the survival of similar circles cut into the stone floor of the nave at Premonstratensian Easby Abbey in North Yorkshire, and by a single circle surviving in the centre of the nave floor at Benedictine Bardney. The origin of these markers is not even monastic. The cathedrals of Lincoln, Wells, and York had similar markers in the nave floors until nineteenth-century reflooring removed them.

BURIALS IN MONASTIC CHURCHES

Though the church was intended solely by the monastic community as their place of prayer it was seen by patrons in a different light. They founded and endowed monasteries for the benefit of their souls, and though most orders were originally reluctant to see their churches taken over as burial places for the laity they were prepared to grant sepulture to their founders. Pressure from outsiders grew throughout the Middle Ages, as did the temptation to accept the benefactions that came with burials. By the mid-thirteenth century even the Cistercians were prepared to accept lay burial at the heart of their churches. Founders and their immediate family might be buried at the focus of the choir or in front of the high altar. At Holy Trinity Priory in London, founded by Henry I's queen Matilda, King Stephen buried his children Baldwin and Matilda on the north and south sides of the high altar in the late 1140s and may have intended his own burial there. As it was, he lost the support of London and chose instead to establish a Cluniac house at Faversham in Kent where he was buried before the high altar in 1154. Abbots and priors tended to be buried in the chapter house, at least until the late thirteenth century, and burial within the church was the exception rather than the rule. That situation did not last, and as chapter houses filled up, and patrons pressed, monastic churches were to become mausolea as well as houses of prayer.

With its well stratified sequence of floors and its evidence for ritual re-planning, it is possible to study the development of burial practise at Bordesley Abbey (47). Here, recent re-examination of the excavation archive shows that burials were normally inserted not at death, but immediately before new floors were about to be laid, implying temporary burial elsewhere until a convenient time for relocation arose, particularly in the liturgically active areas of the choir and transepts. The earliest burials in the south transept begin in the early thirteenth century and in the crossing in the late thirteenth century. The first graves in the south transept were a group of three in the central chapel and one to its west. By the late fifteenth century a further nine graves had been dug before the entrance to this chapel, and the impression given is of a family grouping. A smaller group outside the north chapel also had its origins in the thirteenth century. The transept burials were, with a single exception, either uncoffined or buried in wooden coffins. A single stone coffin occurred at the entrance to the northern chapel, implying a better quality of burial. The burials in the choir and crossing were generally of a better quality, with two stone coffins and one stone-lined grave. Their central position, at the focus of the choir, suggests important patrons and the centrally placed grave in the presbytery which had evidence of a raised tomb above it has been tentatively identified with Guy Beauchamp, earl of Warwick, who was buried at Bordesley in 1315.

Although Norton Priory lacked the deep stratification of Bordesley it did produce good evidence of burial practice relating to its patronal families. The development of a chapel to the north of the presbytery and entered from the north transept provided both a Lady Chapel and a burial place for the Duttons, the dominant benefactors of the house from the thirteenth century. Their burials had, for the most part, stone coffins with fine carved lids. Later burials, some filling the gaps between stone coffins, were in wooden coffins, their graves marked by tile panels or effigies.

Urban monasteries undoubtedly had a greater number of intramural burials, none more so than the friaries and suburban Carthusian houses. At the Coventry charterhouse almost the whole of the church has been excavated, revealing the pattern and placing of burials. There was only a single tomb in the presbytery, but 40 graves were excavated to the west of the choir, either below the tower, in the entry between the rood altars and more generally in the nave. The graves were by and large carefully laid out in rows, generally with the earliest to the east, and most bodies appear to have been coffined. There was a single built grave on the north side of the entry through the rood screen. Where the floor tiles survived there is little evidence that they were marked in any way at floor level, or they were marked by tile settings. All the same, several of the graves were reused, to the extent that parts of the earlier burial had been carefully reincorporated in

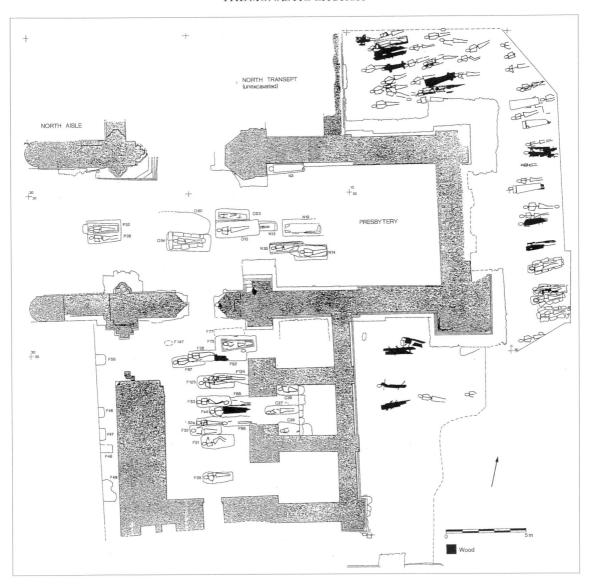

47 The pattern of burial at Bordesley has also been recovered by excavation, with groups of graves within the church and the convent cemetery to the east of the presbytery. *After Rahtz, Hirst, and Wright*

the filling of the later grave. In the north-west corner of the nave two graves had been cut by a third intruded between them, disturbing the skull of one burial and the upper arms of both. The loose skull and crossed upper arm bones were placed on the legs of the child in the later grave. Almost certainly this reflects a family grouping. Another is suggested by the will of Nicholas Fitzherbert who died in 1508 requesting burial next to his mother and father and the provision of a grave stone at a cost of £3 6s 8d to be laid over all three of them. Fitzherbert's grave must be one of the eight or more graves that produced fragments of earlier burials.

Grave slabs are frequent survivors, though it cannot always be assumed that they are now in the locations they were first laid. The church at Bardney Abbey in Lincolnshire retained much of its paving, including 65 grave markers. These are particularly informative because many have inscriptions which give the name and date of death. They commemorate not only local lay folk and abbots but also monks and their families, a late medieval practice judging from the dates that survive. In the third bay of the nave from the west were, side by side, the graves of John Bracy (who died in 1415) and his wife Joanna, parents of brother John Bracy who was the sacrist in 1437/38 and later sub-prior and prior. At Monk Bretton Priory in Yorkshire, areas of the stone flagging of the church survive, and within this floor are 14 grave markers commemorating both monks and benefactors (48). One simply marked with a chalice is that of a priest. Excavation revealed a pewter mortuary chalice and patten in the grave below, while that of Brother Osbert de Gresby has a plain cross, probably a stock pattern bought from the quarry, with the added inscription filled with lead. A third stone, with a cross, shield and sword, and an inscription which reads *D(ominus) W(illemus) (de) Watton* is that of a knight. Most grave stones of the twelfth and thirteenth centuries are anonymous, and the most common marker is a plain or floriate cross. Early grave markers are coffin-shaped, though they do not have to cover a stone coffin. Later stones are rectangular and are more likely to be inscribed, such as the many stones in the nave floor at Bardney, or the grave marker of the cellarer Brother John Ripon in the south transept at Fountains. A note of caution, however, grave stones were useful paving material and in many cases no longer lie over the burial they commemorate. At Monk Bretton some of the stones have their foot ends to the west and have clearly been relaid. In the north transept at Thornholme Priory a fine thirteenth-century grave stone was found set in a fourteenth-century paved floor. Beneath it the floor bedding was unbroken, and it was only when the bedding was excavated that the grave cut was seen, only approximately sited below the stone. The burial was obviously an important one and when the floor was renewed the stone was lifted and relaid as close as possible to where it had come from. More commonly, grave stones were lifted and reused elsewhere, most frequently as door cills.

Grave effigies must have been a common sight in monastic churches, with fine collections surviving at Furness Abbey in Cumbria and the London Temple church, but for the most part they survive only as fragments. One notable survivor is an early fourteenth-century effigy from Fountains Abbey (49). It moved around the site after the suppression and by 1800 was leaning up against the presbytery aisle wall. Overturned and broken by a group of drunken militiamen, its fragments were gathered together and reset in the northern chapel of the south transept. It can, however, be identified with Lord Henry Percy of Alnwick, a major patron of the abbey who was buried at the centre of the presbytery before the high altar in 1315. At Kirkham Priory we only have a description of the tombs of the de Roos family from a family genealogy, made of marble and located to the north, south and before the altar, where there are now only stone-lined graves.

The graves of the community were normally found in an external cemetery around the east end of the church, or to its north. Excavation at Bordesley has recovered a part of the cemetery with graves laid out in well-organised rows (see 47). Some 128 burials have

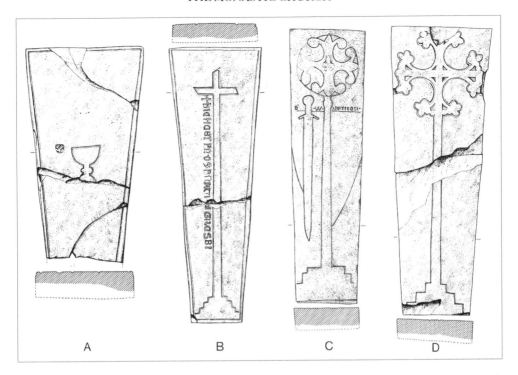

48 A group of four grave markers from the church at Monk Bretton, (A) a priest's grave marked with a chalice, (B) the marker of Brother Osbert de Gresby, (C) a knight's marker, and (D) a plain floriate cross

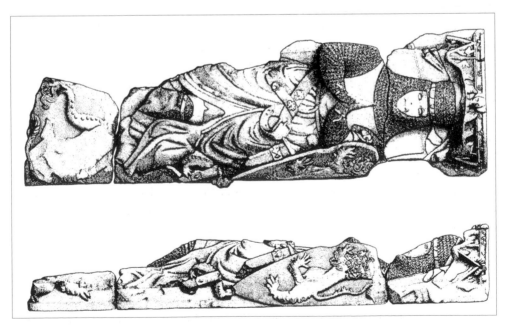

49 The tomb effigy of Henry Percy of Alnwick from Fountains Abbey was placed centrally to the west of the high altar in 1315. *S. Hayfield*

been excavated, including at least three women and five children. The burials could be phased by the interleaving of construction deposits associated with the adjacent church. The earliest burials, all male, were presumably religious and were associated with pieces of reused timber which appear to have come from a carpentered building. One piece gave a tree-ring date of 1150±9, leading to the speculation that the earliest members of the community were buried below pieces of their foundation-period timber church. This is not as strange as it might seem. When the Cistercian monks of Signy in the Ardennes built their first stone buildings they chose ritually to bury the parts of their temporary buildings they could not reuse in their new buildings in the monastic cemetery. Later burials at Bordesley were in stone-lined graves, in wooden coffins, or simply shrouded, and some were marked with stone slabs with head and foot markers.

Bordesley has demonstrated that not all graves in the monastic cemetery need be monks, and there is plenty of documentary evidence to prove that patrons and relatives of the religious were frequently buried with the community. The excavation of the cemetery at Cistercian Stratford Langthorne in east London has demonstrated the extent of mixed lay and religious burial in two areas of cemetery to the north of the church. While there was a heavy male bias in the burial pattern, there were a substantial number of women and some children. Study of the skeletal material suggests that there were family groups through several generations that may have contained both religious and their relations. One of the most notable features of the male burials was the high incidence of DISH (diffuse idiopathic skeletal hyperostosis), a bony growth that affects the spine normally associated with obesity and a distinct lack of exercise. This has been seen as a 'monastic' disease, a marker of overindulgence and a sedentary life which was interpreted as an indication of falling standards in monastic life throughout the later fourteenth and fifteenth centuries. The problem is how to differentiate the religious from the laity, and this is far from easy in cemeteries associated with urban or suburban monasteries. What is desperately needed is the excavation of the cemetery of a small- to medium-sized rural monastery where the pressure of lay burial was low.

The monastic church was as much a mausoleum as the house for the monastic choir in the later Middle Ages. It was often modified and extended, it was divided by screens into 'use areas', and it was normally highly decorated. It is only by a full study of surviving fabric and the examination of archaeological deposits that we can get close to understanding how it functioned throughout time.

3

THE CLOISTER BUILDINGS

From the tenth century in England it was normal for monasteries of both men and women to have domestic ranges built around three sides of a court or cloister, usually on the south side of the church, the innermost enclosure of the monastery. This area was normally referred to as the house. The word 'cloister' (in Latin *claustrum*) literally means a locked or enclosed space, and it remained an area to which access was very carefully controlled. It was a concept that was fully developed by about 820 when the stylised plan of a Benedictine monastery was supplied by an unknown donor to Gozbert, abbot of St Gall in Switzerland, and which came to England from Normandy in the later tenth century.

Although many monastic communities had lived communally since the foundation of St Basil's monastery of Neocaesaria in about 360, a concept which was to spread slowly to western Europe and which was to be encapsulated in the rule that St Benedict developed for his monastery of Monte Casino after 529, there was no regulated pattern of building that dictated the form of domestic buildings on early monastic sites. Monastic life was still developing, and as it did so it split into a series of different traditions. That which spread to Ireland and thence to northern England via Iona and Lindisfarne was at least partially eremitic, with monks and nuns living in individual cells which were not necessarily related to the several oratories that were normally provided. Though several churches associated with the Roman mission of St Augustine have been excavated, no evidence has been recovered of the domestic buildings that should be associated with them before the eighth century. It is only from known monastic sites, that is those listed by Bede in the early eighth century, that we can even be sure we are dealing with monastic domestic buildings at all.

THE DOMESTIC BUILDINGS OF ANGLO-SAXON MONASTERIES

Two monasteries, both associated with St Hild, in Northumbria have provided the clearest evidence for the form of the earliest domestic buildings associated with monastic sites: the monasteries of *Heruteu* at Hartlepool and *Streonshalch* at Whitby. Hartlepool was the earlier, being established in the 640s. Excavation in Church Close has identified two distinct periods of occupation, the first with post-hole and post-in-trench buildings of the seventh century, the second with stone-founded timber buildings of the eighth century. All the buildings were small, typically about 4.5m x 3m, and some were divided by a partition into a sleeping or storage area and a working area, and usually had a single external door. Altogether, there were four phases of timber buildings, which apart from their small size were typical of Middle-Saxon domestic buildings. From the finds associated with them, which included evidence of high-quality metalworking, the excavators concluded that this was a male area of the monastery, which because it was ruled by an abbess would have been a double house of monks and nuns. The early buildings were enclosed by a timber palisade, but the settlement had expanded outside this enclosure and a new enclosure had been established. Whether this was the *vallum monasterii* (monastic enclosure), or simply a function area within a larger site remains to be seen. The change in building technique to using stone foundations is highly significant when compared with the buildings which were excavated at Whitby in the 1920s.

Hild established a new monastery at the headland above the later town of Whitby (a site remarkably similar to that of Hartlepool) in 657, and it was to become a burial site for the Northumbrian royal family. Its accidental discovery in the course of the conservation of the post-conquest monastery which still marks the site, led to a substantial area on the north side of the standing church being stripped between 1920 and 1925 to reveal a mass of buildings, drains, pathways and burials (*50*). The method of excavation was brutal, with the removal of all archaeological deposits that sealed the structures with little supervision, and few of the objects found were adequately recorded. However, the site was critically studied by Rosemary Cramp and Philip Rahtz, and in the light of the Hartlepool excavation of 1984/5 it is possible to understand the site more clearly.

Analysis of finds suggests that the excavated buildings lie in the women's area of the monastery, and that there are two or more phases of development, the earliest with timber buildings, evidenced by burned daub, replaced by buildings with stone footings (and given later documentary evidence) stone superstructure. The buildings are not, as originally thought, a series of free-standing structures but elaborate ranges of rooms served by a complicated network of drains and divided into groups by metalled pathways. The remains of individual buildings are, in many cases, fragmentary, and most show some evidence of modification and reconstruction. Dating from the eighth and ninth centuries on the evidence of Hartlepool, several elements can be identified with a reasonable degree of certainty. Individual cells, each comprising a living room or work room with an open hearth and a bedroom with a latrine can be recognised at A, B, C, and D, while building E was originally identified as a store or guest room, the finds from it suggesting either use was possible. It was at least partly rebuilt when a series of rooms, H, was built on its east side. To the west a series of structures overlay earlier burials and appear to date from the early years of the ninth century. Room F, part of a heavily robbed building extending to the west, was domestic in nature, producing *styli* (writing implements), needles, pins and a quern for grinding grain. Further west still, a pair of buildings Gi and Gii produced 18 loom weights, indisputable evidence of weaving. The more fragmentary range L, to the north of this area, contained a series of rooms used, judging from the artefacts they produced, for spinning, writing, copying

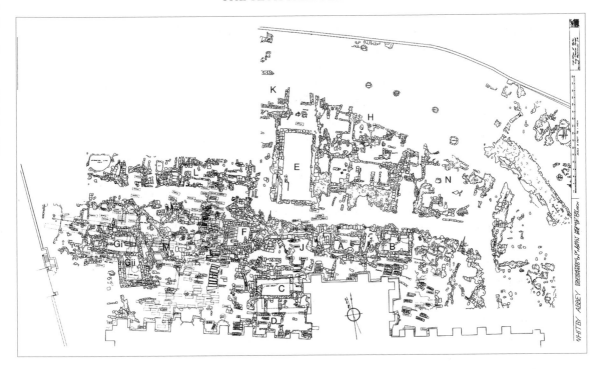

50 Excavation by Peers and Radford revealed the extensive remains of pre-conquest buildings on the north side of the Norman and later abbey church at Whitby

and weaving. There are no traces of communal rooms for eating or sleeping at either Whitby or Hartlepool, though in both cases only small parts of the monastery have been examined. Bede, writing of the monastery of Coldingham, described how the monastery contained both public and private cells and buildings for study and reading, exactly what the excavated buildings at Whitby seem to represent.

Hartlepool, Whitby and Coldingham belong to the Irish tradition of monasticism. There are other monasteries which follow more communal patterns, but it remains difficult to prove that they were monastic. Bede refers to 'unofficial' or 'family' monasteries which he did not recognise because they did not follow a form of rule of which he approved. The precise relationship between Middle-Saxon monasteries and high-status lay settlement is not understood, and some monasteries may well have adjoined or even been part of a princely residence. The obvious signifiers of monastic life, the evidence of literacy and religious symbolism, were not restricted to monks and nuns. Three sites have been claimed as potentially monastic. Flixborough in North Lincolnshire, Brandon in Suffolk, and Fishtoft in south Lincolnshire. What they have in common is not the small cells of the Northumbrian monasteries but a series of rectangular halls, usually indistinguishable from the halls of Middle-Saxon high-status settlements. At Fishtoft (*51*), where pottery indicated settlement between the late seventh and mid-ninth centuries, there was a hall-like building at least 12m long and 7m wide, which lay in a ditched enclosure on the surface of a clay island only 4m above sea level and surrounded by silt

51 Middle-Saxon monastic buildings under excavation at Fishtoft. One of the hall-like buildings is visible in the left foreground

fen, typical of the setting of Middle-Saxon monasteries in Lincolnshire. It is the setting at Fishtoft, deep in the Lincolnshire fens, and a known connection with the contemporary monastery of Crowland to the south that sets it apart.

THE MONASTERIES OF BENEDICT BISCOP

Benedict Biscop was a Northumbrian nobleman who had been professed as a monk in the island monastery of Lerins, had travelled widely on the continent and who had been temporarily abbot of St Peter and St Paul at Canterbury. He returned home to establish two new monasteries, one at Monkwearmouth in 674, and the second at Jarrow in 682. These monasteries are significant for two reasons. The first is that Monkwearmouth was where Bede was professed and where he wrote his *History of the English Church and People*; the second that both sites were excavated by Professor Rosemary Cramp. Biscop had collected books for his planned monasteries when he travelled in Europe, and when he began building he brought masons and glaziers from France. Monkwearmouth and Jarrow (both Tyne and Wear) thus followed the pattern of contemporary European monasticism and not the native Irish or Anglo-Saxon models. They provide an updated version of what is known from Canterbury and the monasteries of St Augustine's mission.

At Monkwearmouth (*52*), excavation failed to find the major communal buildings but did give tantalising clues as to how the monastery was laid out. A corridor-like structure with glazed windows and a slated roof ran southwards from the church, perhaps an enclosed 'cloister' giving access to the communal buildings, for Bede specifically described a cloister there. To its east and also leading to the church was a cobbled path, which ran through an area of burials towards the church. These primary structures were truncated by a wall which was originally pre-conquest in date but which had been reused in the late eleventh-century recolonisation of the site. Sadly the post-conquest development of the site and the limited area available for excavation made it impossible to recover further details.

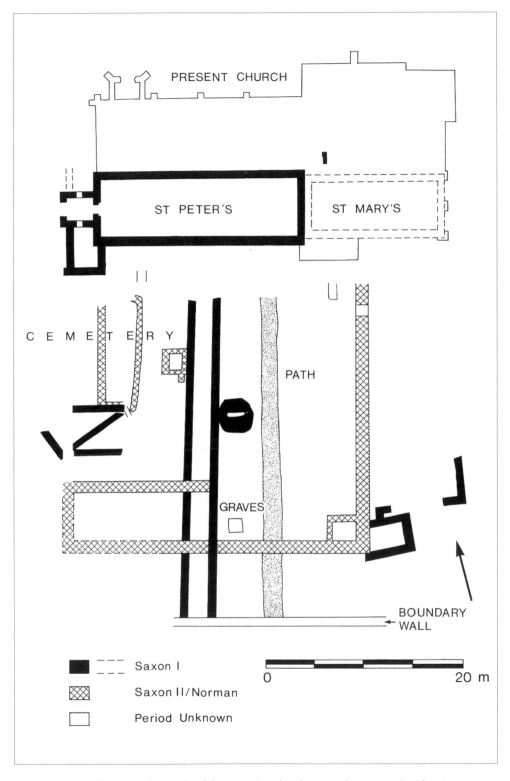

PRESENT CHURCH

ST PETER'S

ST MARY'S

C E M E T E R Y

PATH

GRAVES

BOUNDARY
WALL

Saxon I

Saxon II/Norman

Period Unknown

0   20 m

52 The Saxon buildings to the south of the surviving church at Monkwearmouth. *After Cramp*

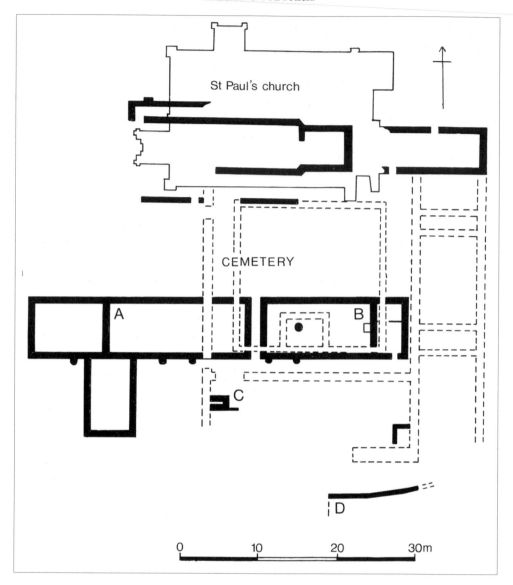

53 Excavation at Jarrow below the cloister of the post-conquest monastery have revealed extensive remains of Benedict Biscop's domestic ranges separated from his churches by a cemetery. *After Cramp*

At Jarrow (*53*), however, in spite of post-conquest reconstruction, Professor Cramp was able to recover good evidence for the layout of the monastic buildings. The area to the south of the two in-line churches was terraced, and on these terraces major stone buildings were found. Some 16m to the south of the churches and sharing their alignment were two substantial structures, A and B, with walls of coursed masonry laid in mortar and faced with plaster. Both had been destroyed by fire. Building A comprised a range of two rooms, each with a floor of Roman-style *opus signinum*, a concrete with high concentration of crushed tile in it that gives it a distinct pink colour. In the centre of the eastern room was an octagonal base associated with fragments of a shaft carved with heavy plant scrolls, interpreted by the excavator as the remains of a stone lectern. It seems that this room, enlarged by the ultimate removal of the dividing wall, was the monks' refectory. To the south was an annex which had a partially paved floor at a lower level than the main building with pebble-lined settings which might have been for standing large barrels or storage vessels. It seems to have been added after the partition wall was removed from Building A, and was the servery associated with the refectory. A small hut to the south of Building A appears to have been a workshop associated with the construction of the annex for it contained quantities of Roman tile which was used as chippings in the floor of the new work. Separated from Building A by a flagged path was Building B, a range of one large and two small rooms. The larger room had a setting for a seat against its east wall and a circular tank or well, placed centrally towards the west end. Fragments of plain and coloured glass found along the south wall indicate that it had glazed windows of the highest quality. Finds included a *stylus*, a pin with a ring-and-dot head and a small whetstone, suggesting that the room had been used as a place of assembly and writing, what would have been the 'chapter house' of a later monastery. The two rooms to the east, in comparison, were not 'public' but comprised a small oratory with an *opus signinum* floor and the base of an altar against the east wall, divided by a timber screen set in a slotted stone base from a larger living room with a sink in its south-east corner and an external door in its south wall. This suite can be directly compared with the individual cells identified at Whitby, but at Jarrow it is associated with a communal building of the monastery, very much in the contemporary fashion of domestic halls and private lordly accommodation. Almost certainly it was the suite of the abbot or a senior monk.

The late Roman-style buildings of the upper terrace at Jarrow were supplemented by wooden buildings on the lower terrace. Several wattle huts produced evidence of glass-working, and there was evidence that the lower terrace was also cultivated. At its east end was a partially excavated building, D, again with painted plaster on its inner wall surfaces and producing some 900 fragments of plain and coloured window glass. Its latest use was as a workshop, but its primary use was perhaps a guest house, placed as it was close to the river that skirted the site and away from the communal monastic buildings. From Bede's written description of Jarrow we know that other buildings await discovery, including a common dormitory, the kitchen and the bake house.

THE DEVELOPMENT OF THE CLOISTER

Neither Monkwearmouth nor Jarrow had what we would recognise as a cloister, a square or rectangular court attached to the church and surrounded by ranges of buildings, and though Bede used the word he meant something different. The cloister as it came to be understood developed on the continent in the late eighth and early ninth century. It was sufficiently developed by about 820 to be the model chosen for the St Gall plan, and it remained little changed into the early sixteenth century.

The introduction of the enclosed cloister to England was part of the reform introduced into England from the mid-tenth century and centred on St Dunstan. The *Regularis Concordia* (see Chapter 2) mentions the provision of a common refectory, a common dormitory, the cloister itself, a room set apart for daily chapter meetings, a warming house, a kitchen and a guest house. This grouping of buildings into a central nucleus was the next stage on from the development of sites such as Whitby or Jarrow, both of which would have been reordered on this pattern had they not succumbed to the Viking raids of the late ninth century. The earliest cloister in England to have been identified by excavation is that of Dunstan's own monastery of Glastonbury (see *21*), to the south of the church but still separated from it by a cemetery. The east range was aligned on the south *porticus* of the church. The cloister garth itself measured some 55m x 37m and was surrounded on three sides by ranges from 6-8m wide. Sadly, little is known about the planning of the ranges themselves. At Canterbury, however, excavation has revealed the layout of not one but two Late-Saxon cloisters on the north side of the church. Although their plans are fragmentary it is possible to identify the earlier layout as that built by Abbot Ælfmaer between 1006 and 1017, now firmly attached to the church and with ranges of rooms on all three sides. It was enlarged, with a new east range aligned on Abbot Wulfric's rotunda which was left unfinished at his death in 1059. Presumably Wulfric was also responsible for the enlargement of the cloister.

Excavation at Eynsham Abbey in Oxfordshire has revealed the south refectory range of the reformed monastery built by Abbot Ælfric before 1005 (when it is mentioned in a letter together with the cloister). Its relationship with the east and west ranges could not be determined, but excavation to the south indicated a second enclosure and further buildings to the west. The second enclosure was interpreted as a garden because its archaeology had been consistently reworked throughout the tenth and eleventh centuries.

At Westminster Abbey, Edward the Confessor planned a cloister on the south side of his new church, following the Norman model which was to become the standard for all post-conquest monasteries.

THE PLANNING OF THE MEDIEVAL CLOISTER

The plan of the domestic buildings of a medieval monastery was redefined after the Norman conquest, and rapidly became standardised. Remarkably little variation in layout occurs regardless of the observances of particular orders. The placing of the house, as it was called, to the north or south of the church was determined by access to drainage, water supply, or the need for privacy, though there was a marked tendency to place them on the south side of the church. Nuns had a preference for northern cloisters and this is particularly noticeable in Benedictine and Cluniac houses. Cistercian nuns, however, almost invariably placed their cloister on the south side of their church, and canonesses seem to have been ambivalent about its location. The Cistercian nuns of Kirklees in Yorkshire had a southern cloister and from a survey taken in 1534/5 its buildings would have been immediately recognisable to the first generation of nuns who colonised the site in 1153 (see *23*):

Item the cloister at the southe parte of the churche conteynyth in length xl ffoote square and in bredith vij foote, and iij partes coueryd w^t slates, and chambers ouer th'other one parte, w^toute any glasse.

(Item the chapiter house at th'este parte of the cloister, xvj foote
(square, vndir the dorter, w^t iij little glasse wyndowes conteyning vj
(foote of glasse.
(Item the dorter ouer the chapiter house, xl foote longe and xviij foote
(brode, coueryd w^t slates.
(Item a parler vndir the dorter xviij foote square, w^t a chimney, ij baye
(wyndowes glasid conteyning xxx foote of glasse.
aboute   (Item the gyle house at the southe parte of the cloister, xx foote square,
the   (vndir the fraytour.
cloister   (Item a larder house vndir the fraytour, xiij foote longe and xiiij foote
(brode.
(Item the fraytour, xxxiiij foote longe and xviij foote brode, stone
(walles, vnglasid, coueryd w^t slates.
(Item a little house at the west parte to ley brede yn, xvj foote longe
(and x foote brode.
(Item a bultynge house at the west parte of the cloister, xvj foote brode.
(Item v little chambres ouer the same at the west parte of the cloister for the
(ladyes and others to worke yn, coueryd w^t slates.

Item a low chamber called the fermery at the nether ende of the fraytour, xviij foote square, old stone walles, a chymney, no glasse.

Item the kychyn, xx foote longe and xviij foote brode, no chymney, stone walles and coureyd w^t slates.

Item the halle at the west ende of the churche, xxx foote longe and xxj foote brode, w^toute glasse, coueryd w^t slates.

Item a parler or chamber at th'upper ende of the halle xxiiij foote longe and xviij foote brode, coueryd w^t slates, no glasse.

Item a little chamber by the same, x foote square, coueryd w^t slates, tymber walles.

Item the buttrye at the upper ende of the halle vndir the chamber, xxj foote longe and x foote brode.

Item a little buttrye by the same.

Although Kirklees was a poor nunnery, its buildings were of stone and it provided the same facilities for the community as richer houses: cloister, chapter house, dormitory, refectory and kitchen, and accommodation for its president. Relaxing monastic discipline and a move towards privacy might have made the buildings more comfortable than they were originally and the uses of some rooms might have changed, but overall the plan is that of the later twelfth century.

Although cloister ranges survive in varying degrees of completeness on many sites, few have been extensively excavated under modern conditions and the greater part of our knowledge comes from exploration in the late nineteenth and early twentieth centuries. An important exception is the Augustinian priory of Norton, a house of reasonably modest means. Excavated for public display between 1971 and 1983, the whole of the claustral area was examined (see *43*). The significance of Norton is that it demonstrated the growth of a small and relatively simple house over four centuries. The first buildings were of timber and lay outside the area of the permanent stone cloister buildings, a reminder that stone monasteries took some time to build and that the founding community required temporary buildings to continue religious life while their permanent home was being built. The first permanent stone buildings provided were typical of a small monastery. The east range contained the monks' common dormitory over a sacristy that often doubled as a library, the chapter house where daily business was conducted and discipline administered, and a long undercroft, the day room, which might double as the warming house. The day room was the place where members of the community could work within the confines of the cloister. The south range had a passage at its east end, often with a private room for the sub-prior above it. The rest of the range comprised the refectory, often at first-floor level. Many monks believed that their dining room was modelled on the upper room of the Last Supper, their president represented Christ, and they his Disciples. Meals were as spiritual as the offices sung in church. The west range contained the outer parlour, where members of the community could meet with outsiders, and cellarage. Above were rooms for the prior, who had business both inside and outside the cloister and for guests. All the ranges were connected by a covered passage, the cloister alleys, which were in effect the monks' living room where they read and meditated, washed before meals and even did their laundry.

The rebuilding of the cloister at Norton followed the growth of the community and the building of an agricultural estate to support the house, both of which would only follow the initial settlement of the site. In the late twelfth century, the dormitory was enlarged and the south and west ranges replaced outside their original sites, substantially enlarging the cloister itself, though the planning of these ranges barely changed. This growth continued into the thirteenth century, with the building of a new chapter house to the east of the east range, a new kitchen, and eventually a new guest house complex, leaving the first floor of the west range free for the prior to build himself a substantial house, a common trend from the later thirteenth century. At Norton, the prior's house continued to expand throughout the later Middle Ages, with the addition of a tower against the west wall of the range in the fifteenth century, after the prior had been promoted to abbot in 1391 and had a new status to maintain. Though all of this can be determined from the excavation of the site, Norton has little standing masonry apart from the lower storey of the west range that was incorporated in a post-suppression house. We have to take the example of Norton's archaeology when we look at the standing remains of cloister ranges elsewhere to understand how they developed.

There is no reason to suspect that Norton is exceptional in the way that its cloister buildings grew and were modified, though the provision of major stone ranges and an enclosed cloister often took a considerable time to develop. Well-endowed communities were better placed to build quickly and often began their permanent buildings within a few

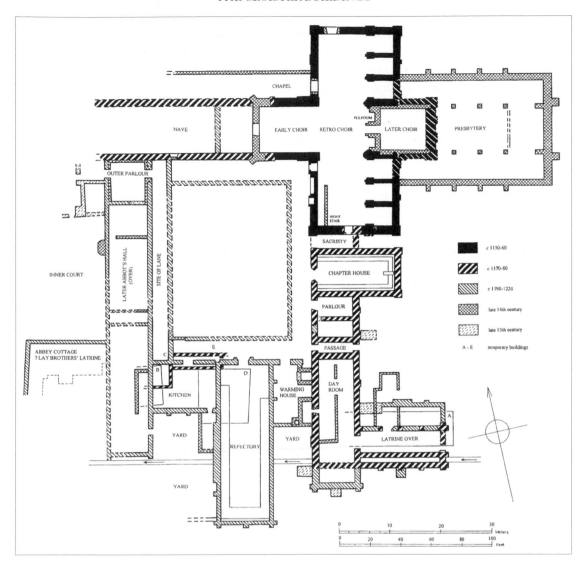

54 The church and cloister at Sawley demonstrate the slow construction of permanent buildings that was typical of a poorly-endowed monastery

years of their foundation. Others were not so fortunate, as the Cistercian abbey of Sawley in Lancashire (before 1974 in Yorkshire) demonstrated. Founded in 1147, Sawley Abbey did not achieve a fully developed cloister until about 1200 (54). Its original temporary buildings provided at the foundation, two great aisled buildings, were replaced in the third quarter of the twelfth century by a new series of timber buildings that incorporated a refectory, kitchen and guest house alongside a stone east range and latrine for the monks. For nearly 50 years there was no cloister or permanent refectory, and the monks had returned to a very early monastic model for their accommodation. Nor was there permanent accommodation for their lay brothers who would have occupied the west range, the last building to be erected.

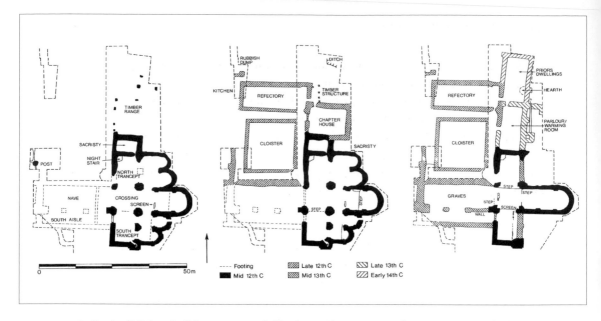

55 At Sandwell Priory building was remarkably slow with progression from (A) a part-built church and timber dormitory in the twelfth century, through (B) a regularised cloister layout in the thirteenth century, to (C) a reduced church and modified cloister in the early fourteenth century. *After Hodder*

Sawley was far from unique. Few small and poor houses have been examined archaeologically, even though they made of the bulk of the monastic settlement, in contrast to the larger and richer houses which are the ones with standing remains. An important exception is the Benedictine priory of Sandwell in the West Midlands. There, excavation has shown a similar development (55). The first buildings were the eastern parts of the church needed for the monks' use, and a timber east range that contained the monks' dormitory. Tree-ring dating demonstrated that one of the posts that framed this building was felled in 1159-60, 70 years after the foundation of the house indicating considerable delay before a claustral layout was begun, even in temporary form. The building of stone domestic buildings did not begin until the end of the twelfth century, when the timber east range was replaced by a stone chapter house with a dormitory above it, to be followed by a stone refectory on the north side. The north wall of the nave and a wall to the west were then built to enclose the cloister and the cloister alleys established. The nave of the church was not built at this stage, and indeed it was not to be completed until the end of the thirteenth century on a much reduced scale. At the same time the chapter house was taken down and replaced with a parlour/warming room with the dormitory above it, with a small pit latrine against the east wall. In the fourteenth century the east range was extended to provide a lodging for the prior, with a ground floor hall and a chamber at first-floor level that communicated with the dormitory. It had taken the monks of Sandwell approximately 150 years to provide the ranges required by their rule and even then on a very basic model.

THE CLOISTER ALLEYS

Excavation alone cannot show how cloister buildings developed for it provides only ground plans and building contents that have survived demolition and stone robbing. It is necessary to combine this information with a study of surviving fabric, which often contains evidence of remodelling that need not extend below ground level, and fallen or displaced architectural elements that often provide a good indication of the appearance of lost buildings. This is particularly true of the cloister itself, the heart of the monastery and the corridor that linked the domestic ranges with the church. The cloister alleys were the monks' regular work place, used for writing, meditation, and study, and surviving cloisters such as those of Norwich, Gloucester, and Durham show that they were places of great beauty and architectural sophistication. Few survive in place and those that do are usually late medieval rebuildings. Cloister arcades were fragile structures, among the first buildings to collapse when the monastic buildings were unroofed (*colour plate 9*). Excavation has revealed considerable quantities of fallen cloister arcade, as at Roche Abbey in South Yorkshire and Fountains Abbey, or elements of earlier cloisters reused in the foundations of their late medieval successors, as at Norton Priory. Because these arcades are reasonably simple it is quite possible to reconstruct them from their displaced fragments.

At Roche Abbey (*56* and *colour plate 10*), the cloister arcade built in 1170-80 survived until the early sixteenth century. Typical of the majority of English cloisters, it was open to the weather, supported on twin shafts with easily recognised bases and capitals. Study by Stuart Harrison of the fragments recovered by nineteenth-century clearance and early twentieth-century excavation has enabled its reconstruction. Remarkably it shows a change of design part way along one of the alleys; the earlier form has two-centred arches, the later with pointed trefoil arches and enrichment with dog-tooth decoration. Neither the monks nor the masons seem to have had any difficulty with the change in design which probably indicates that the cloister building stopped for a while and when work recommenced architectural design had moved on. Heavily moulded towards the garth, it was plain on its inner face, and the whole was painted white with the architectural detail picked out in red paint.

Designed for the warmer climate of southern Europe, the open cloister, just like that of the poor nuns of Kirklees, must have been cold and cheerless in winter. From the fourteenth century there was an increasing tendency to replace the open arcades with glazed windows, as at Lacock in Wiltshire, or to fit glazing in wooden frames into cuts in the masonry. Later cloisters, like that of Mount Grace Priory in Yorkshire, often indicate that they were originally designed with open windows, but that glazing channels were added and the windows filled with glass. The cloister arcade at Mount Grace was built in the 1420s and the glass was added roughly 50 years later, perhaps an indication that the climate was cooling throughout the later Middle Ages.

Though the cloister alleys have every appearance of being corridors that linked the various buildings of the cloister they were much more than that. The alley against the church was traditionally allotted to the religious for reading, study and the copying of manuscripts. It was also there that the monks gathered before bed to hear a reading for from the Collations of St John Cassian. A seat was often provided for the abbot and

56 The cloister arcade at Roche Abbey survives as many fragments recovered by excavation in the late nineteenth century. *G. Coppack and S. Harrison*

the cloister arcade might project into the garth opposite this, allowing the religious to congregate around him. A wall-bench might be provided along the length of this alley, as at Thornton Abbey in Lincolnshire. For study and writing, desks or carrels were provided. At Rievaulx these were of timber, in great abbeys like Gloucester and Chester they were built of stone and were integral with the alley wall. At Thornton, the carrels were in the west alley and their brick-paved base remains inside the alley wall. Books were kept in the east alley, either in wall cupboards, as at Fountains, Rievaulx and Sawley, or in purpose-built libraries such as the three-bay structure that survives at Much Wenlock in Shropshire. The east alley was normally kept clear of fittings for it was the processional route from the dormitory to the church. The floor of the alley was commonly used for burial, especially in front of the chapter house, and this was a favourite burial place for early patrons. The alley opposite the church and fronting the refectory normally contained the laver or washing place of the monks and was thus provided with piped water and drains (see Chapter 5). It was commonly used by the religious as a laundry, fitted up with wooden tubs and strung with washing lines. In houses of the Augustinian canons where the laver was commonly in the west alley, that alley, not regularly used by the religious, might be used as the laundry. In many houses the west alley was the preserve of the novice master and it was there that the novices were taught. As the cloister was a place of silence this must have caused some tension within many communities.

The laver itself, usually placed near the refectory door, was architecturally distinguished to emphasise its spiritual and social importance and was the most elaborate feature of the cloister. Few were as fine as that provided for the Augustinian canons of Southwick in Hampshire. A gift from King John their patron, and probably a second-hand altar reredos from a chapel royal, it was a fine Purbeck marble screen with seven canted niches capped with aisled and pyramid-roofed structures, set within a tall arch inserted into the north wall of the refectory range (57). Below the niches had been a trough that occupied the base of the recess, known from sixteenth-century sources to have been of pewter, presumably lining a stone basin. In the floor of each niche is a circular hole through which a pipe and tap extended, and pipe chases for the water supply can still be seen inside the range.

THE CLOISTER RANGES

The chapter house, which was normally placed close to the church in the east cloister range, was the place where the community gathered daily to hear a chapter of the *Rule of St Benedict* (hence its name), to commemorate the saints and dead brethren, to transact business, and to maintain discipline. It was here, too that the community would here sermons. Accordingly it was second only to the church in importance and displayed the

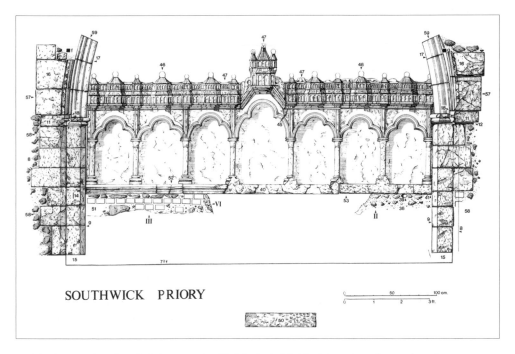

SOUTHWICK   PRIORY

57 The laver at Southwick Priory survived behind a brick blocking when the south and west ranges were converted into a house after the suppression and was only discovered when the ruins of the building were conserved in 1985. *J. Thorn*

importance of the house. Normally, it was vaulted, the vault being carried on pillars as at Cistercian Jervaulx Abbey (*colour plate 11*). Wall-benches were provided for the community along the side walls, returning along both end walls, and a gap in the centre of the east wall was the placing of the president's chair. At his feet was the traditional burial place of his predecessors and such was the desire for abbots to be buried there that they were crammed into tight rows. Nowhere is this clearer than at Fountains Abbey where 19 abbots were buried in the eastern bay of the chapter house between 1170 and 1346, after which abbots chose to be buried in the church. By the head of Abbot Robert of Pipewell's grave is the socket that held the lectern, used for the chapter reading and sermons. The surrounding floor was tiled with the same mosaic tiles as the presbytery of the church. Excavation of the chapter house at Byland Abbey produced the base of a free-standing lectern and the great communal ink pot used for the signing of the deed of surrender in 1539, the last act of corporate business transacted there. At Rievaulx Abbey, a plaited bronze scourge reminds us of the importance of maintaining discipline within the chapter house.

The dormitory was normally on the first floor of the east range and above the chapter house, so placed so that a stair into the church (the night stair) provided direct access to the choir. It also had a stair into the adjacent cloister alley for day use. Its location was further conditioned by the need to provide adequate drainage for the associated latrine block. Its placing in the west range at Durham, Easby and Worcester seems to have resulted simply from the location of suitable drainage. At Benedictine Durham and Westminster the dormitories retain their medieval roofs but have lost their later medieval partitioning. The monastic dormitory was originally conceived as an open space with the beds ranged along the walls, with presses and chests down the centre of the building to hold the community's changes of habit. This pattern certainly held good until the mid-thirteenth century, and survived until the suppression in many houses, but as monastic communities began to get smaller there was a tendency for the religious to favour small chambers partitioned in timber which gave a degree of privacy. In time these chambers became two-room sets, a bed chamber and a study. Some evidence does survive for partitioning. In 1534/35 the dormitory at Esholt Priory in Yorkshire had 'in it for the ladyes vij Celles'. At Jervaulx Abbey (*58*) secondary sockets in the dormitory wall evidence the fixing of the partitions of individual cells. At Durham, the fittings of the dormitory were described thus in the later sixteenth century:

> Vpon the West side of the Cloyster was a faire large house called the Dorter where all the Mounks & the Novices did lye, euery Mounke having a little chamber of wainscot verie close seuerall by them selves and ther wyndowes towards the cloister, euery wyndowe servinge for one Chambre by reasoune the particion betwixt euery chamber was close wainscotted one from the other, and in euery of these wyndowes a deske to supporte there bookes for there studdie. In the weste side of the said dorter was the lyke chambers & in like sort placed with there wyndowes and desks towards the fermery & the water, the chambers beinge all well bourded vnder foute.

1 A late twelfth-century copy of the foundation charter of Rievaulx Abbey. *British Library*

2 One of the mosaic tile roundels from the church of Jervaulx Abbey. *Henry Shaw*

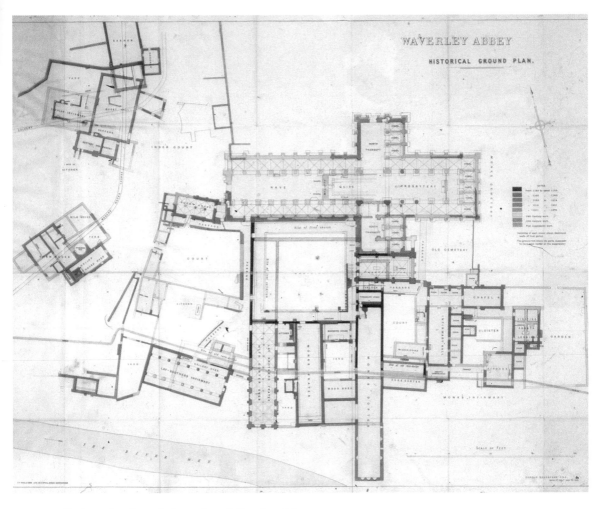

3 Brakspear's coloured phase-plan of Waverley Abbey

4 The presbytery of Bolton Priory in the early nineteenth century. *Richardson*

5 The ruins of the Carthusian's church at Mount Grace Priory. *English Heritage*

Above: 6 and *Below:* 7 The presbytery of Whitby Abbey. *English Heritage*

Above: 8 Reconstruction drawing of the late twelfth-century nave at Byland Abbey. *Simon Hayfield*

Opposite above: 9 The reconstructed cloister arcade at Rievaulx abbey. *Author*

Opposite below: 10 The reconstructed cloister arcade from Roche Abbey. *Stuart Harrison*

11 The chapter house in the east range of Jervaulx Abbey. *Author*

12 The first floor refectory at Easby Abbey. *Author*

13 The kitchen at Fountains Abbey. *Author*

14 The abbot's kitchen at Glastonbury Abbey. *Author*

15 The excavated bake house at Thornholme Priory; the staining on its floor indicating wooden partitions. *Author*

16 The late fourteenth-century grain dryer at Thornholme Priory that lay outside the precinct wall. *Maria Weld*

17 The great gatehouse at Kirkham Priory decorated with the arms of the house's patrons. *English Heritage*

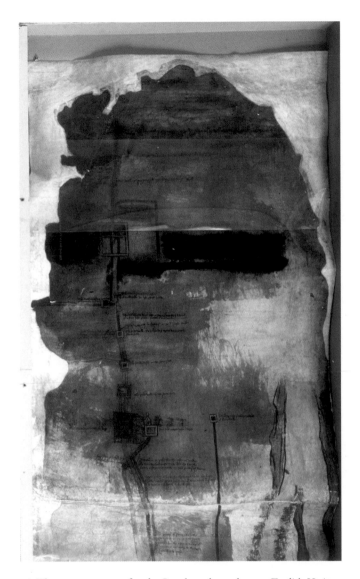

18 The water sources for the London charterhouse. *English Heritage*

19 Ceramic water-pipes excavated to the north of the church at Kirkham Priory. *Rich Williams*

20 The lay brothers' latrine of the 1150s at Fountains Abbey. *Author*

21 Wriothesley's gatehouse range at Titchfield Abbey was little more than the nave of the Premonstratensian church converted. *Author*

58 The west wall of the first-floor dormitory at Jervaulx Abbey with inserted sockets between its windows to hold partitions which divided the originally open dormitory into more private cells for the monks

    Also the nouices had theire chambers seuerall by himselfe not so close, nor so adionynge in the South-end of the said Dorter to the foresaid chambers hauinge eight chambers on either side, euery nouice his chamber seuerall by him selfe, not so close nor so warm as the other chambers was there no windowes to give light but as it came in at the foreside of the said chambers of the said nouices, being all close els both aboue and at either side. In either end of the said dorter was a 4-square stone, wherin was a dozen cressets wrought in ether stone beinge euery filled and supplied with the cooke, and they needed to giue light to the monkes and nouices when they rose to their Mattens at midnight and for their other necessarye uses.

Entered from the dormitory was the latrine, usually with doors to enter and leave by. Between the doors was a small opening that contained the lamp that lit access to the latrine at all times. Examples remain at Fountains Abbey (see Chapter 5) and at Kirkham Priory.

    Below the dormitory, apart from the chapter house, there were usually three other spaces, normally vaulted and fireproof, which were entered from the cloister. The first was the parlour, the only space in the cloister where talking was permitted for limited periods. The early fourteenth-century parlour at Thornton Abbey survives (*59*), a cheerless room with wall-benches, an earth floor and no windows; without a door it took its light from the adjacent cloister alley. Talking was clearly not encouraged. The second space was a passage through the range to the infirmary beyond that was provided for the old and sick

59 The parlour at Thornton Abbey was a finely proportioned but cold and cheerless room that implies necessity rather than sociability

members of the community. The third space was normally a large room at the southern end of the range, often simply called the dormitory undercroft, and sometimes thought to have been used by the novices. Little is actually known about the function of this room, and in sixteenth-century surveys it is often dismissed as a 'chamber' which is far from helpful. At Rievaulx Abbey, this room was excavated in the 1920s and its contents recorded. An impressive room, well lit and vaulted in four-and-a-half double bays, it still contained its fallen vault which had sealed its last contents. Iron rings hanging from the keystones of the vault had held hanging lamps that lit the room in every bay. On the floor were everyday objects: jet rosary beads, pens and *styli*, a wax tablet for writing on, two pewter plates and coins including a gold noble. There were two wall fireplaces, both additions to the original structure of the 1160s. It would appear the room was used for writing and other tasks that the monks would undertake, a sort of common work room. The same room at Byland had open arches in its east wall opening onto an enclosed yard, probably the space where more dirty tasks were undertaken, still within the enclosure of the cloister.

The side of the cloister opposite the church contained the refectory, a building whose importance in the daily life of the community was reflected in its scale and architectural pretensions. It was usually aligned parallel to the cloister alley, and might be at ground-floor level in houses of Benedictines, Cluniacs and Cistercians (*60*), or at first-floor level above vaulted service rooms in the houses of canons, canonesses and nuns (*colour plate 12*). From the 1160s the Cistercians adopted a different ground plan to other orders, placing their refectories at right angles to the cloister alley so that the kitchen which normally lay outside the range could be entered directly from the cloister alley. Whatever the planning, the arrangement of most refectories was the same, with a raised dais at the further end from the entrance where the president and senior officers sat, and raised foot-paces along the side walls on which the benches and tables for the rest of the community sat. The religious sat only on the wall side of the tables. Set in one wall towards the dais was a pulpit from which one of the community would read during meals, and close to the door from the cloister were cupboards set into the walls that contained the napkins and spoons, as at Hailes (Gloucestershire), Haughmond (Shropshire), Kirkham and Fountains. The body of the refectory was open space so that the superior could observe all members throughout the meal as the *Rule of St Benedict* required. Excavation of the early thirteenth-century refectory at Sawley Abbey revealed the foot-paces, wall-benches, and dais, and a small laver or water-fountain in the centre of the refectory floor, with the channel for a lead pipe bringing water to it and a drain taking the waste away to the abbey's main drain. The floor of the refectory at Sawley was plain mortar. Refectories were often tiled, as excavation of the Franciscan nuns' refectory at Denny Abbey, Cambridgeshire demonstrated. There the greater part of the floor survived, covered with Bawsey tiles between the foot-paces. The tables were normally set on stone legs, the bases of which can still be seen in the foot-paces at Fountains Abbey, twin octagonal shafts that are also seen at Jervaulx Abbey. At Rievaulx the table legs were slab-like monoliths, set in a rectangular, slotted stone base. The refectory at Bardney, refitted in the fourteenth century, was altogether more elaborate. There, the tables were set on Y-shaped stone supports, carved with the heads of a monk, abbot, and king on the visible side. The wall-benches had similar supports.

60 At Fountains Abbey the refectory survives to full height though it has lost its central arcade. Around the walls the raised foot-paces and the stubs of stone table legs can still be traced, while the reader's pulpit occupies three bays of the west wall

Between the refectory and kitchen was a hatch through which food was passed. In smaller monasteries this was often no more than a small square hole in the wall. In larger monasteries it could be quite elaborate. The Cistercians in the late twelfth century adopted a revolving dumb-waiter, identified by its curving sides. Examples survive at both Rievaulx and Fountains.

Attached to the refectory or communicating through a short passage but usually outside the cloister ranges was the kitchen, with its great fireplaces and ovens. True to the *Rule of St Benedict* the kitchen was for the preparation of a vegetarian diet. With the gradual adoption of meat into the monastic diet from the fourteenth century, a second meat kitchen was provided, normally associated with the infirmary and a second refectory, the misericord. Excavation of the kitchens at Kirkstall, Sawley, Eynsham (Oxfordshire) and Mount Grace has revealed a complex development of hearths, piped water and drains, indicating that kitchens were frequently rebuilt or modified. Twelfth-century kitchens are rare, but that at Fountains built in the 1160s is substantially intact (*colour plate 13*). Originally it had a pair of back-to-back hearths below a massive chimney that occupied most of the room and passed through the fire-proof vaulted ceiling. In the north wall were cupboards and three open windows below the vault that ventilated the room. The south wall had an open archway, probably filled with wooden louvers, and a door into the kitchen yard where the vast quantities of wood needed to feed the fires was stored. The early thirteenth-century kitchen at Sawley was similar, though it seems to have only a single fireplace set towards the east wall. It was reorganised in the late fourteenth century. The chimney was removed and a timber smoke-hood set on cill walls and in post-holes occupied most of the southern half of the building with a hearth of edge-set tile below it. There was a porch covering the door from the cloister, and a paved area in the north-east corner was the servery from which food was passed into the refectory. Nineteenth-century excavation recorded a turning dumb-waiter here but it did not survive when the building was re-excavated in the 1980s. A passage along the wall of the refectory had a drain running its full length, starting in the servery area and discharging into the main drain. Though no occupation deposits had survived Victorian excavation this narrow room was probably a scullery; the interpretation of a similarly placed room at Kirkstall.

Detached kitchens might be more elaborate, like the first kitchen at Eynsham, designed with circular fireplaces in its south-west and south-east corners, or the great fourteenth-century octagonal kitchen that survives at Durham. The abbot's kitchen at Glastonbury (*colour plate 14*), the finest surviving kitchen in Britain, is essentially a detached Benedictine kitchen of the same size and form as one associated with the refectory.

The west range, which normally lay between the enclosed cloister and the semi-public area of the inner court (see Chapter 4) provided the link between the religious and the outside world. In Cistercian houses it was the preserve of the lay brothers, the ground floor providing cellarage, the outer parlour and their refectory (which shared the kitchen with that of the monks). The upper floor was their dormitory. Other orders normally followed the plan adopted by the Benedictines, with only the outer parlour and cellarage on the ground floor, with the president's lodging and perhaps guest accommodation above. Examples survive at Westminster and Battle, though they have been heavily modified since the sixteenth century. Perhaps more typical is the house of the prior at Castle Acre (*61*). First built in the 1160s, the west range comprised the outer parlour, cellarage and the entry into the cloister. A stair in the corner of the outer parlour provided the only access to the upper floor of the north end of the range. In the twelfth and thirteenth centuries there were two interconnecting rooms: a bed chamber over the outer parlour and a living room to the south. The remainder of the range at this level was probably the guest hall, reached by an external stair. In the late twelfth century a porch had been built outside the cloister entry with rooms at first- and second-floor level above it that did not have a door to the guest hall and must have been entered as it was later from the prior's living room by an angled bridge. The rooms in the tower porch would have provided the prior with a chapel and study. From the early fourteenth century, the prior's house was considerably expanded, a common feature of presidents' lodgings connected with their changing status outside their monasteries. Presidents of major monasteries assumed the status of earls on the basis of their house's landholdings, some had seats in Parliament, and all began to model their houses in the manner of substantial landowners. In a monastic context this resulted in the conversion of existing buildings for the most part. At Castle Acre this began with the building of a two-storey building to the west of the outer parlour. The vaulted ground floor contained three rooms, one with a fireplace, probably to house the prior's secretariat, because a door from here was inserted into his private stair. The upper

61 The prior's house in the west range at Castle Acre Priory survived the suppression and is still partly roofed. Originally built in the 1160s it was largely remodelled and extended in the fourteenth and fifteenth centuries

room was a new bed chamber for the prior, with a door in the north-west corner leading to a latrine tower which survived into the eighteenth century. Next to the latrine door is a very fine wash basin. The old chamber above the outer parlour was converted into a chapel, with an altar against the east wall and an inserted sedile, a seat for the officiating priest, in the south wall. The two rooms were given a new scissor-braced east–west roof that survives, and the chapel retains late fourteenth-century wall paintings. In the late fifteenth century, the wall between the bed chamber and chapel was removed and a new ceiling was inserted in both rooms. Mortises in the ceiling show that they were divided by a timber partition, enlarging the bed chamber at the expense of the chapel. The prior's old living room became his parlour in the late fourteenth century, with a great fireplace inserted into the north wall and a new square-headed window in the west wall. In the early sixteenth century another room was added above the parlour and a stair provided down to the cloister. An angled passage was created to provide access to the tower porch room from the parlour. The south end of the range was rebuilt as an open hall for the prior, reached by a porch and stair from the inner court to the west. In the late fifteenth century, the house was modernised by Prior John Winchelsea who added a great oriel window to his chamber and enlarged the north windows of the chapel. He also removed the timber partition and replaced it with a pair of fireplaces, one to heat his chamber, the other to heat the private pew he installed in the chapel. It was Winchelsea who painted the ceiling of both rooms with Tudor red and white roses.

The prior's house at Castle Acre is remarkable only because so much of it survives to show its development. Sir Harold Brakspear interpreted the excavated remains of the west range and adjacent buildings at Bardney Abbey in very much the same way, stretching credulity in the 1920s but making considerable sense of the multi-period alterations that evidenced a house growing by accretion. The sixteenth-century survey description of Kirklees Priory indicates a very similar arrangement in the west range there.

INFIRMARIES

Small monasteries might set apart one or more rooms in their cloister ranges as an infirmary for the old and sick members of the community. In houses of middle or greater rank, however, separate accommodation was provided for those who could no longer endure the rigours of the cloister. Lying outside the cloister enclosure and usually to the east of the east range away from the disturbance of the inner court and close to the convent cemetery, the infirmary duplicated many of the monastic buildings with its own hall, latrine, refectory, chapel and cloister. It often lay within its own enclosure though it was entered directly from the cloister through an enclosed passage. Fragments of many survive, as for instance at Christchurch cathedral priory in Canterbury, or Gloucester, Peterborough, Rievaulx or Easby Abbeys. Others like Fountains or Tintern (Gwent) have been revealed by excavation. Perhaps the most instructive of these is that built by the Cistercians at Waverley in the early thirteenth century and excavated by William St John Hope and the Rev. T.S. Cooper in 1899.

The Waverley buildings (*62*) replaced a series of timber buildings of which the plan was not recovered. It comprised a hall of six bays with a central hearth and a single aisle on the east side, with a small cloister beyond it. To the south of the infirmary hall was a small latrine, essentially a continuation of the main dormitory latrine. Opening from the north-east corner of the hall was the chapel on the north side of the cloister, on the south side of which was the infirmary kitchen linked to a door in the south wall of the hall by a passage. On the east side of the cloister was a two-storey domestic building, interpreted by the excavators as the house provided for the abbot of the mother house who was to visit annually. In practice, though such houses were frequently provided they tended to be used to house abbots who had resigned or been deposed, and the lower floor would have been the lodging of the infirmarer whose duties required him to be present at all times. The conduit from which water was piped to all parts of the monastery (see Chapter 5) was normally located in the infirmary, for the sick were to have the first use of the water; at Waverley its base was found in the west alley of the infirmary cloister. Associated with the infirmary was a garden for the growing of medicinal herbs. Often this was located within the infirmary cloister, as at Christchurch, Canterbury and at Rievaulx; at Waverley it lay to the east of the infirmary complex.

It is common to find radical changes in monastic infirmaries from the fourteenth century and Waverley was no exception, with its buildings being subdivided and extended. The northern part of the hall was divided off and partitioned into at least five cubicles that provided more privacy than the aisle of the open hall. Significantly each of these rooms had a fireplace. Further rooms were built against the west wall in what had been an open court, and to the south of these was the misericord or infirmary refectory where meat might be eaten, not only by the sick but by all members of the community. The availability of a meat diet led senior members of the community to build their lodging in the infirmary area, and from the early fourteenth century this became a common trend, in spite of papal and episcopal injunctions. The infirmary halls at Fountains, Kirkstall and Tintern were all fitted up with two-room apartments, each with a fireplace and a latrine, providing accommodation for a third of the community. At Waverley it was the abbot who took over part of the infirmary, using the misericord as his hall with his parlour to the north, and his chamber above the old infirmary latrine where he had access to its drain for his own latrine. At Rievaulx, the abbot took over the whole of the infirmary as his house in the early sixteenth century. The abbot of Waverley clearly took some of the community into his personal household and further rooms, probably two-storeyed, were fitted up for them in the aisle of the infirmary hall. The picture that is emerging is that as numbers fell the monks had a tendency to move out of the cold and draughty communal dormitory into more comfortable lodgings. At Byland, this led to the demolition of the infirmary and the use of its materials to build a range of private two-room sets partly inside and partly outside the old day room in the east range and on the site of the infirmary hall, a certain sign that the idealistic communal life of the twelfth and thirteenth centuries had been abandoned in favour of comfort and privacy, a very different form of monastic life that tends to be overlooked.

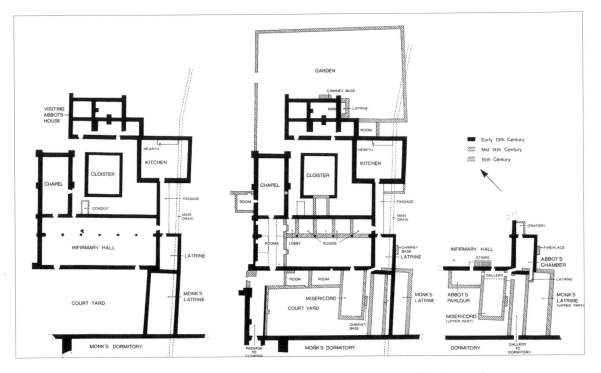

62 The infirmary at Waverley Abbey (A) as it was built in the early years of the thirteenth century, (B) as it was modified in the fourteenth and fifteenth centuries, and (C) the possible layout of the abbot's house attached to the later infirmary hall

ALTERNATIVE MODELS

Not all monks lived communally, and the Carthusians in particular developed a different form of monastic life, that of hermits living together but spending most of their lives in seclusion within their charterhouses. Instead, each monk occupied his own cell (from the Latin *cella*, a room), and these were ranged around three sides of a massive cloister. The Carthusian cell was actually a substantial two-storey house set in its own walled garden (63) and it was probably the inspiration for the private apartments that began to appear from the fourteenth century in the houses of other orders.

The Carthusian plan can best be seen at Mount Grace Priory, the best-preserved Carthusian charterhouse in Britain, though excavations at Witham and Hinton (both Somerset), Coventry, Beauvale (Nottinghamshire) and London have revealed very similar structures. Set within a garden of approximately 15.3m square, each house comprised on the ground floor four rooms divided by timber partitions: an entry passage, a living room, a study, and a bedroom and oratory. The living room had a fireplace and a stair leading to the upper storey which comprised a work room. Every Carthusian monk had a trade and needed space within his cell to work. The garden was bounded by two corridors. One, along the cloister wall, was a private cloister for study and meditation. At least one at Mount Grace, that of Cell 8, had glazed windows and a wooden floor. The

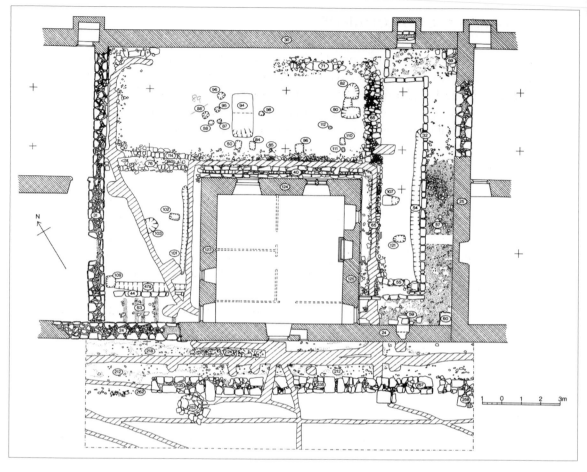

63 Excavation of Cell 8 at Mount Grace Priory has revealed the plan of both the house and garden, with its planting pits and cultivation trenches. *D. Coppack*

second corridor, normally entered from the living room, led to a latrine in the back wall of the garden and to the garden itself. In one of the two corridors, or within the entry passage of the cell, was a tap set in a niche that provided drinking water.

The garden, which provided the monk with the opportunity to undertake manual labour within the confines of his cell, provided the only scope for self expression in the most rigorous of monastic orders. Several of the Mount Grace gardens have been excavated, and no two are alike. That surrounding Cell 8, the earlier of two gardens excavated there, was divided into rectangular beds defined by paths of roof slates, the location of some plants being marked by slots or separate planting pits dug into the heavy clay subsoil and filled with richly manured soil. In comparison, the garden in the adjacent Cell 9 had three square knots edged with stones and divided by turf paths, a much more formal late medieval layout. In the sixteenth century, the garden of delight in Cell 8 was replaced by a vegetable garden, its soil being dug in rows. Unfortunately the soil at Mount Grace was too acid to preserve pollen or seeds from the plants grown there.

GARDENS AND ORCHARDS

Monastic gardens were common. They can be traced in frequent references in suppression-period surveys, and have been noted in excavation at priory St Mary of Clerkenwell, the Hospital priory of St John, Bermondsey Abbey and St Mary Graces Abbey in London. They have a long history going back to the early ninth century St Gall plan. At Wilberfoss Priory in East Yorkshire, the surveyors of 1534/5 noted 'ane orchard where the dovecote standyth ane acre di., fulle of esh trees. Item, gardens'. At Rievaulx, two gardens are mentioned: the Abbot's garden in the old infirmary cloister and the kitchen garden, the location of which was not recorded.

Gardens were invariably enclosed in some way, and in the monastic world were related to the garden of the Song of Solomon. That garden was a metaphor for a virgin bride, which by extension in the medieval monastic church was a metaphor for the Virgin Mary as well as providing an earthly paradise as an aid to meditation. The Cistercians in the twelfth century planted their cloisters. In the mid-1160s, Abbot Aelred of Rievaulx wrote in his *de spiritualia amicitia* (Of Spiritual Friendship) 'the day before yesterday, when I was going round the cloister of the monastery ... as though amid the delights of paradise, I admired the leaves, the flowers, and the fruits of every single tree'. At Christchurch in Canterbury it was the infirmary cloister that was planted in the late twelfth century. The waterworks plan (see *89*) of the monastery, dating to the 1160s or '70s shows a *herbarium* (herb garden) set with rows of plants and wooden trellises.

The plants grown in monastic gardens can be identified from contemporary herbals and plant lists found in monastic libraries from the twelfth century. The records of the abbey gardener at Glastonbury survive for part of the fourteenth century, and the analysis of garden soils is starting to recover the pollen and seeds of individual plants. Few monastic gardens have been fully excavated, and fewer have provided evidence of their layout. This is partly because excavation has concentrated on buildings, and partly because it is very difficult, if not impossible, to recover planting evidence from frequently cultivated garden soil. One of the first gardens to be excavated was the cloister garden at Denny Abbey in Cambridgeshire. Here the results were initially disappointing. No bedding trenches or plant remains were found. The soil had been constantly dug over and manured with domestic refuse. At the centre, however, was a cistern with a wooden cover, presumably the source of water for the garden and a feature of its layout. More instructive was the garden of the Augustinian friary in Hull where deep trenches had been dug into the heavy clay and filled with topsoil and domestic refuse. Waterlogging ensured the survival of the seeds and pollens, though the results of their analysis has yet to be published. The garden appears to have been medicinal. During the course of the excavation, cannabis plants grew from the spoil excavated from the bedding trenches and spread on the spoil heaps! The layout of the bedding trenches shows that the garden was formal in its layout.

Cloister gardens are the least examined of all monastic gardens. Parts of one were excavated at the Gilbertine St Andrew's Priory in York, with bedding trenches for box hedges dividing formal plots and extending the formality of the cloister arcades to the garden itself. For many orders, the cloister garden may have been a late medieval introduction. At Bardney Abbey, Brother Thomas Suthewelle was criticised by the sacrist before Bishop William Alnwick when he visited the house in 1444 for building a garden in the cloister. Presumably it had previously been a grass plot and the older members of the community did not hold with such modern ideas. Suthewelle's garden remains to be excavated and the cause of the sacrist's displeasure disclosed; it was the only part of the cloistral area not excavated before the First World War.

4

THE WIDER PRECINCT

Medieval monasteries were essentially self-contained and self-sufficient institutions depending for their continuing existence on the produce of an agricultural and industrial estate. Although the church and cloister were the heart of the monastery they comprised only a small part of the whole. Many other buildings were needed, either within the monastery or on its estates to service the house and manage its economy. To a medieval monk, the word monastery encompasses every piece of land his abbey owned and not just the buildings he lived in.

THE PRECINCT

In effect, the site of the monastery was a series of inward-turned enclosures designed to protect the community from contact with the outside world. If the innermost enclosure was the cloister, the next was the inner court with its guest accommodation, granaries, stables, bake house and brew house, often with its own gatehouse, the great or inner gatehouse. Access to the inner court was tightly controlled. Beyond was the outer court or yard, enclosed within a precinct wall or bank, which contained the agricultural and industrial buildings necessary for the economic exploitation of the abbey's estates, the great barns, mills, and animal houses as well as closes to pen animals, and orchards. Accommodation for poorer visitors and perhaps even a lay infirmary and the almonry would be placed in the outer court. Normally they would lie between the outer gatehouse and the inner gate. There might also be a chapel outside the inner gate for those not permitted to enter the inner court. Urban monasteries might not have an outer court at all, the agricultural and industrial functions being relegated to a nearby grange. Beyond the precinct estates were managed either as granges, centralised and often specialist farms managed directly by the house, or manors, which were little different from those owned by laymen.

While the cloister buildings were normally constructed to a standardised plan, the same is not true of the inner and outer courts of the precinct. Their planning was dependent on topography and local requirements. The survey of Kirklees Priory (see 23) provides a good description of the most basic provision:

	(	(Item the new chamber at the northe parte of the inner
	(for	(courte, xvj foote square wᵗ a chimney and coueryd wᵗ
	(the	(slates, tymbre walles.
alle v	(chapleyns	(Item ane other chamber by the same, xvj foote
vndir one	(	(longe and xij foote brode, tymber walles, coueryd wᵗ
roofe	(	(slates.

Item ane other chamber by the same of like bignesse

Item ane other chamber therby of like bignesse

Item suche ane other chamber coueryd wᵗ slates.

Item a low house or old parler vndir the said chambers, xviij foote square, wᵗ stone walles and one glass window conteyning x foote of glasse.

Item the Prioress chamber at the northe side of the nether ende of the church, xxiiij foote longe and xvj foote brode, tymbre walles, coueryd wᵗ slates, no glasse.

Item j litle closet and a litle cole house therby.

Item the brewhouse and bakehouse at the south parte of the inner court, xxxvj foote longe and xx foote brode, stone walles and coureyd wᵗ slates.

Item a stable and ane old cole house at the southe parte of the seid courte, vndir the chambers.

Mᵈ that alle the seid houses are aboute the […] inner courte.

The survey then goes on to list the buildings of the outer court:

Item ane old almshouse wheryn a poore man dwellith wᵗoute the gate.

Item ane other old almshouse, xl foote longe and xiiij foote brode, by the bek side.

Item a cowhouse, xxxviij foote longe and xx foote brode, brokyn walls, coueryd wᵗ slate.

Item ane old rounde dove cote in the vtter yard, of stone walles, partely brokyn, decayed.

Item a corne barne of ij storeys, wherof th'one lxxij foote long and xxx foote brode, and th'other xl foote longe and xxiiij foote brode, stone walls, a good stronge roofe coueryd wᵗ slates, v quarter rye.

Item a carte house, xxx foote longe and xvj foote brode, no walles, coueryd wᵗ slates welle.

Item the oxehouse, lx foote longe and xviij foote brode, stone and tymbre walles, coueryd wᵗ slates.

Item the kylne house, xliiij foote longe and xviij foote brode, wherof th'one half old and th'other half late burnyd and new bilded, wherof lakkith xx foote to couer, and the rest coueryd wᵗ slates.

Item the garner, xx foote longe and xvj foote brode, tymbre walles, coueryd wᵗ slates.

Item ij little houses vndir the same, and th'one of them for seruantes to lye yn.

Item a swynecote, xxiiij foote long and xvj foote brode, coueryd wᵗ slates.

Mᵈ that the moste parte are olde houses.

Item ane orchard enclosed wᵗ ane olde stone walle wᵗ few frute trees, conteynyth by estimacon iij roodes of grounde.

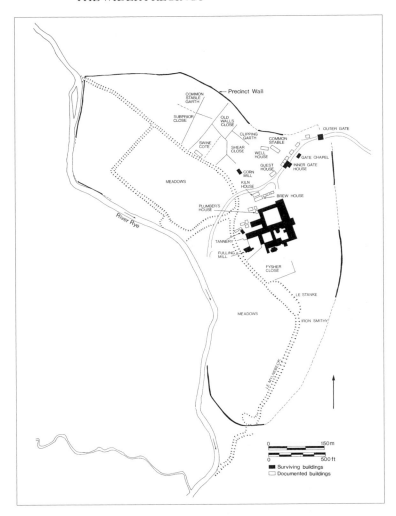

64 The precinct of Rievaulx Abbey in 1538-39, defined by contemporary documents, surviving buildings and earthworks

Remarkably, very little work has been done on the disposition of inner and outer court buildings, often dismissively referred to as the 'outer precincts', though this is being addressed through the survey of surviving earthworks, the analysis of the surviving sixteenth-century surveys and the few surviving buildings, and the publication of three exceptional excavations, at Augustinian Waltham Abbey and Thornholme Priory, and at the Fontevraldine priory of Grove.

THE PLANNING OF THE PRECINCT

The whole of the precinct of the great Cistercian abbey of Rievaulx can be recovered from the evidence of four separate documents dating from 1538-9 (64). These comprise the original grant of the site to its new owner, the earl of Rutland, an inventory made before demolition began, a survey of the site made during its spoliation and an account rendered to the government at the end of Rutland's first year of ownership. Together, these documents detail the church and cloister buildings, 27 other buildings in the inner and outer courts, extensive water meadows and other pasture fields. In particular, they identify three mills, the walk or fulling mill, a corn mill, and the Iron Smiths, a water-powered forge. Additionally there are the extensive offices of the tannery or bark house, the houses of resident craftsmen such as the plumber, tanner and smith, and close to the west range the brew house, bake house and kiln house. In the outer court there is the swine house, the common stable and the houses of six pensioners or corrodians of the abbey. The outer and inner gatehouses are identified, together with the gate chapel that still survives, close to the inner gate. The whole of the precinct amounts to an enclosure of 39ha, 20ha of which was water meadow and pasture, some of which can still be traced from modern field names, and all enclosed within a stone wall that can still be traced.

Rievaulx was a Cistercian abbey and there is good reason to believe that the major Cistercian houses maintained a different form of outer court to monasteries of other orders. There is no mention of barns or animal houses other than the swine cote; Rievaulx had two home granges, those of Griff and Newlass to the north and east of the precinct, and other surveys describe them in detail. Both granges held land inside the precinct, but the great barn and ox house were at Griff and both Griff and Newlass had extensive sheep cotes, buildings and closes which would normally be inside the precinct.

At Rievaulx, no indication is given of which buildings lay in the inner court and which were in the outer court, and this is where the survey of Kirklees is so helpful. The commissioners who surveyed the monasteries in 1534/5 were landowners who knew the houses and how they functioned, and the structure of the service buildings was different only in scale from that of their own farms and manors. Even the names were the same.

THE INNER COURT

The only inner court to have been fully examined is that of Grove Priory, though remains of inner court buildings have been identified at a number of sites. At Lindisfarne Priory it comprised a court to the south of the cloister, with its own gate and the identifiable remains of both bake house and brew house. At Mount Grace Priory the inner court comprised the southern part of the walled enclosure to the south of the church and lay brothers' cells, and it contained all the buildings normally found there: the guest houses, stables, kiln house, extensive granaries and an unexcavated bake house and brew house. It too had its own gate. The inner court at Kirklees had a gate, though it is not described, and the gate was the means of controlling access. Generally, in male houses women were excluded from the inner court because it had access to the cloister. In nunneries this is where the priest's lodging was placed, again a form of controlled access where it was difficult to exclude men from the court. The poor, too, were normally excluded, which is why at Kirklees we find 'an old almshouse wherein a poor man dwells without the gate' and 'an other old almshouse … by the beck side' in the outer court.

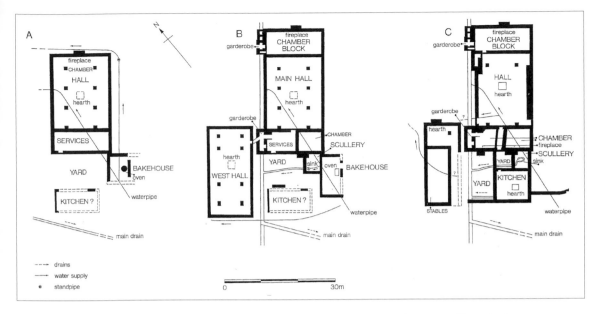

65 The ground plan of the Kirkstall guest halls (A) in the early thirteenth century, (B) in the late thirteenth century, and (C) in the fifteenth century. *After Wrathmell*

A small number of inner court buildings have been excavated, the most frequently studied being guest houses, buildings which were often architecturally sophisticated and which occasionally survive as standing ruins. Excavation of the guest complex at Kirkstall Abbey between 1979 and 1987 revealed an extensive group of buildings centred on a great aisled hall of the early thirteenth century (65). Largely reduced to low walling it was possible for the excavators to identify three principal phases of development in what was a much rebuilt structure. As originally built it was the guest hall rather than a guest house, a place for the feeding and entertainment of guests who would have slept elsewhere. It was a substantial aisled hall of four bays with an open central hearth. At the south end was a service room and beyond that, across a yard, a detached kitchen. Attached to the south-east corner of the building was a fragmentary bake house, probably a part of a combined bake house and brew house that comprised the south range of the inner court. Piped water was supplied to both buildings. At some point, the central hearth went out of use and a fireplace and chimney were inserted into the north wall.

In the late thirteenth century the guest hall was substantially modified. The main hall which may have originally been a timber-framed building, was reconstructed with the addition of a two-storey chamber block at its north end. The service end of the hall was also rebuilt on two stories, and the main drain of the abbey was diverted down the west side of the building to serve latrines attached to both residential blocks. This was now a building provided for the more important guests who could be given private chambers, and a subsidiary guest hall was built to the west for poorer visitors, like the first guest hall an aisled building with a central hearth. As we will see elsewhere, guest accommodation was clearly segregated by status.

The final phase of development dated to the fifteenth century. The hall was rebuilt, its west wall being rebuilt inside its original line and all but two of the aisle pots removed, indicating a new roof structure. A stone stair was provided to the upper floor of the northern chamber block, and a wall-bench provided against the east wall. The southern service block was further adapted to provide additional chamber space, and a new kitchen was built to the south, separated from the main building by a small yard. The secondary or west hall was partly demolished, its nave walled up to create a stable, with a blacksmith's shop at its north end.

The social stratification of guests is nowhere clearer than at Fountains Abbey. In the 1160s, two guest houses were built on the south side of the inner court. Both provide a different form of accommodation to the common guest hall and private chambers at Kirkstall. Instead, each of the two guest houses (66) has separate facilities on both the ground and first floors comprising a hall, chamber and latrine, the lower storey being vaulted. The east guest house is the larger of the pair and provided the better quality of lodging, with both hall and chamber occupying three bays of the building. The vault of the lower floor had finely moulded ribs and a wall fireplace, its now missing head supported on detached shafts with waterleaf capitals. The upper floor, of which only the gable walls survive, mirrored the accommodation below, but being open to the roof and having rose windows in its gables, was of even higher quality. The smaller western guest house was only four bays long and divided equally into hall and chamber, and its architectural detailing was more restrained. Thus four separate suites of differing quality were available for the most important visitors.

These guest houses did not stand alone. Immediately to their north geophysical survey has located a guest hall of the 1170s (67), seven bays long and aisled. The arcades had quatrefoil piers, the base of one survives above ground, and between the piers were tables. The base of one table leg remains in the ground, its upper part lying next to it. In the west gable wall was a wall fireplace. Further buildings remain to be discovered, but Fountains clearly had a range of guest accommodation available for its visitors of all social levels. At its most basic, this was the 'poor men's house' built by Abbot John of Kent in the 1230s and attached to the almonry that stood by the great gate. The Fountains guest houses were modified throughout the Middle Ages, and the guest hall was taken down in the fourteenth century, the drums of its piers being used to floor the abbey's wool house at that date. When it was demolished a smaller hall was attached to the north wall of the western guest house, perhaps a sign that the number of guests had diminished.

Hospitality was central to monastic life, and guest houses were among the first buildings to be provided in a new monastery. St Aelred, visiting Rievaulx within two years of its foundation was lodged in a timber guest house which he miraculously saved from fire. Excavation at Thornholme Priory revealed a stone guest house (68), built around 1160 at the entrance to the precinct. Statigraphically it could be shown to be earlier than the priory gatehouse that stood next to it, a sure indication of the relative importance of the two buildings to the community. Its architectural detail shows it was built at the same time as the canons' own church.

66 At Fountains Abbey, two guest houses of the mid-twelfth century are among the finest surviving domestic buildings of any monastery. Unlike the common guest hall at Kirkstall they provide separate suites of rooms for visitors of the highest rank

Thornholme was a middle-rank monastery of average means, so its buildings are likely to be more typical than those of a wealthy monastery like Fountains or even Kirkstall. Following the near contemporary Fountains model, however, the Thornholme guest house was a masonry building with separate accommodation on two floors, though it had been reduced to low walling by stone robbing. The building was of fine quality but of a different building tradition to the Fountains and Kirkstall buildings, being built of coursed rubble limestone with high-quality ashlar dressings. The walls were plastered inside and out, and painted with limewash. Smaller than the Fountains guest houses it was still substantial, some 12.8m long and 8.3m wide internally. Stone internal thresholds marked the position of opposed doors, and the base of a timber stair against the north wall indicated the location of the door to the upper floor rooms. An internal widening in the north-west corner marked the position of a latrine serving the upper floor, which may have provided better quality accommodation. The ground floor was divided by timber partitions into at least three rooms, the largest of which was a living room with a fireplace in its end wall.

Guest accommodation varied considerably, as the fifteenth-century guest wing at Mount Grace Priory shows. Although Carthusians were not supposed to encourage guests, Mount Grace lay on the pilgrimage route from York to Durham and seems to

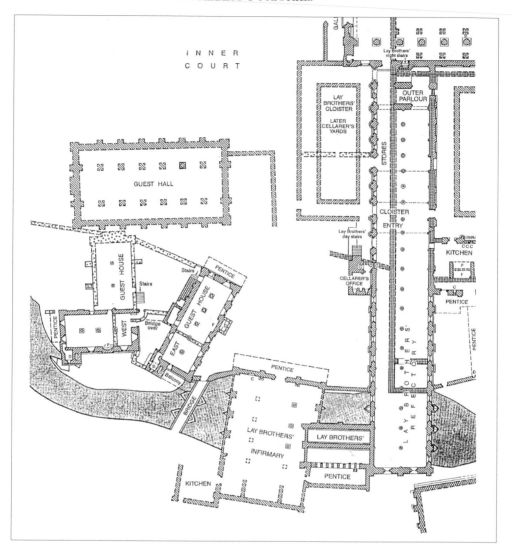

67 The Fountains guest hall was built on the south side of the inner court screening the higher-status guest houses from the court. Its existence was unknown until 1990 when it was located by geophysical survey

have been a major stopping place. In the 1420s a new guest house was built on the west side of the inner court to the north of the gatehouse (*69, 72*). It still survives within a post-suppression house of 1654. Its east wall is intact with doors and windows looking into the court. No trace remains of any internal divisions, which must have been timber-framed, but its plan can still be reconstructed with a fair degree of accuracy. There were four cell-like rooms on the ground floor at the south end of the building, each with its own door and window. Above these individual rooms were two floors that seem to have been a single apartment, entered by a door at the south end of the first floor, providing a very high level of accommodation indeed. The central part of the building was an open hall with large square-headed windows in each side wall, with a screens passage at its north end, clearly the guest hall. To the north of this was a servery on the ground floor with the guest kitchen, containing a great chimney, beyond it. Over the servery were the rooms of the procurator, with the only fireplace and latrine in the whole building. The procurator was a senior monk responsible for the guests and the external affairs of the monastery. If this was the only guest accommodation, Mount Grace would have been very well served. In the 1470s, however, another guest house was provided to the south of the gate, with four further guest-cells on the ground floor. On the first floor was a common dormitory, entered from the outer court by a stair against the outer wall. Thus the house had accommodation for three different social groups. This was not all, though, for sixteenth-century documents refer to a lodging called *le Inne* in the outer court as well.

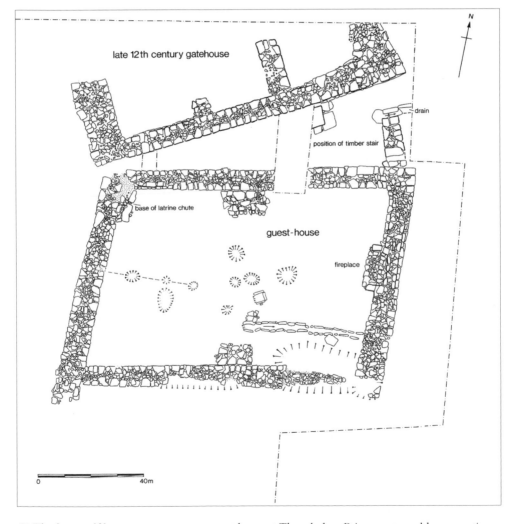

68 The late twelfth-century two-storey guest house at Thornholme Priory recovered by excavation

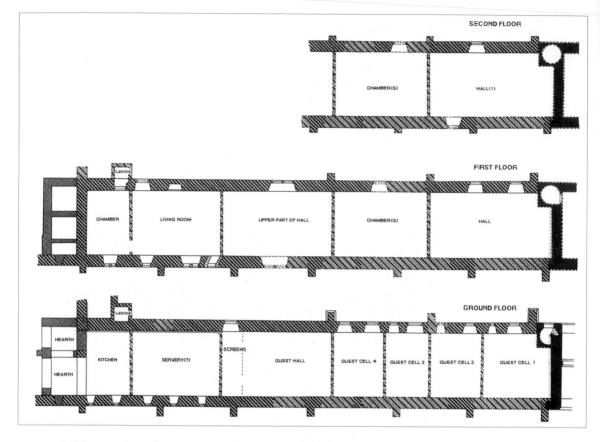

69 The 1420s guest house at Mount Grace, with individual chambers at its south end, a central guest hall and kitchen and servery at its north end, still maintains the separation of guests by rank

Apart from guest accommodation, the inner court normally housed the bake house, brew house and granaries that supplied the monastery with bread and ale, the staples of monastic life, the kiln house that dried the grain for the granaries, and stables for the guests' horses. Kirklees had fuel stores there, too, and two coal houses are listed. Coal was found in large quantities in the inner court at Mount Grace, and it was not only wood and turf that was used for cooking, baking, brewing and heating the rooms.

Few monastic bake houses have been excavated, though a number can be identified from their bread ovens. At Thetford Priory, in Norfolk, a complete oven survives (70), though this is actually attached to the kitchen range. Excavation at Bradwell Priory in Buckinghamshire, at Grove Priory, Fountains Abbey and at Thornholme Priory has revealed complete bake houses of different qualities. At Castle Acre Priory, where the granaries, kiln house, bake house and brew house occupied a separate yard to the main area of the outer court, the bake house and brew house were combined in a single building, converted from an earlier use. The bake house at Thornholme Priory (colour plate 15) began its life as the guest house, but by the earlier thirteenth century the guest had moved elsewhere and the building was refitted with a large sub-circular bread oven built into the earlier fireplace and a substantial floor of pitched limestone. The oven was rebuilt or repaired on at least two occasions, evidence of very heavy use, and the final oven retained many fine layers of wood ash, the residue of numerous firings. The floor was repaired numerous times in mortar, and these patchings retained the evidence of two partitioned rooms at the west end of the building and the setting of a stone water tank with a pipe leading to it and a drain taking away waste. The rooms were for the storage and boulting (or sifting) of flour in a boulting ark or hutch. There was also an internal stair leading to the upper floor against the north wall. The use of the upper floor in not known. At Fountains Abbey, the upper floor of the bake house was the brew house, and this may have been the case at Thornholme too.

70 A brick-built bread oven in the early sixteenth-century kitchen at Thetford Priory. Normally, the industrial ovens of the bake house would be two or three times the size of this example but of the same general form

Brew houses are best known from sixteenth-century documents. At Rievaulx Abbey the brew house remained complete with its fittings in 1537-8, and it had six *kelynge throughs* (cooling troughs) of lead and two copper vessels. Dieulacres Abbey in Staffordshire had three leads, a mashing vat, twelve lead coolers, a brewing vat, a cistern, and a table *before the ouenne* in 1539. Apart from a source of heat for the brewing vats and a supply of water, brew houses are notoriously difficult to identify in the archaeological record. At Castle Acre Priory the brew house occupied the eastern half of a building that also contained the bake house; the bread ovens are easy to identify, brewing facilities are much more problematic.

Associated with the bake house and brew house was the kiln house, a grain dryer associated with the inner court granaries. The basic form of this building was first identified at Lindisfarne Priory, in the south range of the inner court. At Thornholme Priory a late fourteenth-century to sixteenth-century kiln house has been identified by excavation (*71*). The northern room, with its raised floor contained a centrally-placed square kiln heated by a flue which had a segmental vault that carried the working floor. The southern room was used to stoke the kiln, and outside its eastern door the yard was filled up with ash raked out from the kiln flue. The kiln itself retained three stone props that carried the horse-hair cloth on which the grain was dried. Suppression-period accounts frequently refer to the hair cloths remaining in kiln houses, as well as the ladders used to access the granaries that often comprised their upper floors. Kiln houses were particularly susceptible to fire – the kiln house at Kirklees was in the course of reconstruction after a fire in 1534/5.

71 The kiln house at Thornholme Priory was built in the late fourteenth century within parts of an earlier building. Seen from the south, the room in the foreground was used for stoking the kiln which had a raised floor around it

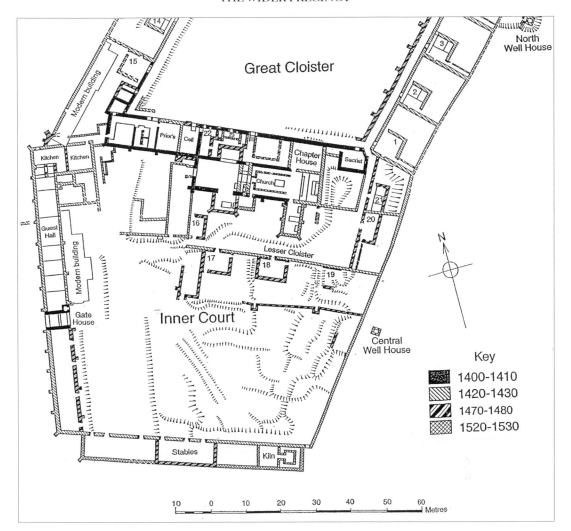

72 The inner court at Mount Grace Priory. The west side comprised guest accommodation, the south range stables, granaries and the kiln house, and the unexcavated building in the east range is probably the bake house and brew house

The best surviving example of a monastic inner court is at Mount Grace Priory where the buildings were ranged around three sides of a large courtyard, the entrance to which was controlled by a gatehouse (*72*). If the west side was occupied by the guest houses, the east side comprised a large bake house and brew house which has yet to be excavated. The whole of the south side was taken up with granaries, the kiln house and the stables associated with the guest house. These had all begun life as timber-framed buildings, replaced in stone from the late fifteenth century on the outside of the enclosing yard wall and with their doors cut through it. From west to east it comprised three separate buildings of which the central one, the stable, was the first to be built. It had stone floors, drains, three wide doors to the inner court and the sockets for three mangers in its south wall. The floor above, of which only the gable walls survive, was almost certainly a granary which must have been reached by a stair from the court, for there was no evidence of a stair within the building. The building to the west is featureless apart from three doors to the inner court and has never been excavated. The use of its ground floor room cannot be identified with any certainty. Again there was an upper floor with no evidence of an internal stair. To the east was the kiln house, usually closely associated with the bake house and brew house, with the ghost of the kiln in its eastern room. The square kiln with its central pedestal was heated from a short but heavily burned flue. The floor around the kiln was raised about 1m above the rest of the building and there was a door from the court that provided direct access to the grain dryer. The western half of the kiln house was a separate room with a floor drain and a mortar floor and a door to the court in its north-eastern corner. It had two single-light windows and a loop in its south wall. It was common for the court servants to be lodged in the inner court, often close to the granaries, and this room may have been their mess-room. This interpretation is greatly strengthened by the room at first-floor level that extends over the western part of the kiln house proper. Only its south wall survives but this has three two-light windows with evidence of bars and shutters. Clearly it was not a granary and it looks domestic, perhaps the sleeping room for the court servants. A latrine in the corner of the inner court was also provided for their use. Over the kiln itself and on the second floor of this substantial building were further granaries. In all the surface area of all the granaries in the south range totalled 218m², a substantial provision but a necessary one for the provision of two loaves of bread and 7-8 pints of ale per day to all the members of the community, their servants and guests. One medieval granary still survives in the inner court at Thetford Priory, a timber-framed building of late fourteenth-century date, with a two-bay domestic building at its west end that mirrors the room for the *seruantes to lye yn* at Mount Grace.

THE OUTER COURT

The outer court which provided the economic base of the monastery was an area which was largely ignored until the 1970s when a number of important excavations took place. The most important of these were at Waltham Abbey, Thornholme Priory, Grove Priory and Fountains Abbey. Together they have revolutionised our understanding of the monastic economy. The buildings of the outer court were both agricultural and industrial and, because the monastic economy developed throughout the Middle Ages, were subject to dramatic change. In their most basic form in the sixteenth century they can be recovered from the suppression survey of Kirklees Priory.

Kirklees was a poor house with the basic minimum, and the first thing to notice is that its outer court contained the kiln house, granary and house for the court servants, buildings that usually lay in the inner court. There was, in fact, some interchange between the two areas which is not predictable, and as excavation at Thornholme Priory has shown, later functions did not necessarily correspond to the earlier use of buildings.

There are some survivals. Watermills survive in recognisable form at Fountains, Jervaulx, Monk Bretton and Abbotsbury (Dorset); barns survive among others at Watton Priory (East Yorkshire), Temple Cressing (Essex), Titchfield Abbey (Hampshire) and Bradenstoke Priory (Wiltshire); and a dovecote survives at Garway Preceptory (Herefordshire). Many more buildings are known from documents, such as the mills, swine cote and tannery of Rievaulx Abbey, which can still be identified on the ground. Most, though, are known from excavation, particularly at Grove Priory where the whole of the outer court, indeed the whole of the site, has been excavated, and at Thornholme Priory where the western part of the outer court has been excavated. At Fountains Abbey the great wool house was the only building excavated to reveal that it developed in parallel with the central monastic buildings, a close connection between the development of religious life and economy that should have been obvious.

Thornholme Priory was the first site to produce evidence for buildings which were neither agricultural or industrial in its outer court. In the extreme south-west corner of the precinct from the middle of the twelfth century to the early years of the fourteenth century a group of high-status domestic buildings were developed. The earliest of these (73) was a two-storey chamber block (A) and a detached hall (Bi), built in the first years of the priory's existence. In the yard between them was a contemporary dovecote. In the 1170s a new building (Ci) was added to the east side of the original chamber block, again on two floors, with a stair against its northern gable entered from the yard on the east side. The upper floor comprised a hall with a wall fireplace (evidenced by a widening of the wall itself) and a private chamber. The ground floor, entered from the west and from outside the ditched precinct, was simply service rooms, the northern one with the base of an oven in the centre of its floor. Fragments of the first-floor windows were recovered, showing that this was a highly decorated building. If it did not lie within a monastic precinct it could easily be interpreted as a manor house of some quality. It was altered in the early thirteenth century when the precinct was walled and its original use was abandoned. It was replaced by an aisled hall to the south (74), which was rebuilt on at least three occasions between the 1220s and the 1320s because it kept subsiding into the original precinct boundary ditch. In its final phase it was a timber-framed building, indicating that either the builders had given up trying to deal with subsidence or, more likely, a more fashionable material was being used for an important building. It was linked at its upper end to the old Building Ci by a corridor along the precinct wall, and a small chamber block was provided at its west end, outside the precinct boundary. The hall had a central hearth in the second bay from the west and it was indistinguishable from a standard manorial hall. From the high quality of the buildings it is obvious that this part of the precinct was neither industrial nor agricultural, and it has been suggested that this was the house of the priory's lay steward who managed the home estates and was responsible for the court servants, the senior of whom would have lived within his household. As Thornholme had a substantial estate in north Lincolnshire the post of steward was a responsible one, and the man would have been recruited from a family of at least knightly status. It is significant that the buildings were converted to agricultural use in the fourteenth century. It was exactly at this point that the priory was

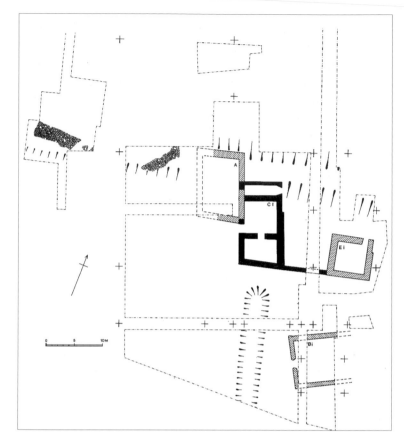

Left: 73 In the late twelfth century the south-west corner of the precinct at Thornholme Priory contained a two-storey building (Ci) of high status, perhaps the house of the priory steward. In the yard to the east is an earlier dovecote

Below: 74 The steward's hall at Thornholme in the thirteenth century was a great timber-framed aisled building of at least four bays (Biii) rebuilt on three occasions before it was finally converted into a granary

restructuring its estates, and putting most of them out to rent. The high-status steward would have been replaced by a more lowly bailiff or reeve.

The Thornholme buildings are far from unique – a similar aisled building of undoubted domestic use was recorded at Elstow Abbey and another domestic hall is known in the Veresmead or outer court of Waltham Abbey, later converted to agricultural use.

Dovecotes providing a source of fresh meat in the winter were a perquisite of manors, and are ubiquitous on monastic sites, though few have been excavated. The Thornholme dovecote, Building Ei, was one of the first stone buildings to be erected in the outer court in the 1150s or '60s (75), contemporary with the guest house in the inner court described above. Rebuilt in the early fourteenth century on a smaller scale, the original building was 7.5m square internally, with plastered walls painted in imitation of ashlar and a hipped, tiled roof with decorated ridge tiles. Within, tiers of L-shaped nesting boxes began just above floor level. The floor itself was of mortar, scoured hollow with the constant collection of guano. A drain leading to a tank outside the east wall also collected this valuable by-product which was used in the preparation of parchment skins used in book production. In the fourteenth century a stone-lined socket was provided at the centre of the floor for the potence, the revolving post and ladder-rests that gave access to the higher level nesting boxes. The reason for the abandonment of this building in the early fifteenth century was very clear. Generally, the building had been kept scrupulously clean but its final floor was covered with dead pigeons, suggesting an avian epidemic. The building was simply dismantled, its interior filled up with rubble, and a new circular dovecote was built to the east of the cloister buildings where it can still be seen as an earthwork.

75 The first of two phases of dovecote excavated at Thornholme Priory, dating to the middle years of the twelfth century

Excavations at Waltham Abbey also produced evidence of two dovecotes in the Veresmead: a fragmentary circular structure of twelfth-century date and a superimposed square building of the fifteenth century. The later building had a socket for a potence like the rebuilt dovecote at Thornholme, but like the early dovecote at Thornholme the circular building did not have one. The undated dovecote at Llanthony Prima Priory in Gwent produced a heavy pivot stone, interpreted as the base of a revolving potence. Given the similarity of this building to the surviving dovecote at Garway, it is almost certainly fourteenth century in date. Apparently the potence was a later medieval development replacing a simple ladder.

The best surviving monastic dovecote is that built by the Knights Hospitlar at Garway in 1326. It has tiers of nesting boxes of L-shaped plan divided into groups of four by plain string courses (at Llanthony each tier sits above a plain string course), extending from floor to roof. Access for the birds was through the upper part of the roof, where a 'glover' or louver was provided. In the floor a central tank 1.5m in diameter was provided to collect guano and stone-built drains ran from this to a larger collecting pit outside the building. The Garway dovecote retains no trace of its potence, but this could have been carried on a timber baulk across the central pit that has not survived the post-medieval use of the building.

Mills were central to the monastic economy, and one of the principal reasons why monasteries chose sites with access to running and manageable water. They were almost always placed in the outer court, and their sites can often by identified, as at Bordesley, by the provision of mill ponds and dams, or by leats taken off the river that runs through or past the precinct. The greatest of monastic mills is a double corn mill at Fountains Abbey, on the face of it an early thirteenth-century building but one which incorporates parts of its predecessor, a building of the early 1140s which was built at precisely the same time as the first cloister buildings. Its recent repair occasioned small-scale excavation and a reappraisal of its surviving fabric. The original mill had been destroyed by a flash flood, often a problem with watermills, and its replacement was placed on a dam that incorporated the remains of the earlier building. The first mill had been fed by a leat, the second one used a mill pond which was more easily controlled.

The early mill was a single-storey building, and its east wall stands almost to full height, and it was a rectangular building some 22m long and 10.4m wide externally, with walls 1.3m thick. The mill race passed through the southern half of the building and drove an undershot wheel, exiting in a vaulted tunnel that took the used water back to the River Skell 50m to the east. The building that replaced it was on a different scale altogether, and was built in the 1230s by Abbot John of Kent who had extended the abbey church and built the monks' infirmary on a scale commensurate with his abbey's importance and wealth (76). Retaining the old mill as a basement for the southern half of its replacement, Abbot John's mill was a vast building on three floors, at least 40m long and 9.5m wide. The upper floor which extended the full length of the building was a granary lit by paired lancet windows on both sides of the building and entered through its south gable. The first floor was the working floor, and a second wheel pit was provided at the centre of the building. The northern end of the building, most of

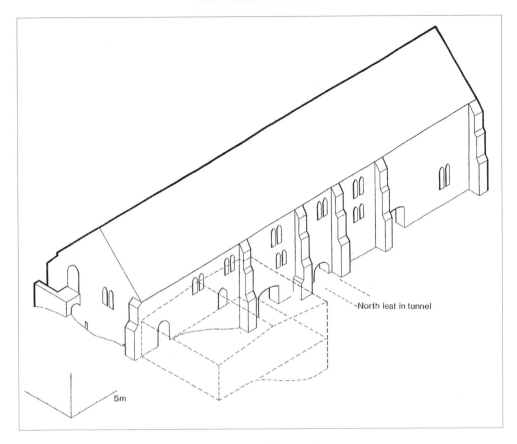

North leat in tunnel

5m

76 A reconstruction of the double watermill at Fountains Abbey as rebuilt in the early thirteenth century. A fourteenth-century extension is shown in broken line

which has been demolished, appears to have been only of two floors. This rebuilding is actually two-phased. While the west wall of the mill is all of the early thirteenth century, the east wall is more complicated. The upper floor is certainly thirteenth century, and the basement floor is retained from the 1140s mill. In between the two is an area of masonry which contains an inserted window of the early thirteenth century at the level of the working floor. The north jamb of this window is reused from an earlier window of the 1160s, and it would appear that the mill had an earlier rebuilding, parts of which were retained. What is not known is when the earlier mill was destroyed – it may not have been wrecked until the early thirteenth century. The Fountains mill is a remarkably complex building, like many other outer court buildings. It was certainly extended in the fourteenth century when a building was placed against its south-eastern corner, and it continued to be modified into the 1930s when it finally went out of use.

Corn mills were not the only water-powered mills in the monastic precinct. Rievaulx Abbey had three watermills in the sixteenth century, a corn mill, a fulling mill, and a water-driven forge called the *Iron Smythes*. The first two were driven by water in a purpose-built leat, the latter by a mill pond that still exists. At Bordesley, excavation of the eastern mill site revealed a water-powered smithy. The first building was raised in 1174-6 according to the dendrochronological dating of its structural timbers It had burned out and been replaced approximately 14 years later. Finds suggested that it was a highly specialised mill, producing nails, tenterhooks (for the stretching and drying of cloth) and arrow-heads, as well as obviously military equipment. It suggests, as does the iron smithy at Rievaulx, that the mill at Bordesley was producing iron objects for sale as well as supplying the needs of the community. At Fountains there were at least two other mills, both on a stream that ran through the southern part of the precinct. One, a smithy, can still be identified as a building whose earthworks still remain across the stream, the other, a fulling mill, was identified within the abbey's great wool house when it was excavated.

The wool house at Fountains (77) was excavated between 1978 and 1980, though it had been partially examined by Hope in the late 1880s and mistakenly identified as the abbey bake house. A remarkably complex building with at least six phases of development between the 1150s and the late fifteenth century, it survived for the most part as low walling. Essentially it was a great barn-like building of five bays with an office for the monk who had charge of its operation attached to the east side. Initially it was approached from the south, and a great blocked round-headed door survived in the south gable wall, the only part of the building to survive above ground before excavation. As the abbey's economy developed throughout the thirteenth century it was enlarged and re-planned, and by the end of the century it had acquired a double fulling mill in its south-west corner, powered by a small undershot wheel. To the south and sharing its gable wall was a second building, erected in the 1230s and replaced by a two-storey bake house and brew house in the 1290s. The fourteenth century saw changes in the use of the building, with the removal of the fulling mill and its replacement with dye vats and a pair of furnaces to provide hot water. The western aisles were partitioned off and appear to have been used for finishing cloth. This was no longer the store of the abbey's wool crop, which had declined seriously after the outbreak of sheep scab in the 1290s, but a multi-purpose building. It did however, keep its original name, for the obedientiary in charge of the building was still called the monk of the wool house and guest house in the mid-fifteenth century.

The final use of this great building came in the mid-fifteenth century when it was partitioned up to provide a series of workshops used in the repair and refitting of the abbey church. Debris indicated glaziers at work in the central aisle of the building, while a small blacksmith's shop was created in the eastern aisle, the smith's tongs and the lead liners of his wooden water boshes still lying in the hammer scale on the floor. To the south of the smithy was a large pit full of bronze-working debris, the product of a bronze smith working somewhere in that part of the building. In the last quarter of the fifteenth century the old wool house had outlived its usefulness and was simply demolished and its site levelled up. Good building stone was removed but most of the door and window dressings still lay where they had been thrown down in demolition.

Forges were a basic requirement of any monastery, not only for servicing the masons involved with buildings and repair and the vast amounts of iron used in building, but to serve the agricultural needs of the house. Not only did horses (including those of guests)

77 The Fountains Abbey wool house was built in the 1160s and was altered at last six times in its three centuries of use. Demolished while the abbey was still functioning, it was carefully levelled to the ground but contained remarkable evidence of its changing uses

and oxen need to be shod, but all the agricultural equipment needed to be made and kept in repair. At Waltham Abbey a substantial blacksmith's forge has been excavated in the outer court (78). A timber-framed aisled building of three bays it had a complicated structural history with evidence of repair and renewal. It appears to have had at least two hearths, with hoods and bellows demonstrated by post-holes in the clay floor. Clay-lined pits in the floor served as water boshes for the quenching and tempering of hot iron, and in several instances had been filled with bloomery waste, indicating that the iron had been smelted close by. One small hearth set in the floor of the eastern room had been used to work lead. At Kirkstall Abbey (see 65) a small smithy was provided in the north end of the second guest hall in the inner court when it was converted to stables in the fifteenth century. There, a single hearth and the settings for a pair of bellows and an anvil indicated the provision made for guest's horses.

Most common were the granaries and barns that occupied the greater part of the outer court, simply because of their scale. If the granaries of the inner court provided for the day-to-day needs of the house, those in the outer court were intended to hold grain and other dry goods from the monasteries estates. Initially, the barns and granaries would be provided normally on outlying granges, but from the early years of the fourteenth century granges and estates were being rented out on an increasing scale, and provision there needed to be replaced within the monastic precinct – often rents were paid as much in terms of crop as cash.

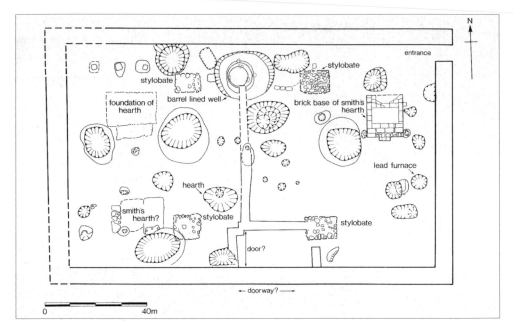

78 The smithy at Waltham Abbey as excavated. Its heavy use, repair and partial rebuilding is typical of outer court buildings. *After Huggins*

At Thornholme Priory this change in monastic planning was demonstrated by the conversion of the high-status steward's hall to a granary in the 1320s (*79*). The north aisle was removed and a wall built on the line of the north arcade. The south aisle was retained but converted to a passage walled off from the main span of the building. Ground floor granaries are infrequently described in sixteenth-century surveys, probably because they had been converted to other uses by the later Middle Ages, but the evidence for such an arrangement survived at Thornholme in the form of shallow depressions in the floor where the timber-framed divisions of the bins could still be traced on excavation.

The storage of grain required the provision of grain dryers, and Thornholme Priory has produced good evidence of two. The first was a large keyhole-shaped dryer (*80*) built into the ruins of the old bake house in the inner court where it presumably served the granaries there; the second (*colour plate 16*), a replacement dating from the late fourteenth century, was an industrial-scale dryer with opposed flues and a loading door on its north side, built partly of brick and still containing part of its final load which had been burned. This drying kiln lay outside the precinct wall close to the outer court granaries it must have served.

The remaining buildings, predominantly animal houses and barns might lie inside the precinct or in adjacent home grange. Thornholme Priory had at least one small barn within the precinct in the early sixteenth century, but its great barn can still be identified by its earthworks half a mile to the west within the home grange. Generally it was the Cistercians and the Augustinians who preferred to keep animals and the great barns separate from the outer court, other orders and all nunneries were happy to keep them within the precinct. These buildings are described below.

79 A late fourteenth-century granary at Thornholme Priory built in the shell of the old steward's hall. The south aisle has become a corridor accessing the grain bins that filled the central space of the building

80 A keyhole-shaped grain drier built within the ruins of the Thornholme Priory bake house in the late fourteenth century

PRECINCT WALLS AND GATES

The precinct of a monastery was normally contained within a wall or bank and ditch which was called the precinct wall, through which access was controlled by gates. Great monasteries like Gloucester or Chester Abbeys or Norwich cathedral priory had several gates leading into different enclosures. Smaller houses, like Thornholme Priory, had only one point of access. At Thornholme, the precinct was entered through a substantial gatehouse, the great gate, that led directly into the inner court to the west of the church and cloister. That gate lay on the boundary of the precinct, which at the time the first gatehouse was built was not enclosed by a wall but simply defined by a bank and ditch. Indeed the precinct was not to be walled until the second quarter of the thirteenth century. At Thornholme the outer court was entered through a second gate in the wall that separated it from the inner court, an identical arrangement to that found at Bardney Abbey.

Gatehouses have survived in greater numbers than any other monastic buildings, as for instance at Alnwick Abbey, St Augustine's Abbey at Canterbury, Kingswood Abbey or Thornton Abbey where they are the principal survivals. This is partly because they could be reused to serve new houses after the suppression, but also because they had a residual legal significance. At Bridlington Priory, the great room over the inner gatehouse was the prior's court and exchequer where all external business was done and it remains the property of the lords feofees who succeeded the prior in temporal matters in the town. One of its flanking guardrooms was the prior's prison, and it remained the town lock-up into the early nineteenth century.

The great gatehouse at Thornholme (*81*) has been fully excavated together with the series of paved roads that led through it, and it was not a single gate but a series of three starting in or before 1202, being rebuilt immediately to the west of its original site in the early fourteenth century, and rebuilt again in the 1380s. Most other monastic gatehouses will have a similar development, though few have been examined archaeologically. The earliest gate comprised a two-bay porch separated from a single-bay gate-hall by an internal wall that carried the gates. The road passed through the northern half of the building. Against the north wall of the gate-hall was the lodging for the gate keeper, a chamber with a fireplace and probably a bed room above. There was no door from the lodging into the gate-hall as one would expect, and the only door led into the yard to the north and east of the gatehouse where there was a latrine for the gate keeper. On the south side of the building was a wooden stair that accessed the upper floor of the gatehouse, probably the site of the gate chapel given subsequent developments in the vicinity of the gate. In the early fourteenth century a new gate was built, its axis turned through 90 degrees. Its east wall more or less sat on top of the foundations of the west wall of its predecessor, and the road still ran through the northern part of the building. In the south-east corner of the building there was a partitioned room for the gate keeper, and a small timber-framed chamber was also provided for him against the north wall. The gate was actually built into the butt end of the precinct boundary ditch, suggesting that its reconstruction was connected with a re-planning of this part of the precinct. The late fourteenth-century rebuilding added guardrooms to either side of the roadway and

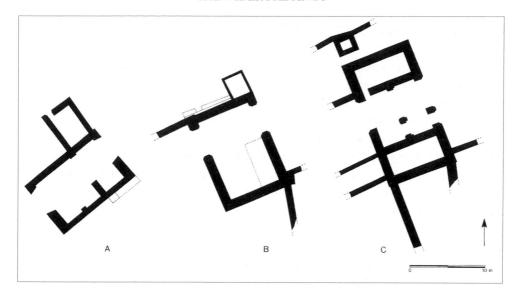

81 The great gate at Thornholme Priory, (A) the gate built before 1202, (B) the new gatehouse of the early fourteenth century, and (C) the extended gatehouse of the 1380s

provided separate pedestrian access from the porch. Only the door into the northern guardroom was found in excavation, and nineteenth-century excavation recorded a wall fireplace and a door into the gate-hall in the southern guardroom which did not survive stone robbing in 1835. The upper floor was a large space or series of spaces served by a detached latrine tower to the north on the line of the precinct wall. The roadway to the west of the gate was enclosed by walls, with a pedestrian path on the south side. Against the west wall of the south guardroom was a timber-framed gate chapel; to the west of the northern guardroom was the almonry, separated from the gatehouse by a small paved yard. At the west end of the enclosed roadway was a small outer gatehouse.

The almonry (*82*) was the lodging for poor travellers who were not normally allowed within the inner court. At Thornholme it took the form of a domestic hall with a central hearth and wall-benches, a screens passage (through which a major drain had been laid), and a pantry and buttery at its south end. A second, heavily robbed, chamber to the north contained ovens and probably had a sleeping chamber above it. Outside the building on the very edge of the island was a latrine for the occupants of the almonry. The almonry had seen considerable use from its first construction in the late fourteenth century, and it was substantially altered on two occasions before 1536. Its contents were unexceptional, though there were a number of needles, evidence for the repair of old clothing patched up and given as alms. Remarkably a small oven had been inserted into the wall-bench of the hall against the timber screens partition.

The concept of a walled precinct, separating the religious from the world outside appears nowhere before the closing years of the twelfth century and it seems to post-date the construction of gates wherever study has been possible. The twelfth-century cemetery gate at Bury St Edmunds was built as a free-standing structure as was the first

82 The almonry hall at Thornholme Priory lay in a wet and unwelcoming area outside the great gatehouse. It was rebuilt at least twice in little more than a century

gate at Thornholme Priory. The precinct wall at Fountains Abbey contains architectural fragments from the eastern arm of the church which was being demolished in the first quarter of the thirteenth century. Until the 1220s, Thornholme Priory was surrounded, at least on its western and northern sides, by a ditch some 2m wide and a little over 1m deep and a timber palisade. There was no evidence of an internal bank and the boundary was little more than a formal definition of the area of the monastery. When a wall was built it simply joined up existing buildings, some of which had doors to the outside world. It was not until the later fourteenth century that precinct walls became a means of exclusion. The troubled times after the Black Death left monastic communities at odds with their tenants and in many cases at risk of attack from them. The Peasants' Revolt of 1381 was led by people of substance in both town and country, craftsmen, jurors, and manorial officials, who were the monks' natural allies in the past. Within a year of the revolt the abbot of Thornton was applying for a licence to fortify 'the new house over and above the gate' and was building a new brick precinct wall with towers and gates on it. At Thornholme Priory, the canons cut off their peninsular site from west by a great ditch almost 2m deep with sharpened stakes in its base, and rebuilt their gatehouse which probably displayed the arms of their patrons, people likely to come to their aid in a crisis. The contemporary gatehouse of Kirkham Priory certainly did this (*colour plate 17*).

THE HOME GRANGE

The buildings of the precinct served the immediate needs of the community and they in turn were supported by a network of agricultural or industrial estates, held either as blocks of land or individual holdings spread across many manors and vills. Their extent and method of management resulted both from the wealth, or lack of it, of individual houses and the policy pursued by particular orders. Whilst the Benedictines and Augustinians were prepared to hold land in much the same way as lay magnates, the Cistercians rejected tenurial farming as late as the end of the thirteenth century in favour of a centralised economy managed by lay brothers. Whatever the system chosen, estates were centred on farms or granges (the name is derived from the Latin *grangia*, a barn). In all but the poorest houses (and the majority of nunneries) the principal centre was the home grange, built close to the house and containing the major barns and animal houses for which there was too little space within the outer court. Richard Pollard described the home grange of Bridlington Priory in 1537 thus:

THE BARNE YARD

It' there ys a great Barne Yarde on the Northsyde of the seyde Pryorye cont by estimacyon foure Acres.

THE BARNE

It' there ys on the Northsyde of the seyd Barne Yarde a very fayre Barne conteynyng in length Est and West cxvij pac's and in breddith xxvij pac's covered well with lede to the value of fyve hundred m'ks, and so it ys offered for.

THE GARNERD

It' on the South syde of the same Barne standyth a Garnerd to lay Corne in, conteynyng in length North and South xxvj yards and in breddith x yards, covered with lede.

THE MALTHOUSE

It' on the Est syde of the same Garnerd standyth the Malthouse cont in length North and South xliiij yards and in breddith xvij yards, well covered w^t lede, and on the North syde of the same Malthouse a prety Howse with a Chamber where the Hervest men dyd alwayes dyne, covered with slatt.

THE KYLNE HOUSE

It'm on the Est syde of the same malthouse standith a Kylne House covered with slatt.

OLDE STABLES & OXSTALLES

It'm on the Est and West sydes of the Barne yarde standyth olde Stables, Oxstales, w^t other olde houses buylded w^t stone, covered with slatt, geatley in decaye.

Only one home grange has been examined in detail. At Waltham Abbey (*83*), rescue excavations in advance of road building in Grange Yard led to the recovery of 10 buildings in less than ideal conditions. The scale and layout of the establishment was very similar to

Pollard's contemporary description of Bridlington and included an aisled barn of 12 bays, some 64m long, the hay barn, the plough house, the ox house and a stable ranged about Grange Yard. The buildings ranged in date from the early thirteenth century to the late fifteenth century and showed considerable evidence for reconstruction and repair. Some had survived the suppression, being used by the new lay owner of the site.

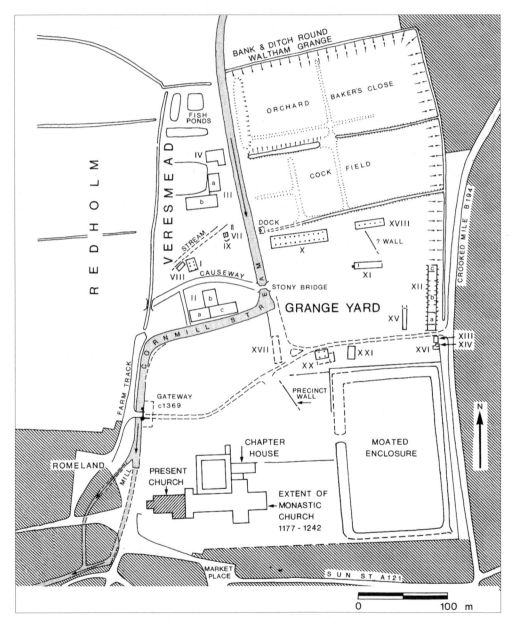

83 Waltham Abbey, showing the extent of the precinct and Grange Yard, the home grange of the abbey. Buildings are known from documents, excavation and the recording of parch marks in the turf. *After Huggins*

The barn (*84*), which was originally only of five bays and dated to the early years of the thirteenth century, was extended by a further seven bays in the course of that century as the abbey's economy developed. Its storage capacity has been calculated at 8300 cubic metres, and it would have been required to store the produce of a demesne estate of 418ha (1033 acres) of arable land, up to a third of which would have been fallow in any year. The smaller hay barn to its east (XVIII), in comparison was supported by 80ha (198 acres) of meadow land. The plough house at the centre of Grange Yard, XI, like the barns was a timber-framed structure on stone cill walls and dated from the fifteenth century. Its use – to store agricultural equipment – could be ascertained only from a suppression-period survey of the grange. The ox house (XII) was also built in the fifteenth century (*85*), and was perhaps the most remarkable of the grange buildings. At the south end was a hall with a large fireplace and a chamber, presumably the lodging of the grange bailiff. The building was aisled, as evidenced by the bases of arcade posts in the hall and by the short walls that ran from the side walls to the line of the arcades. Remarkably, the arcade posts were not aligned with the external buttresses of the building. The stalls for the oxen, the *oxstalles* of Bridlington or *oxehouse* of Kirklees, were ranged down both sides of the body of the building and were roughly a perch (5m) wide, sufficient for two oxen; room for 32 beasts or eight teams in bays 2-9, or the 19 oxen and 13 work horses recorded at the home grange in 1540. At the north end of the building, in bay 1, was a small grain dryer or malting kiln. In all, this was a multi-purpose building of a type common in sixteenth century surveys.

A similar home grange is known from Thornton Abbey, where it was called the North Baile, and had a watermill and a great barn that is recorded as a parch mark from time to time. The home grange of Thornholme Priory lies 1km to the west on the Roman Ermine Street, its great barn neatly bisected by the Scunthorpe to Grimsby railway. The most common surviving buildings on home granges were the great barns, of which the most impressive are those of Glastonbury, Abbotsbury, and Titchfield in Hampshire. Greater houses, and particularly Cistercian monasteries might have more than one home grange. Fountains Abbey had three: Morker, Fountains Park and Swanley ringing the site on the south, west and north, each with a specialist function.

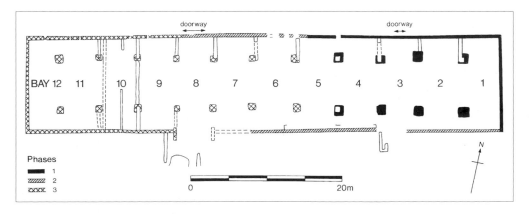

84 The great barn in Grange Yard, Waltham Abbey. *After Huggins*

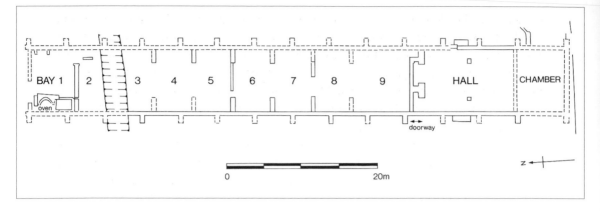

85 The ox house in Grange Yard, Waltham Abbey. *After Huggins*

DISTANT GRANGES

Most monasteries that derived their wealth from the land had several granges at a distance from the house which acted as self-contained estate centres. It has long been assumed that these granges were designed as monasteries in miniature with a chapel and domestic ranges in one enclosure and the agricultural buildings in a second. Such an arrangement certainly suited the Cistercians who ran their estates with lay brothers under monastic discipline. Few early grange sites have been examined archaeologically. An exception is the Gorefields grange in Bedfordshire (*86*) of the Cluniac nuns of Delapré outside Northampton. Here, stone-built domestic ranges around a cloister-like yard had been added to a twelfth-century chapel by the end of the thirteenth century, which might support the tradition view of granges. However, granges might become monasteries in their own right, and some abandoned monasteries certainly became granges, and it has been suggested that Gorefields was perhaps intended to become a daughter house of Delapré. The Rievaulx grange of Laskill in Bilsdale had at least one major stone building from the twelfth century, of two storeys with a vaulted undercroft barely distinguishable from the contemporary cloister ranges of the abbey itself, and when Pipewell Abbey's grange of Cawston on Dunsmore, Warwickshire, was damaged by fire in 1307, the cloister, chapel, dormitory, latrine, refectory, kitchen and private rooms, including one for the abbot, were mentioned. While this might be an appropriate Cistercian model, field survey and the study of surviving grange buildings indicates it is not the norm, even for the Cistercians. Deserted sites commonly show an outer enclosure with barns, granaries, and animal houses and an inner enclosure with domestic ranges. The central component of the domestic ranges was a hall with living chambers at one end and a kitchen and services at the other, usually with an attached chapel. These buildings were barely different from the houses of the lay landowning classes and, indeed, the average monastic grange was little different from a lay manor. Often, the abbot or prior would appropriate the domestic quarters of a grange for his own use from as early as the first quarter of the thirteenth century – Abbot John of Kent at Fountains died at his grange of Thorpe Underwood on the Derwent in 1247 – and the quality of many surviving buildings suggests that this was not uncommon. While a steward would need housing and room for the manorial court was required, the scale and elaboration of some buildings such as Glastonbury Abbey's manor house at Mere in Somerset, rebuilt in the 1320s for Abbot Adam Sodbury, indicate the assimilation of religious landowners with the laity in the later Middle Ages.

The Knights Templar house of South Witham in Lincolnshire is one of the few grange sites which have been substantially excavated (87). Established between 1164 and 1185 and abandoned before the transfer of the site to the Knights Hospitlar in 1311, it was essentially a grange of the London Temple. Built to exploit the southern limestone heath in Lincolnshire, the site developed over the century and a half of its existence before its estates were taken over by the greater preceptory of Temple Bruer. Excavation demonstrated the development of its buildings through several phases as the house's economy developed. Planned as a series of courts in the same way as a monastic precinct, the domestic ranges lay at the centre, more manorial than monastic in nature. To the north and west was a walled yard bordered by barns (1, 4 and 11) and animal houses (2, 3 and 6) with stone walls and thatched, tiled or slated roofs. The yard also contained other service buildings including a forge (10), and access was controlled by a gatehouse (C). Outside the enclosure was a small watermill fed by a leat from the River Witham, a series of fish ponds and a dovecote, which has recently been identified by geophysical survey. The site itself was surrounded by paddocks that are still apparent in the landscape.

What is most apparent about South Witham is the provision of great barns and granaries, and the scale of these buildings is indicative of the extent and productivity of the estate serving the house. A number of grange barns survive to show that there is nothing unusual about South Witham. At Temple Cressing in Essex, the wheat barn and barley barn both survive from the 1220s, again in a Templar context. At Great Coxwell in Berkshire Beaulieu Abbey's grange barn survives intact, its timber-framing related to the Cistercian grange barn of Ten Bogaerde and precinct barn of Ter Doest, both in West Flanders, Belgium, and indicating the international connections of monastic orders. A second Beaulieu grange barn at St Leonards, Hampshire, survives as a fragment, and at 224ft x 67ft is the largest surviving barn in England. Pershore Abbey's grange barn at Leigh Court in Worcestershire is the country's largest cruck barn.

Mills were an important source of income to religious houses, for all tenants were obliged to use them, and corn mills were a common feature of granges. Granges with access to a major river such as the Fountains grange of Bradley used their power not only for milling, but for industrial processes. There, water power was used too, for an important iron-working site which remains as a fine series of earthworks and extensive scatters of waste material. Elaborate precautions were taken to ensure that Fountains controlled both banks of the River Colne both above and below the mill. An earlier site on the River Calder had to be abandoned because the poor nuns of Kirklees worked a mill upstream of it and controlled the availability of water.

Water was not the only source of power for milling. Many monasteries owned windmills, their sites identified by their mounds or by charter evidence. They first appear towards the end of the twelfth century, when Jocelin of Brakelond recorded a dispute between Abbot Sampson of Bury St Edmunds and Hugh, Dean of Bury, concerning the erection of a windmill which was a threat to the abbey's monopoly on milling. Monasteries were slow to take up windmills, probably because their well-established watermills were more productive and though more expensive to build easier to maintain. Timber-built post mills were portable, and in the late thirteenth century Abbot William of Meaux in East Yorkshire moved a windmill from Beeford to a new site at Dringhoe about a mile away to replace a defunct watermill.

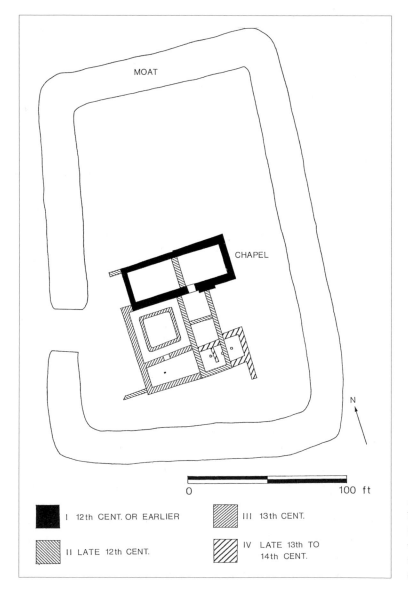

MOAT

CHAPEL

N

0   100 ft

I 12th CENT. OR EARLIER

II LATE 12th CENT.

III 13th CENT.

IV LATE 13th TO 14th CENT.

86 The central buildings of Gorefields Grange were laid out like the claustral ranges of a monastery

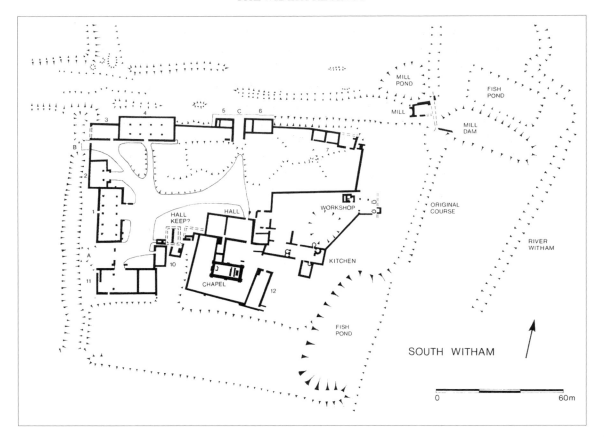

87 The plan of South Witham recovered by total excavation demonstrates the most common layout of grange buildings and shows them to be every bit as complex as the buildings of the outer court

While the majority of granges practised a mixed economy, some were specialist in their function. Fountains Abbey encouraged pottery production on its granges of Sutton (the Winksley pottery) and Bradley (the Upper Heaton pottery), and Rievaulx had a specialist iron-working granges at Sitlington and Flockton near Wakefield. Fountains and Rievaulx both maintained large stud farms in the Tees valley to provide draught-horses for their extensive estates, while Barlings Abbey operated a major fishery and smoke-houses on the River Witham in Lincolnshire. In upland areas, most orders maintained large sheep runs or *bercaria* and cattle-ranches or *vaccaria*. One of the finest to survive is Old Malton Priory's bercary on Levisham Moor above Pickering in North Yorkshire (*88*). The site is defined by a series of earthworks which suggest several phases of development. This ranch included pasture for 1000 sheep, 120 beasts, 12 mares with their foals and 2 stallions.

Excavation has yet to demonstrate how any grange functioned through time, and what little work that has been done on monastic estates has tended to concentrate on the early years of development. Because the monastic economy developed from farming in hand to a rentier economy from the early years of the fourteenth century, the same

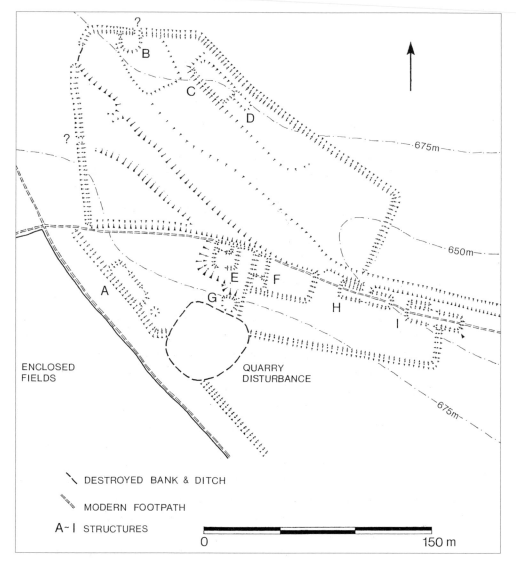

88 The earthworks of Old Malton's sheep-ranch on Levisham Moor are a reminder that much of the evidence for monastic agriculture remains unexcavated and largely unexamined

degree of change is apparent within the precinct itself. As a note of caution, it should be remembered that the Fountains grange of Cowton, rented out from the early fourteenth century, lost its great timber buildings in the course of the fourteenth century to be replaced by a courtyard farm indistinguishable from many non-monastic farms, and that the tenant was responsible for the grange buildings, though the abbot would supply the timber for building and slates for the roof. All the same, the stock the tenant managed was the property of the abbey and if an animal died the production of its skin at the abbey tannery got the tenant a replacement. Even when monastic control seems to have been lost, there were often special deals for monastic tenants.

5

SANITATION AND THE USE OF WATER

One of the most remarkable aspects of monastic life was the preoccupation with the provision of a plentiful water supply, not only for drinking and washing but also to flush drains, fill fish ponds, and service the buildings of the outer court. Separate sources were needed, for potable water, water used to flush the drains and water used for industrial purposes were seldom mixed except as waste. The vast quantities of water needed even by a small monastery was an important factor in the initial siting of the house, and the failure of an expected supply might indeed cause the abandonment of a site. The Augustinian priory of Wigmore in Herefordshire was first established at nearby Shobden in about 1141, but moved to a place called Eye at Aymestrey because the canons found they were 'too far from the water they sorely lacked'. Patrons tended to forget the essentials, and the canons were next uprooted from Aymestrey where they has access to the River Lugg and transferred to a new site adjacent to the church at Wigmore, high on a ridge above the village though convenient for the Mortimers of Wigmore Castle. This new site was 'above all ... very short of water'. It was not until the 1170s that a suitable site in the marsh below Wigmore Castle was granted to the house.

Ideally, a monastery would be placed on a river, as at Fountains, Roche or Waverley, and the river made to work for the house. At Rievaulx, the River Rye that ran down the centre of the valley divided the lands of the founder Walter Espec from those of Roger de Mowbray. Both established monasteries in the vicinity, Espec a Cistercian monastery and Mowbray a house of Savigniacs, a situation with which both found great difficulty. It took 30 years for the abbots of Rievaulx to negotiate an agreement with their neighbours of Byland to realign the river and permit Rievaulx to use its water effectively. Suitable rivers were not always available, particularly for urban houses, and an alternate supply had to be engineered, often at great expense and with remarkable ingenuity. Great vaulted drains (the source of many stories about tunnels linking monasteries with other buildings) flushed by distant watercourses were built to serve latrines, rivers were diverted or leats canalised to serve mills and industrial buildings of the precinct, and clean, potable water was brought from wells or springs and piped to every part of the monastery. Even engineered supplies could not be guaranteed, as the monks of Waveley discovered in 1215. The aqueduct that brought water from the spring of *Ludwelle* dried up 'not without astonishment', and it was only after 'great difficulty, enquiry, and invention, and not without much labour and sweating' that the monk Symon located a new spring some 480m to the east of the abbey buildings and brought its waters to the house by underground conduits.

Excavation and ground survey has demonstrated that such major undertakings were not restricted to the wealthiest houses but even poor nuns and especially friars could expect a clean water supply and efficient drains. Because clean water and good sanitation were a necessity of monastic life the majority of religious houses were provided with both at a time when the only other buildings to be supplied with either were royal and episcopal palaces. It is only the scale and complexity of hydraulic engineering that varies from house to house, and because good drainage and clean water were central to religious life they tended to be supplied from the earliest years of development though they would undoubtedly be modified as the needs of the community developed.

MONASTIC PLUMBING AND MEDIEVAL DOCUMENTS

The starting point for the archaeological study of the monastic water supply is the surviving collection of medieval drawings that show how water was supplied. Of these, the most useful are two late twelfth-century drawings of the great cathedral priory of Christchurch in Canterbury and a much amended waterworks plan of the early fifteenth century from the Carthusian charterhouse of London (which survives as two slightly different versions). The Canterbury drawings can be dated from associated documents to the priorate of Wybert, 1153-67, and show in remarkable detail the total water system of the house.

Canterbury had begun its life at the very end of the sixth century on a site within the Roman city without ready access to water. The Saxon monastery and its successor built by Archbishop Lanfranc after a fire in 1067 had relied on wells, and it was only the granting of a source of spring water 1.2km to the north-east of the city by either Archbishop Theobald or more likely St Thomas Becket that guaranteed a sufficient supply for a convent of perhaps 200 monks. The first drawing shows the mechanics of bringing water from the source, a large spring-fed pond. The water was collected in a conduit house or tower and brought along the line of the current Military Road in a pipe, past a cultivated field, a vineyard and an orchard. Five settling tanks were provided to filter the water, the supply pipe entering through the base of the tank and leaving from the top. Each settling tank had its own tap or cock by which it could be drained off for cleaning. Remarkably, this system, which was protected by Act of Parliament in 1545, is still running. The supply pipe was brought across the city ditch on a bridge of three arches, and then through the city wall and the precinct wall of the monastery. From there its course is better followed on the second drawing (*89*), a combined plan and elevation drawing of the whole monastery. The water-pipe is shown in blue and it ran first to the infirmary and then to a great first-floor laver in the infirmary cloister, passing a well which was perhaps an earlier source, for next to it was a hollow column with a caption which says that water poured in here was distributed to all the officers of the house. From here the water was taken to the great cloister laver outside

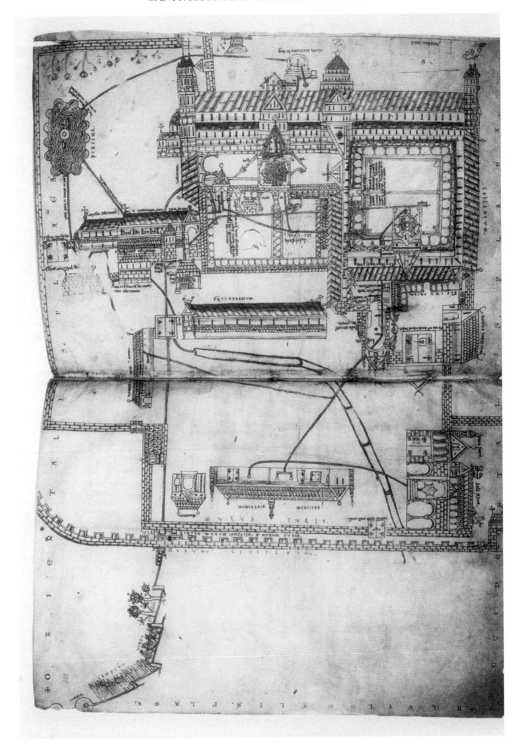

89 The installation of a piped water supply at Canterbury was recorded in remarkable detail on an accurate drawing of the house that shows not only how the water system worked but also how the buildings of the monastery appeared in the 1160s. *Trinity College, Cambridge*

the refectory door. The lavers were all buildings of remarkable architectural sophistication, marking their importance to the community. The colour coding of the pipes changes from blue to red once water has left the great *lavatoria* or washing places, showing that they were the primary sources of clean water. Here is perhaps a clue to the significance of the monastic water supply, for the lavers in the infirmary and great cloisters had great spiritual significance and the sick and old were given the first use. They also used great quantities of the purest water which was then recycled into the system. From the great cloister laver water was distributed throughout the priory, with a pipe carried below the refectory to the kitchen, from where a further pipe led to the bake house and brew house. A branch off this fed a building labelled 'bath house and chamber', and a pipe from the bake house took water to the court house in the inner court, the *Aula Nova* or New Hall where there was another monumental laver. A second feed from the laver in the great cloister to a laver outside the infirmary door, and from there a supply was taken to the prior's chambers. From this main supply, a branch-pipe led below the church to feed a fountain in the lay cemetery, alongside which was another well with a bucket and counterbalance to draw water, presumably associated with the earlier supply of water in the monastery. Once water had been distributed to all the major offices of the house, the waste was used to feed a great and decorative fish pond in the court and was then channelled back to flush the drain of the monks' latrine or *necessarium*. From there the waste was taken away in a great vaulted drain that debouched into the city ditch close to the court house but away from the monks' buildings. Surface water from the great cloister and the church roofs was collected in drains, coloured yellow on the drawing, and used to help flush the latrine drain.

The scale and sophistication of Prior Wybert's supply is immediately apparent from the two drawings. Excavation has confirmed that the pipes are of lead and that they follow the lines shown on the plan. As yet we have little information on how the supply system was modified as the monastery developed, for the free-standing lavers were swept away and wall *lavatoria* substituted. The plan shows taps on the great lavers but none have survived, and we have to look elsewhere to understand exactly how the system functioned.

The London plans, in comparison, are highly detailed. Drawn up after the house was first given a distant water source in Islington 1430, 61 years after its foundation, and altered at least twice before 1512, they are very much working drawings for the convent's plumbers. Deletions and insertions in the manuscripts show how the system was adapted, and how exactly the water was collected, filtered and directed to the house. Originally four springs were enclosed and linked by a stone gutter, but by 1512 two further enclosed springs and two open springs had been added to the system. From the closest spring to the house, around 1.5km to the south of the furthest springs, a lead pipe carried all the collected water to a conduit house, the White Conduit, which survived in modified form until 1831 in Denmark Road, Islington (*colour plate 18*). Two pipes led from the conduit house: a waste pipe carrying off any surplus and the 'home pipe'. The home pipe ran through a series of settling tanks, described on the plot as 'wells', first as a single feed, then doubled and finally trebled, to a second conduit house which was shown in detailed elevation. To prevent the pressure of water bursting the pipes a series of vents or 'suspirals' were provided, and these also acted as drain cocks for servicing the system.

From the second conduit an enlarged home pipe ran directly to the house, skirting two mill mounds and passing below the highway from Islington to London, where the pipe 'goth in a pece of oke kev(er)ed w^t a creste of oke ovyr the diche'. Running with the home pipe are the supplies of the Clerkenwell nunnery and the priory of St John of Jerusalem over whose lands the Carthusians' pipe ran by agreement. Once within the charterhouse, the home pipe ran to a water tower or 'age' at the centre of its great cloister, from which water was piped in ring mains to every monk's cell, the cloister laver and the buildings of the inner court, including the meat refectory of the guests.

WATER SOURCES

Monastic water supplies were often retained after the suppression to serve new mansions built out of monastic ruins, with many surviving well into the post-medieval period. Remarkably little attention has ever been paid to them, and only one source has been examined archaeologically, though others are known. Excavations in Canterbury have revealed the spring house that supplied St Augustine's Abbey from the twelfth century (90). Lying just east of the source used by Canterbury cathedral priory a series of springs fed an open pond. Early in the thirteenth century the pond was replaced by a polygonal tank of flint and Caen stone dug into the hillside on the spring-line This tank was fed by no less than 25 separate springs, each of them tapped by a vaulted stone-lined channel and, where examination was possible, the springs themselves rose within little vaulted chambers. This source survived the destruction of St Augustine's Abbey in 1540, being retained to serve the palace that Henry VIII established on the site, and it was repaired and refitted in the later seventeenth century. Unfortunately this work removed any evidence of how the water was led from the spring house and destroyed the medieval covering of the tank. It must have been completely covered to ensure an uncontaminated supply.

A more usual form of supply was an open collecting tank within an enclosure that kept it clear of animals. Two survive at Fountains Abbey in the southern part of the precinct. That which served the monks supply was a pair of connected rectangular tanks, the first 40m x 20m in the south-east corner of the precinct and the second to its north 65m x 20m. The first, which still contains water, was fed by one or more springs, the second was a holding tank fed by gravity from the first and some 115m from and 20m above a spring house, known since the Middle Ages as Robin Hood's Well in the valley bottom. A similar collecting tank of identical form to the Fountains example has recently been recorded on the South Common in Lincoln, the source for the Gilbertine priory of St Katherine that lay to the south of the city.

In comparison, close sources are very well known and individual spring or well houses are more common survivors. Perhaps the finest well houses are to be seen at Mount Grace Priory where three separate buildings survive. Like their brothers of London they enjoyed a piped supply direct to their cells, but did not have to go so far to find a reliable source of clean water. Natural springs on the hillside immediately above the house were tapped, each with its own well house. Two were excavated in the 1960s during the general clearance

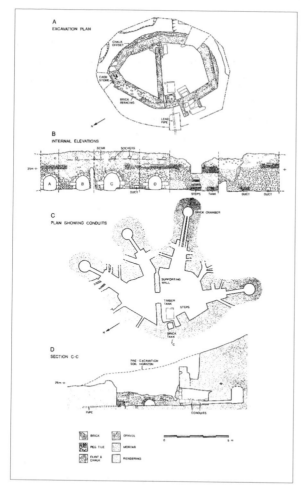

Left: 90 The spring house that served St Augustine's at Canterbury survives more or less in its thirteenth-century form. *After Canterbury Archaeological Trust*

Below: 91 The northern well-house at Mount Grace that supplied the great cloister with clean water

of the site and were found to have been dismantled to recover their valuable lead tanks and pipe-work. Now reconstructed with some additional stonework they match the third which survived in use until 1900, serving the post-suppression house built on the site, square or rectangular buildings with a tank sunk in the floor, with a water inlet in the back wall, and a lockable access door in the front wall. The spring that supplied the monks with water (Carthusian monks actually drank water on their fast days) lay to the north-east of the great cloister (*91*). It contained a lead tank 1.5m long, 0.9m wide and 0.6m deep, and from this a pipe, 0.5m above the base of the tank, had been laid in a pear-sectioned channel between two layers of stone flags to lead the water to a water tower at the centre of the cloister, very much on the model of the London charterhouse plans.

Well houses survive at Cistercian Valle Crucis in Clwyd and Beaulieu in Hampshire, Augustinian Haughmond in Shropshire and Canons Ashby in Northamptonshire, and at Cluniac Monkton Farley in Wiltshire.

THE CLOISTER LAVER

If the purpose of supplying clean piped water was for washing, the focus of water use was the *lavatorium*, the washing places that feature so prominently in the Canterbury drawing. These take two forms in England, a detached laver that stands in its own building that first appears in the mid-twelfth century (the continental model) and a wall-mounted laver (almost exclusively British) that first appears towards the end of the twelfth century.

Several attempts have been made to identify and date the provision of piped water to cloister ranges by excavation. One of the earliest was the excavation of the laver in the great cloister at Durham by William St John Hope in 1903. Like the Canterbury monks of Christchurch the Benedictines at Durham had a piped supply that fed among other offices:

> Within ye cloister garth over against ye fraterhouse dour ... a fair laver or counditt for ye mouncks to wash ether handes & faces at, being made in forme Round covered with lead and all of marble saving ye verie uttermost walls. Wthin ye wch walls yow may walke rownd about ye laver of marble having many little Cunditts or spouts of brasse wth xxiiij Cockes of brasse Rownd about yt, havynge in yt vij faire windowes of stone woorke, and in the Top of yt a faire dovecote, covered over about wth lead ....

The 1903 excavation set a very high standard for its day, with the examination of the whole structure to reveal a series of building phases (*92*). Hope resolved the sequence logically with reference to the exceptional documentary evidence available at Durham, and so meticulous was his reporting that the site is still capable of reinterpretation.

The earliest laver, dated by its recovered architectural components to the late twelfth century, lay in the south-west angle of the earliest cloister garth, and comprised a free-standing circular structure 2.5m in diameter set within a square enclosure, apparently the foundation for an open arcade. This was clearly secondary to the cloister arcade itself for its footings butted against the foundations of the cloister. The circular base of the laver, sections

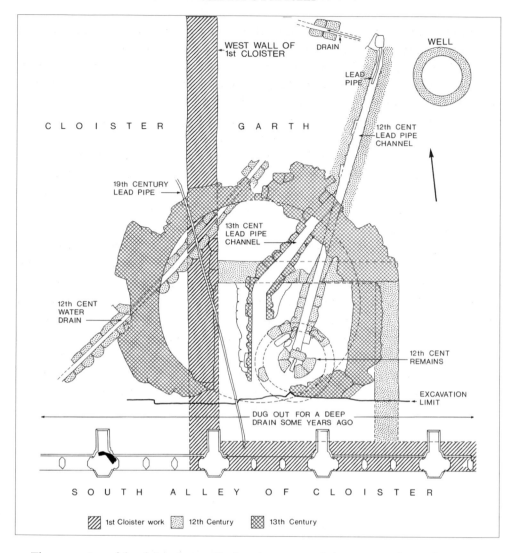

92 The excavation of the cloister laver at Durham in 1903 revealed two major phases of construction. *After C.H. Fowler with reinterpretation*

of which had been reused in later work, was decorated with an arcade of 15 blind arches and had supported a basin which was not recovered. At its centre a lead pipe rose up from a stone-lined channel to feed the basin in the same way as the rising pipes are shown in the Canterbury drawing. The pipe itself was traced for some 12.5m towards the centre of the cloister where it terminated against a stone base, and a narrow drain ran off to the west from the same point. The water-pipe was turned up towards the base, and 1.5m to the east was a stone-lined well that appeared to be of twelfth century date. Hope drew the obvious parallel with the well and pillar in the infirmary cloister at Canterbury which was captioned 'Pillar into which, when the water supply fails, water from the well can be poured and will be supplied to all the offices'. At Durham this appears to have been the original arrangement.

Early in the thirteenth century the great cloister was extended to the west and the old laver and its house were demolished. It was replaced a little to the north and west by the octagonal, buttressed laver house so graphically described in the late sixteenth-century source quoted previously. This rebuilding coincided with an engineered water supply brought from outside the precinct to the south, and the supply from the old well was redirected towards the centre of the new structure, though the main supply came in a stone-lined channel that came from below the refectory to meet the realigned pipe from the well. No trace of the thirteenth-century laver survived, From the Bursars accounts for 1338/9 and the following year it is clear that the engineered supply could not always be guaranteed: 'to women carrying water from the Wear to the abbey for the bake house, brew house, and kitchen at divers times when the pipe was frozen', and 'in drawing water from the draw-well in the cloister and for work about the pipe'.

A third phase in the development of the laver is apparent from the surviving laver basin now lying at the centre of the cloister, which can be identified as the basin of the sixteenth-century description (93). An octagonal pedestal rose from the centre of the octagonal bowl and it was drilled to take a rising pipe that fed a fountain and water was drawn off from the basin through 12 pipes with double taps, the *xxiiij Cockes of brasse*, to feed a lower trough. The level of water in the basin was controlled by an overflow pipe, allowing the fountain to run continuously. All the plumbing was evidenced by pipe holes drilled in the stone. According to contemporary accounts, this new laver was provided in 1432/3, the year in which the single stone of the basin and two stones of the trough were quarried at Egglestone on the Tees.

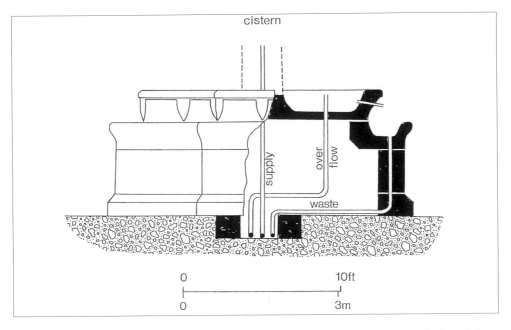

93 A reconstruction of the fifteenth-century laver at Durham, based on the surviving basin and the sixteenth-century description

Related to the early laver at Durham is the late twelfth-century laver of Wenlock Priory in Shropshire which was reconstructed in the early thirteenth century, and from which large elements survive (*94*). Being Cluniac it is highly decorative. As first built, it comprised a central hollow column of fine ashlar very much like that at Durham that carried a massive 40-lobed basin of Wenlock marble, and was surrounded by a ring of curved limestone and carved marble slabs with a rebate in their inner upper edge that carried a trough. Fine lead tubes in the mouths of 20 faces carved around the base of the basin constantly ran water into the trough. No remains of the trough have been recovered but it is identical in its seating to the trough of the great laver built by Henry II outside Westminster Hall in 1182/3 and excavated by Brian Davison in 1973. There must have been a fountain above the basin but none of its remains have been found. The laver can be dated from its carving to the 1170s or '80s, making it closely contemporary with Henry II's laver.

Early in the thirteenth century the Wenlock laver was reconstructed to provide a wider, oversailing basin. Because the basin was raised above the supporting structure of limestone and marble slabs the original plinth was removed and the slabs set in a circle of rebated stones that hid the lower margins of the two surviving carved panels. A small bowl of Wenlock Marble with a series of lead spouts emerging from the mouths of bishops and carved to match the original bowl was added to replace the original fountain, and the whole of the laver was enclosed in an octagonal laver house attached to the south alley of the cloister. As at Durham, water was piped in from the south, with a door provided below the trough to access the pipes and to permit the constantly flowing fountain to be turned off.

The Benedictines and Cluniacs appear to have favoured the free-standing laver, and a number that survived into the later Middle Ages can be identified from the remains of the laver houses that contained them. The finest is at Sherborne in Dorset, a rebuilding of the early sixteenth century, taken down at the suppression and re-erected as a market cross in the town. Both Battle Abbey and its cell of St Nicholas in Exeter retained free-standing lavers, the former in an octagonal house built after 1172, the latter in a circular one of which a number of elements survive. Though the free-standing *lavabos* of Canterbury Christchurch were swept away in the thirteenth century, the neighbouring abbey of St Augustine retained its free-standing laver in a hexagonal adjunct to the cloister up to the suppression. The Cluniacs of Lewes had a circular laver house, and excavation has recovered a single fragment of the laver, a curving slab of Sussex marble decorated with arcading supported on attached shafts and waterleaf capitals of the 1160s. Peterborough Abbey, which built a fine wall laver in the thirteenth century, still retains large parts of the trough of its free-standing laver, now displayed in the northern triforium of its presbytery.

From the 1170s, a new model of washing place was introduced, apparently by the Cistercians, with continuous troughs to one or both sides of the refectory door. Fountains Abbey had a square laver house in the south-west corner of its cloister in the 1160s, but acquired a new wall-mounted *lavatorium* in the 1170s when the south range of the cloister was reconstructed. It is the earliest example which can be dated with any

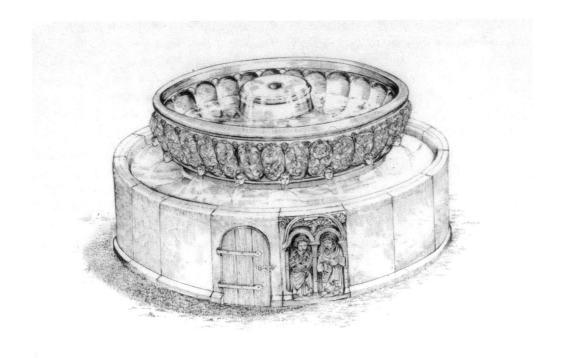

94 The Much Wenlock laver (A) as originally designed, and (B) as rebuilt in the early thirteenth century. *B. Byron*

certainty. Rievaulx followed suit (*95*). The reason for this development has been debated for years. The free-standing laver was fine for the warmer climates of the Mediterranean, but had a serious risk of freezing up in northern Europe, particularly as the fountain houses had open arcades to the cloister. Why the English should abandon the continental model is not known, but it was an idea that caught on rapidly. The canons, in particular, readily adopted the idea and their *lavatoria* tended to be elaborately decorated, as at Southwick (see *57*), Haughmond, or Kirkham Priories. Few of these lavers have survived to show how they functioned, though several are described in suppression-period surveys. At Rievaulx Abbey the laver is described as being 'of lead overcast with pewter' in a document of 1538, yet the evidence of the surviving structure shows that it had a stone trough or tank, fragments of which survive, supplied with water by a single pipe to each half of the laver which was punctuated by the refectory door. Reconstruction is virtually impossible until the fragments of the marble tank at nearby Byland Abbey are examined (*96*). The trough was indeed metal and lead strengthened with a coating of pewter would be ideal; the carved marble that survives was the facing of a tank with holes drilled to take fine lead pipes to run water continually into the metal trough below. At Mount Grace Priory, the tiny cloister *lavatorium* had a lead-lined wooden tank above a stone trough, with presumably a single tap to draw water from the tank.

THE ARCHAEOLOGY OF WATER SYSTEMS

Excavations at Kirkstall Abbey in the 1950s, more recently reconsidered by Stuart Wrathmell and Steven Moorhouse, recovered exceptional evidence for a developing water system of which the earliest phase was contemporary with the first phase of building, that is the early 1160s. More recently still, excavation at Sawley Abbey has identified a piped water system that is contemporary with the provision of temporary buildings between about 1150 and 1180. The earliest water system identified in England is not actually monastic, but was found in the Bishop of Winchester's see palace of Wolvesey by Martin Biddle. Dated to the 1130s and associated with the buildings of Bishop Henry of Blois, the technology was imported directly from Rome. Within 20 years it was to become the norm in British monasteries, and forms the basis of what has been recorded in the earliest water supplies at Kirkstall and Sawley.

The Cistercians, with their fundamentalist interpretation of the Benedictine rule, might be expected to have provided only water that was strictly necessary for spiritual and social needs, and this seems to be confirmed by the evidence of Kirkstall (*97*). Not all of the pipe runs were originally identified, as robbing of the lead had confused the situation. In spite of this, enough was recovered to show how the supply originally functioned. As at Canterbury, water was first piped to the infirmary, and from there a lead pipe was taken into the cloister through the parlour in the east cloister range. The pipe here was protected by a casing of pitched stones contemporary with the footings of the east range and it ran to a stone-lined cistern in the cloister outside the parlour door. The tank was lined with finely cut stone, with a step on its east side below which

95 The cloister lavers at Rievaulx Abbey, originally with lead troughs overcast with pewter, were placed to either side of the refectory door within a decorative arcade. They date to the 1190s when the south range of the cloister was reconstructed

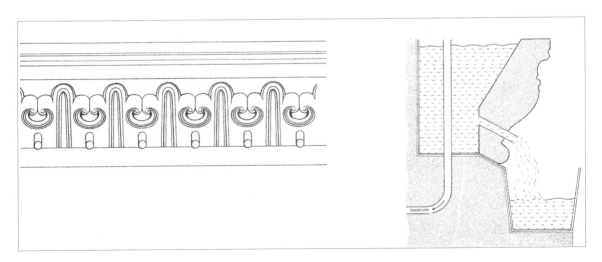

96 The form of the Byland Abbey laver, with its marble tank and metal trough, can be reconstructed from fragments recovered at the clearance of the site. *After S. Harrison*

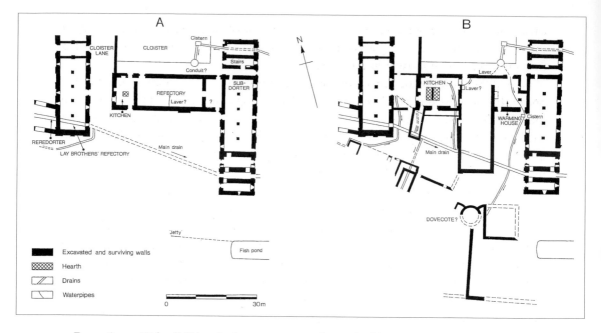

97 Excavation at Kirkstall Abbey in the 1950s recovered considerable evidence for the development of the water supply and drainage. *After Wrathmell and Moorhouse*

the pipe entered and must originally have been lined with lead. Any lining and all of the pipes had been removed, but the tank must have served as a filter or silt trap for the level of the outlet pipe was 300mm higher than the inlet, and this led to a circular feature on the line of the south cloister arcade wall. Though this was never properly examined it appears to have been the site of a free-standing laver. The pipe was extended from there to serve an early thirteenth-century wall laver in the south wall of the cloister. Additionally a drain for waste water ran from the putative laver through the south range and this too was reused to serve the wall *lavatorium*. At the centre of the original refectory in the south range, a short section of water-pipe was traced only from its clay packing, running from the south wall to the site of a possible laver in the middle of the room. As there was a similar feature in the early thirteenth-century refectory at Sawley Abbey, this is possibly a fairly common occurrence. Further excavation is needed at Kirkstall to discover where this pipe came from, but what is certain is that it comes from a separate source to that supplying the cloister laver.

The initial layout was extended from the last quarter of the twelfth century when the east–west refectory was rebuilt on a north–south axis. The link between the old and new lavers was not examined but new lengths of piping were found. The new pipe-work was not protected by stone covering or puddled clay but was simply set in deep and rather irregular trenches. A new supply was brought from the west range to a scullery to the south of the kitchen, a completely separate supply from that which served the laver. That supply was extended through the warming house to a tank in the yard to the south, and from there water was taken not in a pipe but in a stone culvert which passed below the latrine drain to serve buildings in the inner court. A small laver against the west wall of the refectory, apparently a replacement for the twelfth-century fountain there, was fed by a pipe from the wall laver in the cloister alley.

One of the most obvious effects of supplying piped water to the cloister ranges is that once it has been used it has either to be recycled or disposed of. Stone-built drains were therefore provided to carry away waste water from the kitchen and scullery, and from the west range. At Sawley Abbey, the starting points of drains were recognisably the location of taps or standpipes. The usual means of removing waste water was to direct it towards the main drain that skirted the cloister ranges.

Although the technology for piping water in lead pipes was available from the 1130s, few water systems predate the 1150s. This seems to be a result of an under-developed lead smelting industry. Indeed, lead, the common roofing material for churches and cloister ranges in the later Middle Ages was rarely used before the late twelfth century for anything other than flashings. Tile or shingle was the usual material and, indeed, it was not until 1179-84 that the tile roofs of the church of Waltham Abbey were replaced by 290 cart-loads of lead brought from Yorkshire and Derbyshire 'for the work of the church'. Once lead was available, casting it into pipes was relatively simple, using technology developed by the Romans some 12 centuries earlier (*98*). Close examination

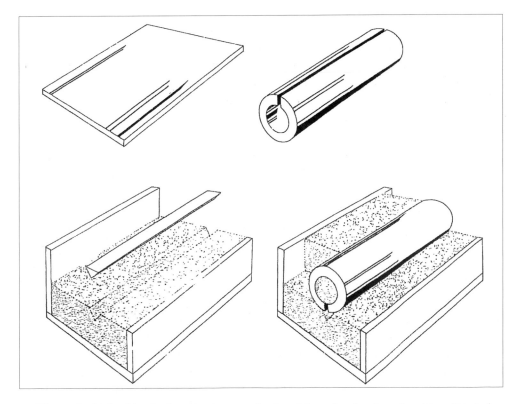

98 The method of making lead water-pipes was developed from that first introduced into Britain by the Romans, using simple but effective technology

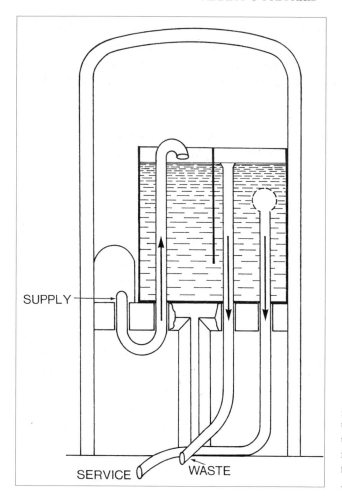

SUPPLY

SERVICE   WASTE

99 Cleanliness required water to be filtered as it passed around the system, achieved by building in settling tanks such as this one from Westminster Abbey. *After Micklethwaite*

of medieval lead pipes reveals how they were made from cast sheet. The pipes themselves were made in lengths of about 3m, and of varying internal diameters from 25mm to 100mm, joined by cast collars. Each section was cut from sheet lead and formed around a wooden mandrel to leave an open seam on the upper surface. The mandrel was then withdrawn and the pipe filled with casting sand. The next operation took place on the casting table, a long tray of damp sand, where a wooden template was used to form a triangular depression over which the open seam on the top of the pipe was placed. Molten lead was poured into the depression to seal the seam and form a distinctive ridge on the upper surface of the pipe. Any bending was done next while the pipe was still full of casting sand. Once the pipe had cooled it was cleaned up, and the individual sections were joined together by soldering on cast collars. Because of the need to shape pipes the plumbers probably made some of the sections close to where they were used.

The collars were the weakest part of the system because joints could fail under pressure, and this was allowed for in the way pipes were laid. One method was to lay the pipes in a stone conduit on a bed of clay and below a second bed of puddled clay which effectively sealed any potential leak. The conduit protected the pipe from accidental disturbance. The most common method of pipe-laying dispensed with the stone channel and the pipe was simply laid in a bed of clay which prevented leaks while leaving the pipe more easily recoverable. The cheapest option was to lay the pipe in a simple trench and only pack clay around the joints.

Water supply did not consist only of pipes, and archaeology has provided evidence of sophisticated filtering systems. In some cases this comprised a tank with a pierced lead grill that removed the most obvious impurities, and lead filter plates are a common find on monastic sites. Less common are the tanks themselves, though a complete example was recovered by excavation in the east guest house at Fountains Abbey. An almost identical filter-tank was discovered in the west range of Westminster Abbey (99), set on a shelf in a purpose-built cupboard in a service passage. All the lead-work had been removed in the sixteenth century when the building was derelict, but a study of the surviving pipe holes cut in the masonry, and the excavation of the debris lying on the passage floor recovered enough information to recover the original arrangements. A lead tank, supported by an internal wooden frame was placed on a shelf in the recess with three pipes entering through its base, one a feed from the water system, one the service pipe that led to a tap, and the third an overflow pipe that restricted the level of water in the tank and returned surplus water to the system. Impurities would settle on the floor of the tank which could be cleaned out periodically. A fine lead grill found in the rubbish on the passage floor was thought to have covered the end of the service pipe to stop any floating debris getting as far as the tap. As the wall it was set in dated to the fourteenth century the filter cannot be any earlier. The Fountains tank, which retained short lengths of pipe of differing diameters, came from a suppression-period context but was likely to date from the fourteenth century.

TAPS

Allied to the technology of the pipe-work was the provision of taps to control the flow of water. The Durham laver in its late medieval form with its 24 brass taps was not particularly unusual and cloister lavers were provided with cast taps of brass or latten from the late twelfth century. Remarkably a number of these early taps survive, an indication that once fitted they were rarely replaced. Richard Walbran's excavations at Fountains Abbey recovered a complete two-piece bronze tap which appears to have come from the cloister laver (100). Made in the 1170s, the water originally came out of the lion's mouth when the key pointed forward, but it was later modified by drilling a hole through the front of the tap body and brazing on a spout. Similar taps are known from Kilburn Priory, London, and Lewes Priory, and a hollow tap key in gilt bronze and with the face of a lioness from the nuns' cloister at Sempringham Priory comes from a similar tap. Waltham Abbey has produced two taps of a different form. The key had a hole drilled through it, and when the hole aligned with the body of the tap water came out of a spout on the front of the tap. Tap keys from Kirkstall Abbey come from a third type of tap, where the water was directed through the base of the key and out of the bottom of the tap.

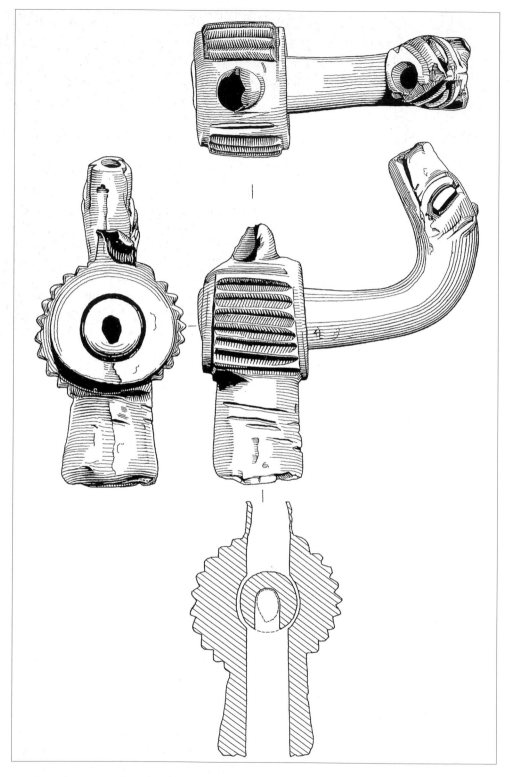

100 A cast bronze tap from the cloister laver at Fountains Abbey and dating from the 1170s

CERAMIC AND WOODEN PIPES

Although the use of lead for pipes is almost universal, alternative materials were used and have been identified in excavation. The most common alternative was ceramic sectional pipes. Excavation on the north side of the church at Kirkham Priory in 1978 revealed a pottery water-pipe carefully laid in puddled clay that could be dated to the period 1160–70 by parts of the church that sealed its construction. Only a short length of the pipe was exposed (*colour plate 19*), but seven near-identical pipe sections were recovered. The pipe passed below the church and into the cloister towards the laver, and it was substantial enough to have been the principal supply for it traversed the hillside on which the priory stood from the spring line above. Supply pipes to the laver and other cloister buildings were of lead as evidenced by the size of the holes cut in the masonry to take them, and the system at Kirkham must have been a mixed one. Fragments of ceramic water-pipe are not always recognised, though they have been recorded at Whitby Abbey from the area of the church and cloister ranges, and at Skendleby Priory. More significantly, a length of pottery supply pipe has been observed running across the outer court at St Augustine's Abbey in Canterbury, and another was found associated with the conduit house of the Franciscan friary in Lincoln. Small pipes, probably of late twelfth-century date, were recovered from a late medieval context at Thetford Priory in Norfolk.

Far less common are wooden pipes, for unless they were jointed with iron collars they are unlikely to survive on most sites. Rare examples are known from Beaulieu Abbey where they were used to feed water to the abbey from its distant conduit house; the wool house at Fountains Abbey, where a length of wooden water-pipe was reused as a drain, its end closed with a lead cap; and at Thornholme Priory, where a fragment of square-sectioned oak pipe drilled out to a diameter of 110 mm was found in an early fourteenth-century but residual context.

MONASTERIES AND WATER MANAGEMENT

Hydraulic engineering for drainage and industry, though it did not demand clean water, was if anything more extensive, requiring massive earth moving that has left its traces on the landscape. The Cistercians particularly are associated with dramatic exploitation of natural watercourses for they more than any other order invested in monumental schemes of water management. This is seen at its best in the earthworks of Bordesley Abbey, in which the development of water management can be identified. A similar development can be read in the earthworks of the precinct at Rievaulx Abbey with the added bonus that they can be related to a series of charters and closely dated.

In 1131 the founder Walter Espec granted the Cistercians a site on the east bank of the River Rye, a deep valley on the edge of the Yorkshire Moors. Land on the west side of the river belonged to Roger de Mowbray who granted it to his own Savigniac foundation of Byland. As a result, the Rievaulx monks did not have full control of the river and could not exploit it to their advantage, though they were able to take a sewer off it to serve their latrines (*101*). Before 1150 an agreement was reached with Byland allowing Rievaulx to divert the river to the west side of the valley. This diversion was only partial but part of an ongoing plan, for by 1160 a second diversion had been agreed with Mowbray's tenant Hugh de Malbis. The extra land that these two diversions gave Rievaulx virtually doubled the size of the precinct. The old course of the river was then recut to form a leat that drove three mills, a corn mill, a fulling mill, and a water-driven smithy, a dam being created in the river close to a small island on the north side of the precinct to raise its level and ensure the leat had a reliable supply of water. A further grant from Hugh de Malbis' son Richard allowed the realignment of the river to the south of the precinct. Effectively the Rye had changed from estate boundary to a workable resource at the very time that the abbey was building and expanding.

While Rievaulx was negotiating control over its water resources Byland Abbey was busy developing a new site. It became Cistercian in 1147 and the community began to expand rapidly. The site chosen was a marsh that had to be drained. There was no powerful river, but by the creation of massive ponds to the north and south of the site sufficient water was available for driving mills and servicing the latrines. This monumental water engineering is still visible in the landscape around the ruins of Byland Abbey, and though the ponds are drained their existence is well recorded in post-medieval field names.

Sanitation was as important as providing water to drive mills and the availability of an existing river could dictate the planning of the church and cloister buildings. The cloister was placed on the north side of the church at Buildwas Abbey (Shropshire) simply to enable the latrines at the north end of the east range to be flushed by a channel in the flood plain of the River Severn, and the canons' dormitory was placed in the west range of Easby Abbey in order that the adjacent communal latrine was able to take advantage of the River Swale. Both sites had occupied early Christian sites, and their planning had to be adapted to suit the topography in the twelfth century. Normally monastic latrines did not discharge directly into the river, but into a purpose-built drain that provided better control of water and separated sewage from water that was being made to work elsewhere. Many of these great drains, often tall enough to walk along, with slabbed tops or tunnel vaults, were reused by the houses that often replaced monasteries in the sixteenth century. Local knowledge of such drains is the source of the many stories about tunnels leading from monasteries to unlikely places, often the local nunnery. The tunnel that served the latrines at Easby survives, some 1.5m high and with a flagged base and roof. Few have been properly examined archaeologically, though the main drain of Norton Priory is a valuable exception (see *43*). There, the sewer was traced for some 120m and was found to flow from east to west. In its original late twelfth-century form, to the east of the latrine block the relatively small drain was stone-lined and square in section. Within the first phase latrine, however, it fed a timber drain, not lined with boards as might be expected, but hollowed from tree trunks 710mm wide. These had survived because the subsoil was waterlogged and because when the latrine block was rebuilt in the late thirteenth century it was moved a little to the south and the drain realigned. The base of the new latrine drain comprised a stone lining, and the redirected drain to the west had a base of sandstone blocks hollowed out to semi-circular profile. To the east of the new latrine a sluice retained a head of water to ensure a head of water.

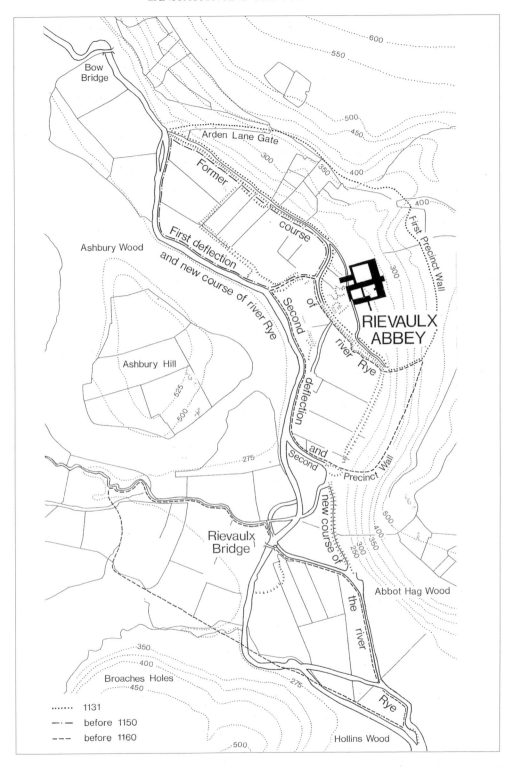

101 The developing system of water management at Rievaulx Abbey can be identified from surviving earthworks and a series of twelfth-century charters detailing land grants

Where the latrines discharged into a river, as they did at Fountains Abbey, they actually had their own channel, separated from the main body of the river by stone walls that segregated clean and dirty water. Though not apparent today, the dividing walls can still be seen in the bed of the River Skell, associated with both the lay brothers' and monks' latrines.

LATRINES AND SANITATION

The mid-twelfth-century monks' latrine block at Rievaulx Abbey survives in places to the height of its wall-plate, and was 26m in length (*102*A). An eastern extension of 11m served the adjacent infirmary. Its scale is enormous, every bit as impressive as the *necessarium* of the Canterbury drawing (see *89*). Built in the original flood-plain of the river it was three storeys high, and only the upper floor was the latrine that communicated with the dormitory. Along the south wall was the drop into the drain almost 10m below the floor, over which there would have been a continuous bench with seating for perhaps 25 monks. Sockets in the masonry suggest that the individual privies were partitioned, though many have been blocked in the course of conservation and the precise number can no longer be calculated. At Christchurch in Canterbury there is evidence of 55 cubicles, at Lewes 30, and at Worcester cathedral priory 23. The latrine has two doors into the dormitory, one to enter by and one to leave by, suggesting an orderly procession through the building. Normally a light was placed in a niche between the doors, and remains at both Kirkham Priory and in the first monks' latrine at Fountains, but does not occur here. The drain, tiny in comparison to the building, was taken off the original course of the River Rye, and after it had passed through the latrine it returned to the river and its successor leet as an open channel.

The way latrine drains functioned is not as clear cut as it might seem. Many latrines have sluices to both sides of them and the drain only has a stone floor within the building. A sluice upstream would serve to build up a head of water, but one downstream would actually maintain the water level within the latrine and prevent sewage washing away. Excavation at Humberstone Abbey in Lincolnshire, where the latrine had a sluice that maintained standing water within the building, indicated that the drain was full of faecal material and domestic rubbish, including many pottery urinals, all dating to the early sixteenth century. Urinals are a common find on monastic sites and their use was not simply for convenience. Urine was collected for tanning and for bleaching cloth, and urinals were placed in the latrines to collect it. The chance loss of one down the privy is hardly surprising. The faecal waste in the latrine drain was also useful fertiliser, and it was often deliberately allowed to accumulate, to be dug out and carted away as manure. The latrine drain at Kirkstall Abbey has a series of footholds on its north side to make access for cleaning out the waste easier. The reason for paving the floor of the drain within the latrine was simply to provide a sound surface to shovel off.

The same provision was made where the latrine stood in a river. When the first cloister buildings were raised at Fountains Abbey a drain was taken off the River Skell

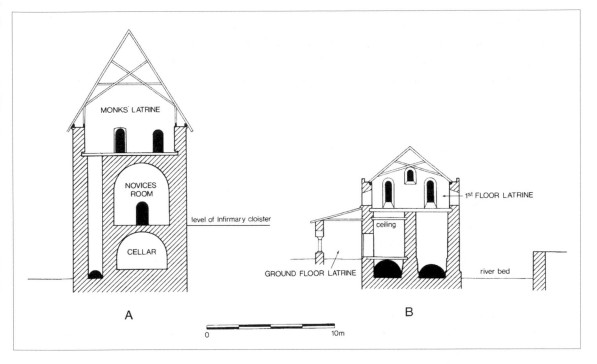

102 Cross sections of (A) the monks' latrine at Rievaulx, and (B) the lay brothers' latrine at Fountains, showing how the buildings functioned

to serve both the lay brothers' and monks' latrines in exactly the same manner as the drain at Rievaulx. When the cloister buildings were extended from the 1150s this drain was partly abandoned and the latrines were built in the river, with their own segregated watercourses and sluices. The river itself had been diverted around the monastic buildings in the 1140s and what is visible today is very much an artificial arrangement. The lay brothers' latrine (*102B* and *colour plate 20*) survives intact except for its roof and floors, showing precisely how it functioned. Here, there were two separate drains, divided to first-floor level by a solid spine wall. In the south wall are nine tall, round-headed arches, each a ground-floor privy set over the river on massive timber joists and divided by wooden screens. Entered from a cloister-like corridor, these were ultimately the latrines of the adjacent lay brothers' infirmary built in the 1170s but were originally conceived as day latrines serving the outer court on the south side of the river. The northern channel served the upper floor and had a single door from the lay brothers' dormitory. The joist sockets for this floor which spanned the whole building survive, though no trace remains of the seats which must have been ranged along the north wall. The provision was not as generous as for the monks at Rievaulx – this latrine had to accommodate at least 200 lay brothers.

Few latrines have been excavated to a modern standard, and most of those have had their drains cleared out beforehand. Two recent excavations, at Cistercian Dundrennan Abbey in Dumfries and Galloway, and Cluniac Bermondsey Abbey, demonstrated that large water-flushed latrines of the late twelfth and thirteenth centuries had ceased to function in their original fashion by the end of the fourteenth century. Watercourses were not maintained and were eventually abandoned, and the stone-lined drains within the latrine building simply functioned as pit latrines that were dug out as necessary. The number of monks in these houses was greatly reduced, and it is quite possible that the communal dormitories were no longer used as such. As monks withdrew to small apartments the great communal latrines were not heavily used, and the stench of the latrine pit was bearable. Where individual late medieval monks' apartments have been identified it is normal to find that they have their own pit latrine.

As well as the latrines provided in the cloister ranges, it is common to find latrines provided in all parts of the monastery. At Kirkham Priory, for instance, the fourteenth-century sacristy provided against the north wall of the north transept had its own pit latrine. At Fountains, outer court buildings such as the wool house, brew house and bake house were provided with obedientiaries' offices that had water-flushed latrines from the late thirteenth century. Similarly, the guest halls at Kirkstall and Tintern were provided with sophisticated water-flushed latrines from the early thirteenth century, and the guest houses at Fountains had their own latrine towers discharging into the river from the 1150s or '60s. Pit latrines, because they did not require engineered drains, were more common. At Thornholme Priory, the late twelfth-century guest house and the late almonry had pit latrines, and the late fourteenth-century gatehouse had a detached latrine tower. The contemporary gatehouse at Thornton Abbey, with accommodation on three floors, was provided with no fewer than eight pit-privies, plus a further latrine in its secondary barbican. Within the average monastery, nobody had to go very far to find a toilet, a degree of sanitary control that was not to reappear until the nineteenth century. Clean water, good drains, and water for motive power were central to the monastic ideal.

6

THE SUPPRESSION
AND AFTER

In April 1536 there were still more than 800 abbeys and priories in England and Wales, though largely with reduced communities, who between them enjoyed a cash income from their collective estates valued by the commissioners for the *Valor Ecclesiasticus* in 1534/5 at more than £160,000. This corporate wealth was far from equally spread, for while Glastonbury Abbey had a net income in excess of £3,000, the nuns of Kirklees had an annual income of less than £30. Kirklees was far from being the poorest monastery in the kingdom. Many houses were in debt and were having difficulty in supporting even small communities, making the continuance of monastic life harder than it had been in previous centuries. It is fair to assume that many of the smaller houses, which made up two thirds of the total, had never accrued vast estates or wealthy patrons and had fewer than 15 religious, did not enjoy an unnecessarily worldly lifestyle. They were simply ticking over. The standard of spirituality they enjoyed varied immensely. In some cases it was virtually non-existent, in other houses discipline was good and regularly found to be beyond reproach when the diocesan bishop visited.

On the whole, however, it could not be said that monastic life, with certain important exceptions, was in good order in the early sixteenth century. Cardinal Wolsey had begun to prune the dead wood, suppressing with papal authority no fewer than 29 houses such as Bayham and St Frideswide's at Oxford to fund new foundations, educational rather than monastic. Before him, John Alcock, Bishop of Ely, had secured papal consent to use the nunnery of St Radegund's in Cambridge to house and endow Jesus College in 1497. Society was changing, and monks and nuns were seen as less important, indeed largely irrelevant, to the functioning of the Church. Religious communities were secluded and rumoured to enjoy a better life than many actually did. They held extensive estates at a time that society was land hungry, and Wolsey's suppressions of the 1520s had shown the potential for the government to extract a substantial income, even from the estates of small monasteries.

It was the problem of the Tudor succession which was to prove the catalyst for the end of monastic life. Henry VIII's first wife Katherine of Aragon had not provided a male heir and he sought a divorce that the Pope was not able to grant for political reasons. The solution was to break with Rome, and for Parliament to establish Henry as 'the only supreme head of the Church in England' in 1534. Convocation, the Church council, which included many abbots and priors, had accepted Henry as Supreme Head 'so far as the law of Christ allowed' as early as 1531, but its ratification by Parliament enabled the government to get to grips with the Reformation of the Church officially. Henry appointed Thomas Cromwell, previously Wolsey's secretary who had handled the earlier suppressions, as his Vicar General.

THE BEGINNING OF THE END

The first actions in what was ultimately to become a general suppression of the monasteries began as a genuine attempt at reform. Following the valuation of all Church property in late 1534 and early 1535, the *Valor Ecclesiasticus,* a Bill was placed before Parliament for the suppression of all religious houses with small communities and a net income of less than £200 a year, where 'manifest sin, vicious, carnal, and abominable living' was daily practised. The displaced monks and nuns were to be licensed to leave the cloister but maintain their vows or be transferred to 'divers and great solemn monasteries of this realm wherein, thanks be to God, religion is right well kept and observed'. The Parliament which passed this Act contained no fewer than 30 abbots and priors whose own wealthy houses were, naturally, not included. Poor friaries were not included in the Act, and provision was made for exemptions. The number of monks and nuns who chose to remain within the cloister effectively meant that some of the poorer houses, all those of the Gilbertines and Carthusians, and the cells of greater monasteries had to be retained to house them. In all, less than a third of the total were suppressed. The process of closure and asset-stripping took place throughout the spring and summer of 1536 and established a process which was to become highly organised over the following years. The Court of Augmentations (of the Revenue of the King) was established to deal with the process of spoliation, the selling of contents, leasing of lands and paying off the staff as many centuries of monastic life were disassembled.

In spite of the care that the government took to make the case for reform, the suppression of houses known for their piety, charity and hospitality, and a distrust of the government's motives caused hostility, particularly in the north and in Lincolnshire, contributing to popular rebellions, the Lincolnshire Rising and the more serious 'Pilgrimage of Grace' that began in October 1536. The rebels were not entirely motivated by the loss of their monasteries, but the return of monks and nuns to their empty cloisters rapidly became their aim, much to the concern of the new tenants and the king himself. In Lincolnshire, the suppression of the lesser houses had begun, the Cistercian abbey of Louth Park had been closed and the prioress of Cistercian Legbourne Priory, who did not consider her well-ordered community to be guilty of 'manifest sin, vicious, carnal and abominable living' had written to the nunnery's patron Thomas Cromwell begging continuance. Mathew Mackerell, abbot of the wealthy Barlings Abbey could see that the writing was on the wall for his own community, and the townspeople of Louth and Horncastle, fearful for the future of their churches and guilds marched on Lincoln seeking assurance. Cromwell's suppression commissioners were not, as was normally the case, drawn from the local gentry and seem to have gone out of their way to be unpleasant, but it was the commons that drew the great abbeys of the Witham valley into the rebellion. First Mackerell was forced to join the host with his brethren, and then the abbots of Bardney and Kirkstead were drawn in, somewhat unwillingly. Charles Brandon, the king's ex-brother-in-law and Duke of Suffolk, was dispatched to deal with the rebels. The rebellion collapsed before Brandon arrived but in the tidying up that followed, the abbots of Barlings and Kirkstead among others were attainted for treason, and their houses seized for the king in 1537. Suffolk became viceroy of Lincolnshire, according to the king 'one of the most brute and beastly shires in our realm', and one of his first acts was to build houses at Barlings and Kirkstead. Among the gardens of these two houses were the unroofed churches and cloister buildings, and anyone who had dealings with the viceroy soon understood what it meant to oppose the government in Church affairs.

The Pilgrimage of Grace had similar origins. Again, the religious had to be forced to join with the commons, and in some instances the rebels reintroduced monks back into suppressed houses. This certainly happened at Sawley Abbey, where the king instructed the Earl of Derby to remove them and to 'cause the said abbot and certain of the chief of the monks to be hanged upon long pieces of timber … out of the steeple'. The scale of the revolt extended throughout the north, and when the rebels met with the Duke of Norfolk at Doncaster they achieved a general pardon while the government bought time. While Henry prevaricated, smaller revolts broke out and the abbots of Whalley, Jervaulx, an ex-abbot of Fountains who was living at Jervaulx, and the Prior of Bridlington were attainted and the houses of Whalley, Jervaulx and Bridlington seized. The convent at Furness decided it was wisest to voluntarily surrender their house before anyone looked too closely at their involvement. While the lesser monasteries which had been suppressed brought the crown small profits, the riches of these great houses were a different matter. The lead roofs of Jervaulx and Kirkstead alone were valued at £1000 and at Bridlington only slightly less. All these houses had valuable and extensive estates which would be a major source of income to the crown. It is arguable that the two risings persuaded the king that reform was not the answer, and that the total suppression of monastic houses became the intention from early in 1537.

Following on from the seizure of 'rebel' houses the government's approach changed. Communities were persuaded to surrender in the manner of the Furness monks. Both abbots and monks who had no black marks against them for dubious behaviour in 1536-7 were offered reasonably generous pensions and often allowed to take their books and even the contents of their cells. This process continued throughout 1537 and was finally legalised in 1538 by Act of Parliament, only ending with the suppression of Waltham Abbey in March 1540.

MONASTERIES INTO CATHEDRALS

The suppression of the monasteries was the first significant act in the restructuring of the English Church. Its first affect was the re-establishment of those cathedral priories that had been served by Benedictine monks. The prior was replaced by a dean and the monks by a chapter of canons, in many cases the previous monks. In this way, the cathedrals of Canterbury, Durham, Worcester, Winchester, Rochester, Ely, Norwich and Carlisle were recreated out of existing buildings, altered to suit the needs of a secular clergy who no longer lived a common life. Six other monasteries were retained to increase the number of cathedral churches – Westminster, Bristol, Oxford, Gloucester, Peterborough and Chester (*103*) ensuring the preservation of not only their churches but also a proportion of the other buildings required by the new chapter. Westminster was later reduced to the status of a collegiate church but retained many of its buildings.

THE EXPLOITATION OF MONASTIC SITES

The sites which were not retained for Church use were normally sold to laymen, and indeed many patrons sought to purchase the houses their families had supported for generations. Though they were not always successful, there are many cases in which the provider became the despoiler, converting newly-acquired buildings and lands to capital in order to fund his purchase. It was a requirement of sale, following the experience of the Pilgrimage of Grace where monks had been reinstated in their suppressed houses, that the commissioners, or failing them the new owner, should 'pull down to the ground all the walls of the churches, stepulls, cloysters, fraterys, dorters, chapter howsys etc', though this did not always happen. The portions of the church that were parochial were by and large retained, though they might have been stripped of their contents and of their lead roofs, and had to be purchased from the crown if they were to continue. In this way, the naves of Bridlington, Wymondham, Bolton, Malmesbury, Leominster (Herefordshire), Binham and Bourne (Lincolnshire) survived the wreck, and on a lesser scale the north nave aisle at Crowland was preserved. It was not just the parochial nave that survived; at Swine (East Yorkshire) it was the nuns' church that the parish sought to acquire, whilst at Boxgrove Priory it was the presence of the de la Warre tombs in the presbytery that ensured that the late patron and new owner retained that part of the church in favour of the smaller parochial nave. More rarely, whole churches were purchased for parish use – at Christchurch and Romsey (Hampshire), Dorchester (Oxfordshire), Selby (North Yorkshire) and Hexham (Northumberland). These however were the exceptions. The degree of destruction was variable. Many churches were simply unroofed and left to the elements, but others were thoroughly demolished, even to the removal of their foundations. At Jervaulx and Bardney, Hailes (Gloucestershire) and Norton, the churches were levelled soon after their closure, partly to comply with the condition of purchase and partly to provide building materials for houses created within the cloister ranges. At Lewes Priory, for which contemporary accounts survive, one Giovanni Portarini and a gang of 25 Italian engineers working for Thomas Cromwell were

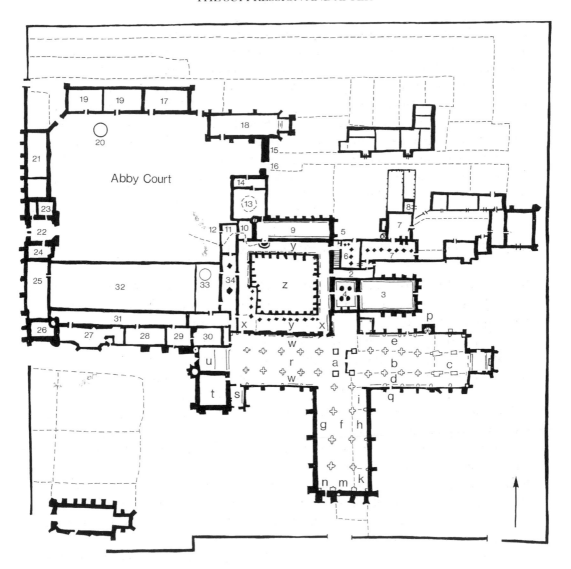

103 Randal Holmes' plan of Chester Cathedral made before 1626 shows most of the buildings that had comprised St Werbergh's Abbey had survived to serve the dean and chapter of the new foundation

employed to level the church quickly using mines and gunpowder. In this way the great Cluniac church of St Pancras with its high steeple and vaults 28m above its pavements was reduced to low walling in less than four weeks in March and April 1538, before Cromwell's son Gregory took possession of the site. The cost of such demolition was one of the principal reasons for the policy of total destruction not being carried out. In Lincolnshire, a county where the level of destruction was greater than most, John Freeman, who was charged with the task of demolition, estimated that it could be done only at a cost of more than £1000 and was content simply to make the churches unusable and let stone robbers do the rest.

There were, however, cases where specific monasteries were earmarked to provide stone for royal works. Meaux Abbey (East Yorkshire), for instance, was largely demolished to provide stone for the king's new fortifications at Hull, and excavation there on the site of Henry VIII's citadel and its flanking walls has produced clear evidence of worked medieval stone in the core of the surviving structure. Similarly, the transepts and presbytery of Bridlington Priory were sacrificed for the building of a new quay in the harbour there that fell into royal hands in 1537 along with the priory itself.

There are many documented cases of monastic buildings being broken up, but one of the most instructive cases is that of Rievaulx Abbey and its home estates purchased by its 'founder' or patron, the Earl of Rutland, in 1538. There, no demolition had begun, and the site came intact to its new owner, though the crown had retained the bells, the lead from the roofs of the church, chapter house, dormitory, refectory, kitchen, cloister, charnel chapel and gatehouse, together with the timber of the cloister roofs to burn it down. There was to be no orgy of destruction, and the dismantling of the site was carried out in such a way as to maximise profit. First, the king's lead was cast down into 'sows' of half a fother (*104*), perhaps in the cloister garth. Four pigs, each weighing approximately 9 hundredweights (half a short ton) and marked with the crowned Tudor rose to prove its ownership, were found below tons of fallen masonry at the west end of the nave, lost when the twelfth-century building collapsed of its own accord. An identical lead sow was found at Kenilworth Priory (Warwickshire). Although the furnaces to melt the lead have yet to be found at Rievaulx, they are well evidenced by excavation at Hailes, Croxden (Staffordshire), Bordesley, Muchelney (Somerset), Sopwell (Hertfordshire), Durham, Pontefract (West Yorkshire), the Franciscan church in Northampton and Monk Bretton (South Yorkshire). From Walbran's description of the stall-bases at Fountains, they must have been in the choir area there. Next, the screen-work in the church was sold, followed by the timber roof and its lead covering of the west range to tenants of the Earl who had previously been tenants of the abbey. Then, the window glass was to be taken out and sorted, the best to be kept, the second quality to be sold in panels, the poorest to be taken from its leads which were then to be melted down. The thousands of pieces of glass recovered by excavation must represent only what was felt to be worthless in 1538/9. Even the scrap iron was to be sorted and sold before it rusted and lost value, down to the nails that fixed the boarding below the lead on the roofs. Such was the desire to maximise the profits that even 'the lede of the joyntes of the pyllers and other placys, of as much as is defasyd of the ppremysses there, now is fastenyd within stonys not lose' was sold speculatively. To judge from the vast quantities of lead and iron left among the heaps of demolition rubble that Peers removed in the 1920s, the interest in recovering the total value of the scrap was soon forgotten.

The destruction at Rievaulx, as on so many other sites, was not complete, and useful buildings were retained undamaged. Unwanted buildings were simply made unusable and slowed quarried, the intention being that the monasteries

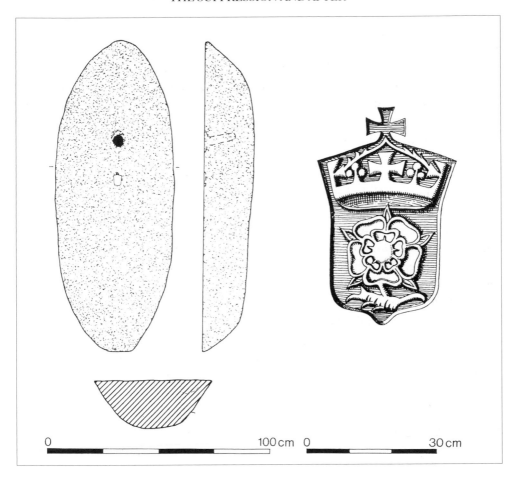

104 One of the four half-fother 'sowes' of lead from the spoliation of Rievaulx found in the north aisle of the church and marked with the king's badge. *After Dunning*

could not be easily restored. To conform with the condition of purchase, the piers that supported the clerestory of the chapter house and the vault of the east range were cut to take wedges that were driven in until the monolithic shafts cracked and could be pulled out thus bringing down the superstructure, which was left where it fell. Iron wedges and sledge-hammers were found amongst the fallen debris, and the bodies of two workmen, crushed when the chapter house was felled, were recovered in 1921.

The church itself did not need this treatment. The steeple on the central tower had already fallen before the suppression and was lying on the floor of the south transept, and the nave actually collapsed in the course of its being dismantled. Though the Earl had given instructions that the fine west window, perhaps only 30 years old, should be removed and stored in his castle at Helmsley, glass, iron, and stonework complete, the masonry of the window was found in the collapsed debris of the west end of the nave in 1920.

THE SURVIVAL OF INDIVIDUAL BUILDINGS

Provision was, however, made to save something from the destruction. No fewer than 18 tenanted buildings remained untouched within the precinct at Rievaulx, though the church and cloister ranges were dismantled in 1539. These were to form the nucleus of the village that succeeded the abbey and was largely built from its remains. In addition, the three abbey mills, one for corn, a fulling mill, and a water-powered smithy, remained a valuable asset. By far the greatest survivor, though, was the abbot's house (*105*), retained as a suitable house for a tenant or 'farmer' (not necessarily employed in agriculture). It was less than 40 years old, of sound construction, and retained its lead and slate roofs, floors, doors and wainscot panelling. The hall even retained its tiled floor and furniture. A substantial house, with its hall and chambers above cellarage, the great chamber over a fine parlour, together with a chapel, a private dining chamber and a substantial kitchen, it provided better domestic accommodation than the Earl's castle of Helmsley 3km away and survived until it was replaced by a large farmhouse in the eighteenth century. This house itself survived until the 1950s when it was finally demolished.

Sound buildings were in any case saleable, and where possible they were spared. In Gloucester, the remarkable survival of the Dominican priory was the result of the extensive reuse of its buildings. The site was sold intact to Alderman Thomas Bell, who converted the church into a grand mansion, Bell's Place, and the cloister ranges into a weaving factory, ensuring their survival to the present day. The suppression commissioners were charged with selling the movables of any monastery they closed, and the buildings that remained to be sold off must have been stripped bare. The interpretation of movable objects was broad, including not simply the furniture and household goods but also paving stones, floor tiles, grave stones, and any iron and lead work that could be easily removed. This process has been graphically demonstrated in the north range of the lesser cloister of the Dominican priory at Beverley (*106*). Though the building was not finally taken down until the seventeenth century, its latest medieval floor retained the evidence of the suppressors at work. Discarded window glass was scattered throughout the building, and the window leads recovered had been melted down in bowl hearths cut into the floors of each room. Fuel for melting down the lead and the brick to line one of the hearths had been taken from internal partitions that had been stripped out for the purpose. Lead water–pipes were systematically removed, and even the lead lining of the gulley that took water from the cloister alley roof was recovered. Scoops in the floors of both principal rooms seem to have been used for casting the lead into small ingots, and considerable quantities of lead runlets and dross from the melting process were spread about the building. On the completion of this work, the bowl hearths were carefully plugged and the scrapes in the floor filled up, leaving the building a useable shell once more.

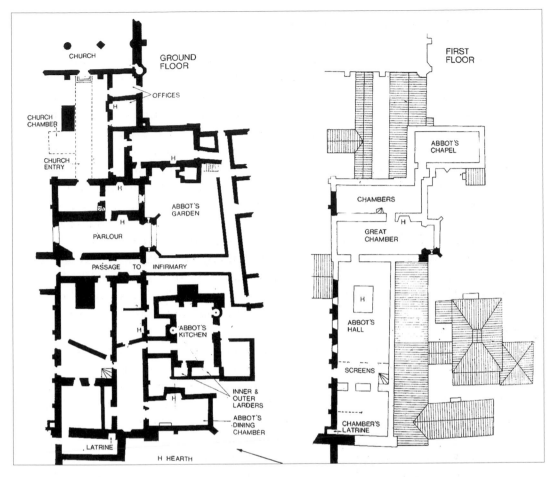

105 The plan of the new abbot's house at Rievaulx can be reconstructed from its ruins and suppression-period surveys. It was retained to house a tenant farmer and was only replaced in the eighteenth century by a new farmhouse

MONASTERIES INTO MANSIONS

Cloister ranges might easily be converted into a house for the new owner with little effort. In the most basic cases the president's lodging, and in some cases the guest accommodation, survived little-altered well into the post-medieval period. At Norton and Hailes, Bardney and Waverley, this has been demonstrated by excavation and by eighteenth-century illustrations to be in the west cloister range, with all the unwanted buildings swept away and buried beneath gardens. In the case of Hailes, Bardney and Waverley, the cloister walls themselves were retained to enclose a garden, a continuing use of the garth. On the last two sites the medieval doors in the surviving walls retained evidence of their blockings when they were excavated. In many ways, the cloister garth at Norton was much more interesting archaeologically for it contained a rubbish dump associated with the post-suppression house.

175

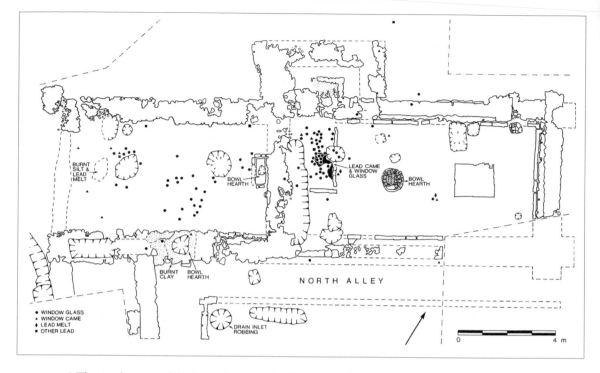

106 The north range of the lesser cloister at the Dominican friary in Beverley retained traces of small-scale spoliation by the suppression commissioners, though the building itself was to survive into the seventeenth century. *After Foreman*

A significant number of monastic buildings survive because they were reused in this way; either great houses, such as those built by the abbots of Battle or Ford (Dorset) and the prior of Watton (East Yorkshire), that required little alteration to make them suitable residences for new owners of rank, or buildings of manorial status like the west range of Lanercost Priory, or the refectories of Horsham St Faith or Syningthwaite which required little work to turn them into simple houses.

Occasionally, the greater part of the claustral nucleus was retained to form a major house. At Netley Abbey, which was acquired by Sir William Paulet, later Marquis of Winchester, the only cloister building to be demolished was the refectory which was replaced by a modest gatehouse. The cloister became a courtyard with a central fountain, the transepts and nave became the hall and kitchen, the presbytery became the chapel, and the east and west ranges were partitioned to form a series of private apartments. So little work was required to effect this change of use that the only clues surviving today are inserted windows. Excavation in 1860 resulted in the unfortunate removal of many post-suppression walls and the bases of three great kitchen fireplaces in the nave to 'reveal better its peculiarities as an ecclesiastical edifice'. This was a sad loss because the Paulet house, which survived in use until 1790, would have told us a great deal about the method of conversion from monastery to mansion.

At another Hampshire site, sufficient fabric and a remarkable series of contemporary documents survive to demonstrate the process, though on a more destructive scale. Thomas Wriothesley, a close associate of Cromwell, petitioned for the site of Titchfield Abbey, which was suppressed on 18 December 1537. Four days later he was advised by the suppression commissioners who continued to act as his agents that the cost of conversion of the monastic buildings to a suitable house would be in excess of £200. On 30 December he was finally granted the site, and three days later the commissioners advised him of their scheme to create a mansion fit 'for the King's grace to bate & for any baron to kepe his hospitalite in'. Such speedy action was consistent with the commissioners' instructions to prevent the return of the canons who had been dispossessed. They were also keen to demolish the church with the exception of the north transept to ensure that the abbey was effectively defaced, but Wriothesley would have none of this.

Although the work of conversion began immediately there were constant changes to the plan between January and April 1538. Initially it had been planned to put the hall on the first floor of the east range, but the final scheme placed it more sensibly in the old refectory, which was largely rebuilt and provided with a porch into the cloister garth which became a courtyard with a central fountain. The great chamber and parlour were then placed in the east range above cellarage and a chapel which seems to have occupied the chapter house, whilst servants' quarters were contrived within the west range, which was extensively rebuilt. Arguments continued throughout the summer about the refitting of the church. Wriothesley finally accepted that the crossing tower and south transept should be demolished, though the presbytery and crossing were to form the shell of three lodgings. The final phase of building was the gatehouse range that closed the south side of the courtyard (*colour plate 21*), constructed from the nave of the abbey church through which a striking gatehouse with octagonal turrets was driven. Sadly all but the gatehouse range was demolished in 1781, though what survives shows that the conversion work was skilfully contrived and that it would have been difficult to tell that the sixteenth-century mansion of Place House was for the most part a Premonstratensian abbey of the thirteenth century. The house was finished by 1542 when its owner sought the royal pardon for crenellating it without licence, almost certainly because of the new gatehouse, and when John Leland wrote in his Itinerary that 'Mr Wriothesley hath builded a right stately house embateled and having a goodly gate and conducte (conduit) casteled in the middle of the court of it, yn the very same place where the late Monasterie of Premonstratenses stoode, caullyd Tichfelde'. It is only with its ruin that the origins of the site have become truly apparent. Wholesale conversions was not a rare occurrence. At Lacock, for instance, Sir William Sharington's new house made use of the Augustinian canoness' cloister ranges and inner court but required the demolition of their church, very much on the same model as Newstead Priory where only the south aisle of the nave and south transept were included in the house created at the suppression. At Mottisfont

Priory and Buckland Abbey, it was the church that formed the basis of a house, though the greater part of the remaining monastic buildings were demolished. Where the church and cloister buildings were swept away or remodelled it was still common to retain the gatehouse to serve new buildings, explaining the survival of the great gates of Thornton Abbey, and St Osyth's Priory (Essex). In some cases, it was the gatehouse itself which became a house, with fine surviving examples at Beaulieu, Butley (Suffolk), Kirkstall and Bolton.

Although the method of converting the main monastic buildings into new houses is well established, little attention has ever been paid to other changes brought about within the remainder of the precinct. At Thornholme Priory, where substantial outlying areas have been excavated, it was possible to demonstrate that most of the service buildings were thoroughly demolished immediately after the suppression, to the extent that virtually all their masonry was removed, though the same destruction was not apparent in the cloister ranges and the gatehouse had not been demolished until the nineteenth century.

At Stainfield Priory (Lincolnshire), the earthworks of the precinct (*107*) show without doubt that they were modified after the suppression to serve as the park for Stainfield Hall, giving lie to the assumption that all earthworks on monastic sites need be medieval. In some cases, the post-suppression modification of the landscape was just as drastic as that caused by the building of the monasteries in the first place. In the case of Southwick Priory, the extent of the precinct is completely obscured by the earthworks that defined the building and garden terraces of a great seventeenth-century house which has been as effectively demolished as the priory buildings themselves.

RUINS IN THE LANDSCAPE

Those monastic sites that were not reused as houses were simply abandoned or served as quarries, and the survival of their ruins has been very much a matter of luck. At Whitby, the abbot's house survived as a residence, but the church was simply stripped of its roof, windows and bells and left to serve as a seamark. Its subsequent fate is indicative of how the simple forces of nature could be just as destructive as the suppression commissioners. It is fortunate indeed that the ruins of the church at Whitby have been so well recorded in the past, for the losses have been dramatic. The earliest known record was engraved by Samuel Buck in the first quarter of the eighteenth century and shows the thirteenth- and fourteenth-century church tolerably complete together with the greater part of the chapter house (*108*). Though the major windows appear to have lost their tracery, the gables remain intact as do a number of pinnacles. Whilst Buck's engravings cannot be regarded as a totally accurate record later drawings of a much better quality do show a number of features recorded by Buck that no longer survive, confirming the broad outlines of his record.

107 The earthworks of Stainfield Priory, a small Benedictine nunnery, detail several phases of settlement, the latest of which is a post-medieval park associated with Stainfield Hall. *P. Everson/RCHM(E)*

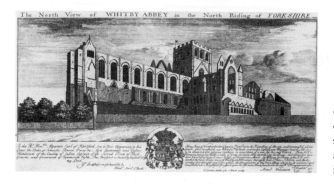

The North View of WHITBY ABBEY in the North Riding of YORKSHIRE

108 Samuel Buck's engraving of Whitby Abbey taken from a drawing of 1711 by P. Combes shows the masonry of the church and chapter house to be largely intact

Another engraving of 1789 after Gibson shows a very different state of affairs (*109*). Two-and-a-half centuries of neglect and the harsh climate of the Whitby headland had caused major falls of masonry. The arcades and clerestory of the nave had fallen in 1762, to be followed by the south transept the following year, their tumbled remains lying where they had fallen. While the ruins were the subject of Romantic curiosity, as is evident from the group in the foreground, no attempt was made to repair them, for the greater part of the west front was to fall in 1794, a victim of continuing decay. The Gibson drawing is extremely useful because of its great attention to detail, evidencing the date of masonry that no longer survives. The tower, which remains intact to the string course below its parapet, was built in the fourteenth century and was contemporary with the completion of the nave, although it stands above a crossing of thirteenth-century date. The west window, a perpendicular window of eight transomed lights to judge from its stubs, was an insertion of the fifteenth century, clear evidence that the fourteenth-century nave was altered and improved, though the scale of this work is no longer apparent.

When the ruins of Whitby Abbey were taken into the care of the Office of Works in 1920, they were much less extensive than the ruins shown in the Gibson drawing (*110*). The crossing tower had fallen on 25 June 1830, and part of the presbytery fell during a storm in 1839. In comparison shelling by the German navy on 16 December 1914 did little serious damage to the ruins. Without intentional demolition or the depredations of stone robbers more than half the abbey church had simply collapsed before any attempt was made to halt the decay and preserve what remained for posterity. The removal of hundreds of tons of fallen masonry in the early 1920s (*109*) has done something to recover the plan and elevation of what was a remarkable building, but it cannot restore what was lost through three-and-a-half centuries of neglect. The course of events seen at Whitby was by no means unique. The north-west or Ethelbert tower at St Augustine's Abbey in Canterbury for instance fell in 1822. Although the repair of many of the most important monastic ruins from the late nineteenth century has ensured that the loss of fabric is largely a thing of the past there are still sites which continue to decay. One tragic loss of the last 20 years has been the crossing tower of Maxstoke Priory (Warwickshire), and without proper attention other monastic sites remain at risk.

109 Gibson's view of Whitby Abbey in 1798, after the fall of the nave and south transept but before the fall of the tower

110 The ruins of Whitby Abbey after their conservation and clearance in the 1920s comprise less than a third of what was recorded by Buck

ROMANTIC RUINS AND EIGHTEENTH-CENTURY PARKS

It was the image of ruin and natural decay that brought the best preserved of our abbeys and priories to the attention of their owners in the eighteenth and early nineteenth centuries. What had ceased to be strictly practical now became art to be appreciated. A good abbey ruin was a fine feature for a gentleman's park. In the eighteenth-century interpretation of the picturesque a real ruin was infinitely preferable to a manufactured one, and several of the northern abbeys were particularly suited to this use. The finest of all monastic ruins, those of the great Cistercian abbey of Fountains, lay in the valley of the River Skell to the west of the gardens created at Studley Royal by John Aislabie, the Chancellor of the Exchequer disgraced in the South Sea Bubble scandal of 1720. Though he was unable to purchase the site, his design was to use the ruins as a vista at the west end of his water-gardens, for according to the traveller Arthur Young 'ruins generally appear best at a distance'. His son acquired the Fountains estate in 1768, incorporating the ruins in an extension of his father's gardens which was conceived not in the classical formality of his father's designs but in the picturesque romantic style which 'Capability' Brown was bringing to Roche at about the same time. Undoubtedly, it was the bringing of the ruins into the gardens that ensured their future well-being, though at the time this was questioned.

The ruins were not quite to William Aislabie's taste so they were improved, not simply by selective demolition but by the addition of new features. Gilpin, who visited in 1772 was not at all impressed by Aislabie's treatment of the ruins:

> A few fragments scattered about the body of a ruin are proper and picturesque. They are proper because they account for what is defaced; and they are picturesque because they unite the principal parts with the ground in which union the beauty of composition in a good measure depends. But here they are thought rough and unsightly, and fell a sacrifice to neatness…. In the room of these detached parts, which are proper and picturesque embellishments of the scene, a gaudy temple is erected, and other trumpery wholly foreign to it. But not only the scene is defaced, and the *outworks of the ruin* violently torn away; *the main body of the ruin itself* is at this very time under the alarming hand of decoration. When the present proprietor made his purchase, he found the whole mass of ruins – the Cloisters, the Abbey Church, and the Hall – choked with rubbish. The first work therefore was to clear and open. And something in this way might have been done with propriety, for we see ruins sometimes so choked that no view of them can be obtained…. But the restoration of parts is not enough: ornaments must be added, and such incongruous ornament, as disgrace the scene are disgracing also the monastery. The monks's garden is turned into a trim parterre and planted with flowering shrubs; a view is opened through the great window to some ridiculous I know not what (Anne Bolein I think they call it) that is planted in the valley; and in the central part of the abbey, a circular pedestal is raised out of fragments of the old pavement, on which is erected a mutilated heathen statue!

Whilst Gilpin's complaints were largely a matter of taste, it is obvious that Aislabie did considerable damage to the archaeology and structure of the site. He swept away the remains of the elegant late twelfth-century cloister arcades, and removed the arcades from the presbytery. He also spread fallen masonry about the site to establish levels for his all-pervading lawns, removing architectural detail from its original context.

If this was the negative side of Aislabie's contribution to Fountains Abbey, there was a positive element which far outweighed the damage done. Aislabie, his daughter Mrs Allanson and her niece Mrs Lawrence conducted a long-term campaign of repair and resetting of fallen masonry. It was Mrs Allanson who permitted the excavation of the chapter house by John Martin, and Mrs Lawrence who first allowed Richard Walbran to excavate in the church. Her successor, the Earl de Grey, in turn was responsible for the clearance of the ruins to the state in which they can be seen today. He was also responsible for opening the ruins to the public and for sponsoring the recording of the site by J.A. Reeve. The worst excesses that Gilpin complained of were effectively reversed as scholarly interests came to influence the noble owners.

THE MONASTIC LEGACY

Without doubt it was the growing interest in monastic sites throughout the nineteenth century described in Chapter 1 that led to the survival of so many sites. Many others have not survived above ground but remain a future reserve of buried knowledge. Their excavation and the continuing study and analysis of those buildings which survive above ground, will continue the growth of our knowledge and interpretation of our monastic past. Though considerable progress has been made, our knowledge of monastic life in medieval England remains imperfect and there are many avenues of research that remain to be followed up. One of the most important is, quite simply, to discover what happened to our monasteries and their estates after they ceased to be corporations of piety and workshops of prayer.

FURTHER READING

There is a vast amount of literature on the subject of monasteries, much of it site specific and most of it dated in the extreme. There are exceptions. Good general introductions are: J. Patrick Greene's *Medieval Monasteries* (Leicester: University Press 1992); Roberta Gilchrist's *Gender and Material Culture: the archaeology of religious women* (London: Routledge 1994); Mick Aston's *Monasteries in the Landscape* (Stroud: Tempus 2000); James Bond's *Monastic Landscapes* (Stroud: Tempus 2004), and Tim Pestell's *Landscapes of Monastic Foundation* (Woodbridge: Boydell 2004). Their bibliographies are extensive and provide the best available access to individual areas of research. For the archaeology of monasteries and the developing approach to research good summaries are provided in Roberta Gilchrist and Harold Mytum (eds) *The Archaeology of Rural Monasteries* (Oxford: British Archaeological Reports 1989) and *Advances in Monastic Archaeology* (Oxford: British Archaeological Reports 1993).

For the development of individual orders, David Robinson's *Geography of Augustinian Settlement in Medieval England and Wales* (Oxford: British Archaeological Reports 1980) remains the best treatment of the black canons, while for the Cistercians his edited *Cistercian Abbeys of Great Britain* (London: Batsford 1998 and 2002 (paperback edn)), my own *The White Monks: the Cistercians in Britain 1128-1540* (Stroud: Tempus 1998), and Terryl Kinder's edited *Perspectives for an Architecture of Solitude* (Turnhout: Brepols 2004) provide the background for this heavily researched order. For the Carthusians, the only modern treatment remains *Christ's Poor Men, the Carthusians in England* (Stroud: Tempus 2002) by Mick Aston and myself.

For individual sites there are two sources of information: the guide books provided for those sites in the care of English Heritage, the National Trust, and private owners that are open to the public, and which summarise recent research; and the ever growing series of site-specific reports which are published either in archaeological journals or monographs. The Museum of London's growing monograph series on monastic sites in the capital is particularly significant.

For the use of water in medieval monasteries, the standard work is Léon Pressouyre's edited *L'hydraulique monastique* (Grâne: Créaphis 1996), but a useful introduction to English sites can be found in James Bond's 'Water management in the rural monastery' in Gilchrist and Mytum's *Archaeology of Rural Monasteries* (above).

INDEX

Page numbers in **bold** refer to illustrations.

If you are interested in purchasing other books published by Tempus,
or in case you have difficulty finding any Tempus books in your local bookshop,
you can also place orders directly through our website

www.tempus-publishing.com